An Inside Story of Modern Syria

An Inside Story of Modern Syria

The Unauthorised Biography of a Damascene Reformer

Omar Imady

PEN & SWORD
HISTORY

First published in Great Britain in 2023 by
Pen & Sword History
An imprint of
Pen & Sword Books Ltd
Yorkshire – Philadelphia

ISBN 978 1 52678 046 1

A CIP catalogue record for this book is available from the British Library.

Typeset by Mac Style
Printed in the UK by CPI Group (UK) Ltd, Croydon, CR0 4YY.

MIX
Paper | Supporting responsible forestry
FSC® C013604

Pen & Sword Books Limited incorporates the imprints of Atlas, Archaeology, Aviation, Discovery, Family History, Fiction, History, Maritime, Military, Military Classics, Politics, Select, Transport, True Crime, Air World, Frontline Publishing, Leo Cooper, Remember When, Seaforth Publishing, The Praetorian Press, Wharncliffe Local History, Wharncliffe Transport, Wharncliffe True Crime and White Owl.

For a complete list of Pen & Sword titles please contact

PEN & SWORD BOOKS LIMITED
47 Church Street, Barnsley, South Yorkshire, S70 2AS, England
E-mail: enquiries@pen-and-sword.co.uk
Website: www.pen-and-sword.co.uk

Or

PEN AND SWORD BOOKS
1950 Lawrence Rd, Havertown, PA 19083, USA
E-mail: Uspen-and-sword@casematepublishers.com
Website: www.penandswordbooks.com

To Mildred Elaine Rippey

Contents

Preface

In the *New York Time*'s review of George W. Bush's *41: A Portrait of My Father*, Peter Baker writes: 'The author makes no pretensions to objectivity and, in truth, this is more Hallmark card than biography.' Though *An Inside Story of Modern Syria: The Unauthorised Biography of a Damascene Reformer* is also a work written by a son about his father's life, my intention in writing this book was far more about trying to understand my father's legacy than with a desire to celebrate it. My life-long dilemma has been trying to reconcile my conviction that my father is one of the most honest, hard-working, principled people I have ever known with the fact that he spent more than half a century working for a regime which I regard as directly responsible for the systematic unlawful imprisonment, torture, dispossession, displacement, and exile of millions of Syrians.

My father was deeply aggrieved by the resistance of the Syrian regimes he worked under to his stubborn attempts to introduce changes that would enhance the quality of life for his fellow Syrians. Yet, when it came to addressing the fact that he worked for a system that was willing to do just about anything to remain in power, my father appears to have mastered a sophisticated form of dissociation. It is as though he took for granted that all regimes were this ruthless, and that if he and others like him were to choose to leave, to refuse to work for the regime on strict ethical grounds, the country would effectively be abandoned to those who desired only to use their positions to enrich themselves rather than the people they were supposed to serve. There was nothing I could share about how criminal some of the regime's practises were – regardless of the 'good' that people like my father were able to smuggle through the net – that he did not already know. In fact, he would often respond to such objections with deep silence, a silence that implied that he knew far more about these things than I ever could.

It was from March 1960 onwards that my father's professional life became intertwined with Syria's ever-evolving political saga. He held official and ministerial positions throughout at least four major phases of the country's political history, the legacies of all of which were in some way morally questionable: from the United Arab Republic to the Secessionist Regime, the early Ba'th leadership following the 1963 coup to neo-Bath rule under Hafiz al-Asad, and finally to the early years of the regime in place today under his son. As such, my father's life provides a fascinating and significant lens onto this period of Syrian history, and his position as a non-Ba'thist, western-educated technocrat operating in a world of largely secular, socialist, Syrian politicians shines a unique light on the events of the years from 1960 to 2000. I have always felt that there are aspects of my father's professional life that are worthy of being shared. And though my father has written several works, including one that focuses on his long professional career, these are not easily accessible to readers in the West, not only because they are in Arabic, but also because he was ever mindful of how his words would be interpreted by a security apparatus that is trained to detect even the faintest hint of opposition in the words and actions of all those it monitors. I don't recall once being encouraged by my father to write this book. In fact, when the idea would come up during our telephone conversations, he would always emphasise that he had already shared what he was willing to share in his own works. But I was certain that not only was almost every major story he shared himself carefully and necessarily censored, but that the personal dimension of the events he described was consistently omitted.

The challenge before me, therefore, was this: how to write a book which reflected a man to whom I am existentially connected and yet a world to which I am so intensely averse. As I began to write this biography, I found myself instinctively sharing my father's story as he would have wanted it shared: carefully and cautiously, focusing more on what he had been trying to achieve, what he called 'reforms', and the various obstacles he had to overcome to realise these. I grappled with a way to resist this voice taking over. In doing so, however, I eventually came to the conclusion that the story of Dr Muhammad Imady was, in fact, best and most authentically told in the way he would tell it. The main chapters of each section, therefore, present a researched and documented account of his life through his own lens.

At the same time, my own personal convictions and intentions in writing this book were also inescapable and overwhelming. In this respect, my desire was twofold. First was my need to come to terms my with father's life and legacy by collecting and, more importantly, processing the events in his life, seeking answers to the many problematizing questions I had concerning my father's role in Syria's political and economic structures. Second was my desire to articulate my understanding of Syria's recent history, having been subject to its regime and having escaped from it.

In 2012, I began my work with the Centre for Syrian Studies at the University of St Andrews and came face-to-face with the way in which information on Syria and its political system is produced and disseminated by the machinery of academia. I have often felt that this process is far more about perpetuating the factories that produce this information – the theories and terminologies – rather than the actual attempt the capture something meaningful about the lived experiences of those being written about. My voice was often alien within these scholastic settings. I was neither interested in defending a certain theory or fitting my narrative into a specific framework, nor able to depersonalise my intellectual reflections on the subject of Syria, despite constant reminders that to personalise is to undermine one's scholarly credentials, however robust otherwise. As such, this work presented a cathartic opportunity to articulate so much of what I've been wanting to share about Syria in the last decade, which I was seldom able to express in an academic context.

This book, therefore, constitutes an 'unauthorised' biography in the fullest sense. It records my father's experiences – as he would have, and indeed often did share them – and my own experience of these accounts. I have woven together the fragments I heard from him with my own research of and reflections on the events involved. It represents the life of Muhammad Imady as I saw, heard, understood, and reflected upon it. I alone, therefore, can be held responsible for any biases, interpretations, and conclusions herein.

Though I am a historian by training, this is not an academic study of Imady's life. Whilst the events described are fully documented and referenced in this work, this book is designed to be accessible to a wide audience, from those interested in this period of Syrian history, politics and economics from an academic perspective to those delving into the philosophical and ethical issues surrounding power and those who wield, and yield to it, to those simply curious about a man who was at once a product of his time and place and yet so obviously removed from it.

The book is divided into sections, each documenting a period of Imady's life. Rather than with his birth, the biography begins with an exploration of the Imady family origins, tracing back our ancestral line to the earliest known Imady, unpicking the mystery behind where and when this family began. The biographical sections are intertwined with in-depth 'Profiles' of the lives of some of those with whom Imady interacted, as well as 'Under the Microscope' sections containing detailed examinations of significant events. These also reflect my own personal investigative research into perplexing dilemmas, anomalies, and historical 'mysteries' in Syria's past and present. Included in each section, too, are 'Post-Uprising Introspections' – these contain my personal, often satirical, reflections on more recent related events in Syria following the start of what began as an uprising and eventually became a drawn out civil war. These were originally published as regular blog and opinion pieces during the time I spent as Deputy Director of the Centre for Syria Studies.

The reforms my father was able to introduce during his long career were notable. His ability to maintain his pragmatic, reformist approach over four decades of less-than-democratic rule is remarkable. I knew him to be a man of the deepest integrity, firmly committed to leaving the world a better place in the best way he knew how, through his skills as a gifted and talented economist. And yet, his biography raises inevitable, unavoidable questions. At what point is the good one can do outweighed by the consequences of working within a corrupt and brutal regime? Is change worth pursuing if it inadvertently affords such a regime a veneer of respectability? Are the men and women I call 'Damascene reformers' to some degree 'Damascene facilitators', inevitably complicit in the crimes they are attempting to mitigate? While conclusive answers to these questions will not be found in this book, readers are provided with an account that makes it possible for them to draw their own conclusions. Even now, I am still attempting to draw mine.

List of Abbreviations

AIU	Arab International University
ESCWA	Economic and Social Commission for Western Asia
FNA	Federal News Agency
FSA	Free Syrian Army
IMF	International Monetary Fund
MENA	Middle East and North Africa
NYIT	New York Institute of Technology
NYU	New York University
PLO	Palestine Liberation Organisation
SP	Syrian pounds
UAR	United Arab Republic
UK	United Kingdom
UN	United Nations
UNDP	United Nations Development Programme
US	United States
WB	World Bank
WFP	World Food Programme

Timeline

1530: Birth of ‘Imad al-Din al-Hanafi in Damascus, the earliest documented ancestor of the Imady family.

1578: Death of ‘Imad al-Din al-Hanafi at the age of 48.

1641: Death of ‘Abd al-Rahman al-‘Imadi (henceforth written as Imady), the first member of the Imady family to be designated Grand Mufti of Damascus.

1758: Death of Hamid Imady, the most famous grand mufti from the Imady family.

1860: Massacre of Damascus during which ‘Abd Allah Imady protects Christians from the violent mobs by offering them sanctuary in his home.

1882: Jawdat Imady, the father of Muhammad Imady, is born in Qaymariyyah, Old Damascus, to Sa’id Imady and Kulthum Mardini.

1893: 14 October – The Grand Mosque of Damascus catches fire, and the structure suffers severe damage. Sa’id Imady and his son Jawdat take part in the collective Damascene effort to extinguish the fire, and in clearing the mosque after the fire was put out.

c.1900: The Imady family moves out of Old Damascus to a large walled-in compound in Salihiyyah, on the lower slopes of Mount Qasiyoun.

1907: Sa’id Imady dies.

1912: Jawdat Imady marries Yusra al-Hawasili.

1919: 26 September – Last Ottoman formation leaves Damascus.

3 October – Prince Faisal enters Damascus. Jawdat Imady is amongst the crowd gathered to receive him.

5 October – Arab Constitutional Government announced.

26 November – Arab Emirate announced.

1920: 8 March – Kingdom of Syria established.
24 July – Battle of Maysalun between the Arab Syrian army and French forces. 400 Syrians are killed, including the Minister of Defence, Yusuf al-'Azma, and 42 French soldiers.
25 July – Siege of Damascus by French forces.
25 July – King Faisal formally relinquishes the throne and departs Syria.

1925: Jawdat Imady secretly supports the 1925 uprising against French occupation with wheat from land owned by the Imady family.

1926: Jawdat Imady and his wife move out of the Imady home in Salihiyyah to a home owned by his father-in-law in Bahsa.

1930: Sunday, 31 August – Muhammad Imady is born to Jawdat Imady and Yusra al-Hawasili in Bahsa, outside Old Damascus, at a home owned by his maternal grandfather.

1931: 9 August – The Imady family moves to Muhajirin.

1942: Fall – Muhammad Imady, henceforth Imady, is enrolled in Tajhiz al-Ula, established in 1936 and later to be known as Jawdat al-Hashimi school.

1943–46: Imady participates in school demonstrations against the French Mandate.

1946: 17 April – The evacuation of the last French troops at the end of the French Mandate.

1948: Imady graduates from high school and is enrolled in the Faculty of Law at the University of Damascus.

1953: Imady graduates from the Faculty of Law.

1953: Imady is employed by the Ministry of Finance. Six months later he begins his mandatory army service.

1955: Imady completes his army service and is offered a scholarship to pursue his graduate studies in economics in New York.

1955: 3 November – Imady arrives in New York on a TWA flight to pursue his graduate education at New York University (NYU).

1955: December – Imady meets Mildred Elaine Rippey, a student of English literature at NYU.

1956: 24 August – Muhammad Imady marries Mildred Elaine Rippey. The marriage ceremony is held at her home in Palisades, NY.

1957: 5 July – Imady's first daughter, Susan Sahar, is born in New York.
1958: 22 February – The United Arab Republic (UAR) is formed.
1958: Jawdat Imady dies.
1960: Muhammad Imady obtains his PhD in Economics from NYU and departs New York for Damascus with his family.
1960: 1 March – Imady, his wife and daughter arrive in Damascus.
1960: Imady begins to teach at the University of Damascus, a position he maintains until 1979, when he departs to Kuwait.
1961: 28 September – End of the UAR – beginning of the Secessionist Regime.
1962: 18 February – Birth of Muna, Imady's second daughter.
1963: 8 March – Military coup ends the Secessionist Regime and brings the Ba'th party to power.
1966: 21–23 February – Radical wing of the Ba'th party, headed by Salah Jadid, takes over, and forces the old guard of the Ba'th into exile.
1966: 8 July – Birth of Omar, Imady's son and youngest child.
1967: 5–10 June – Arab-Israeli War.
1967: June – Syria breaks relations with the US.
1968: Imady is designated Deputy Minister of State for Planning Affairs.
1970: 13 November – The 'Corrective Movement' – a military coup formally begins the reign of Hafiz al-Asad as the undisputed ruler of Syria.
1972: 22 March – Imady is designated Minister of State for Planning Affairs in a cabinet headed by 'Abd al-Rahman al-Khlayfawi.
1972: 23 December – Imady is designated Minister of Economy in a cabinet headed by Mahmud al-Ayyubi.
1973: 6–25 October – Arab-Israeli War.
1974: 26 February-31 May – Kissinger's shuttle diplomacy between Syria and Israel culminates in the signing of the Agreement on Disengagement between Israel and Syria.
15–16 June – President Nixon visits Damascus.
16 June – Diplomatic relations between the US and Syria are restored.
1976: 7 August – Imady remains Minister of Economy in a new cabinet headed by 'Abd al-Rahman al-Khlayfawi.

1977: Imady is elected to the People's Council for a four-year term.
1978: 30 March – Imady remains Minister of Economy in a new cabinet headed by Muhammad 'Ali al-Halabi.
1979: April – Imady is elected by the Board of Governors of the Arab Fund for Economic and Social Development as the new Director General and Chairman of the Board of Governors for a five-year term.
30 August – Imady arrives in Kuwait.
1982: 2–28 February – Hama Massacre.
1984: April – Imady is unanimously re-elected by the Board of Governors of the Arab Fund for Economic and Social Development for a second term (1984–1989).
1985: 8 April – Imady designated Minister of Economy in a cabinet headed by 'Abd al-Ra'uf al-Kasm, and returns to teaching at the University of Damascus, a teaching position he retains until 1996.
1986: 17 April – The 'Hindawi Affair' becomes public.
24 October – Britain severs relations with Syria.
1987: 1 November – Imady remains Minister of Economy in a new cabinet headed by Mahmud al-Zu'bi.
1991: 4 May – Law No. 10 issued.
1992: 29 June – Imady remains Minister of Economy after Mahmud al-Zu'bi's cabinet reshuffle.
1994: 21 January – Basil al-Asad, the eldest son of Hafiz al-Asad, dies in a car accident.
1996: October – Agreement signed with Airbus for purchase of six A-320 planes.
2000: 7 March – Mahmud al-Zu'bi's cabinet resigns.
13 March – Imady retains his position as Minister of Economy in the new cabinet formed by Muhammad Mustafa Miru.
10 May – Mahmud al-Zu'bi is ousted from his positions in the Ba'th party and is referred to court on charges of corruption.
21 May – Mahmud al-Zu'bi commits suicide after learning that the Damascus police chief had arrived at his house to serve a judicial notice to appear before an investigating judge to answer allegations of corruption and other violations.
10 June – Death of Hafiz al-Asad.

17 July – Bashar al-Asad is sworn in as Syria's new president.

2001: 13 December – Mustafa Miru's cabinet is reshuffled, and Imady is replaced by Ghassan Rifa'i.

2002: Imady designated as Head of the Board of Trustees of the Dar al-Na'im Orphanage.

July – Imady publishes *The Concerns of Development – Events I Will Not Forget.*

November – Imady publishes *Syria and the March Towards Arab Economic Integration.*

2004: May – Imady publishes *The Evolution of Approaches to Development in Syria.*

2004: Imady elected Charmain of the Board of Trustees of the Arab International University.

2006: February – Imady designated Chairman of the Board of the Commissioners of the Syrian Commission on Financial Markets and Securities.

2010: February – Imady designated for a second term as Chairman of the Board of the Commissioners of the Syrian Commission on Financial Markets and Securities.

2011: 15 March – The Syrian Uprising begins.

2012: 18 July – Bombing of the National Security headquarters in Damascus. A number of top military and security officials are killed.

2013: 8 April – Imady is injured when a bomb explodes outside his office in central Damascus.

21 August – The Ghuta chemical attack. Estimates of those killed range from at least 281 people to 1,729.

2014: February – End of Imady's second renewal as the Chairman of the Board of the Commissioners of the Syrian Commission on Financial Markets and Securities.

3 June – Bashar al-Asad elected for a second seven-year term.

29 June – Abu Bakr al-Baghdadi, the leader of ISIS, announces the establishment of a 'caliphate'.

2015: 4 April – The Friends of Damascus Society honours Imady for a lifetime of service.

30 September – Russia's 'formal' military intervention in Syria begins.

Imady publishes his last book, *Selected Studies on University Teaching*.

2016: 23 April – Muna, Imady's second daughter, dies from complications related to a heart operation in Damascus at the age of 54.

2017: 4 April – 89 people killed and more than 541 injured in Khan Shaykhun, the deadliest use of chemical weapons since the Ghuta chemical attack in 2013.

7 April – The US launches 59 Tomahawk cruise missiles aimed at the Shayrat Airbase.

June – Imady and his wife travel to Beirut where they meet their son, Omar, for the first time since January 2012.

30 October – ISIS defeated, and Raqqa is liberated.

2018: 7 April – A chemical attack is reported in the city of Duma, with 70 people killed and 500 injured.

14 April – The US, France, and the United Kingdom carry out a series of strikes against multiple government sites in Syria in reprisal for the Duma chemical attack.

2019: 27 October – Abu Bakr al-Baghdadi is killed by the US Delta force.

2020: 17 June – The Caesar Syria Civilian Protection Act comes into force.

2021: 26 May – Bashar al-Asad is elected for a third seven-year term.

2022: 29 June – Muhammad Imady passes away at his home in Damascus, aged 91.

Family Tree

Kasbay

'Imad al-Din al-Hanafi [Abu al-Fida'] Isma'il

Shams al-Din [Abu 'Abd Allah] Muhammad

Kamal al-Din Muhammad

Muhibb al-Din Muhammad

Shams al-Din Muhammad

'Imad al-Din al-Hanafi Muhammad
Born: 1530 – Died: October 19, 1578

'Abd al-Rahman Imady
Born: 14 September 1570 – Died: 25 August 1641

Ibrahim Imady
Born: 1603 – Died: 8 October 1667

'Ali Imady
(Mufti of Damascus)
Born: 12 December 1638 – Died: 8 April 1706

Muhammad Imady
(Mufti of Damascus)
Born: April 1684 – Died: 20 May 1754

'Abd al-Rahman Imady
(Mufti of Damascus)
Born: 1707 – Died: 1762
married
Sa'diyyah bint Hamza al-Hamzawi al-Husaini
Born: 1708 – Died: 1810

Muhammad Imady
Born: before 1762 – Died: before 1810

Ibrahim Imady
Born: before 1810 – Died: 3 November 1839
married:
Hamidah al-Manini

Muhammad Imady
Died: 1861
married:
Fatimah al-Hamwi
Born: 1839 – Died: ?

Sa'id Imady
Born: 1856 – Died: 1907
married:
Kulthum Mardini
Born: 1865 – Died: ?

Jawdat Imady
Born: 1882 – Died: 1958
married:
Yusra al-Hawasili
Born: 1898 – Died: 1969

Muhammad Imady
Born: 31 August 1930 – Died: 29 June 2022
married:
Mildred Elaine Rippey
Born: 16 April 1934

1 – Susan Sahar Imady
Born: 5 July 1957

2 – Muna Imady
Born: 18 February 1962 – Died: 23 April 2016

3 – Omar Imady
Born: 8 July 1966

Introduction

When people share the story of Syria's recent history, much information can be garnered as to their perspective and political leanings based on where they begin their narrative. Some may begin with the departure of the last of the French troops in 1946 and the end of the French Mandate. Others will begin in 1963 when the Ba'ath party takes over, others in 1970, when Hafiz al-Asad assumes power. Others still, will begin with the Syrian Uprising in 2011. Inherent within the choice of each of these milestones is a *Weltanshauung*, a mindset, an outlook, each of which also entails a vision for the future. When I was asked in 2016 to provide an overview of Syria's recent history for a UN report on the country, I made the daring decision to begin with what I believe constitutes the most important unifying reference point in the modern history of Syria, the Syrian National Congress of 1919. Today, I still regard this historical moment as the ideal foundation for a new vision of Syria that can bring together the multitude of conflicting Syrias: regime and opposition, urban and rural, Sunni and Alawite, Muslim and Christian, and religious and secular. What follows is the introduction I once wrote for the UN report, revised and adapted for the purposes of this book.[1]

After the collapse of the Ottoman empire in 1918 and the arrival of King Faisal and the Arab army in Damascus, the first general Syrian conference was held in May 1919. It constituted the foundation of what would come to be known as modern Syria. In March 1920, that same body declared Syria's independence and four months later, eighty-five delegates from four regions adopted a constitution. In it, Syria was proclaimed an administratively decentralized state with a civil constitutional monarchy in which executive, legislative, and judicial powers were separated. The equal treatment of all citizens, irrespective of their religion, sect or ethnicity, was enshrined in its articles and women were guaranteed the right to vote and run for office. In the Constitution, Islam was specified as the religion of the Hashemite Monarch but there was no reference to religion as a basis for legislation. The civil nature of the state was thus ensured.

This progressive experiment in state-building was brought to a swift end in July 1920 by the arrival of French forces. Moreover, the authorities of the French Mandate, which lasted until April 1946, deliberately sought to accentuate differences between various ethnic and religious groups in Syria, often playing one group against the other. The allocation of a distinct, often autonomous, status to groups that had been marginalised during the Ottoman era did not contribute to the creation of a cohesive state, nor did it foster harmony among Syria's citizens.

Democratically elected post-independence governments failed to appreciate that, against this background, they had to reach out with a comprehensive economic and social programme to Syria's rural areas, where the majority of its marginalised groups lived in poverty, without education or infrastructure and exposed to disease. By 1950, it had become apparent that the attention of those governments was caught up in urban elitist interests. They simply could not see the importance of offering all Syrians equal opportunities for political and economic empowerment. The unintended message was that democratic elections were bound to produce governments indifferent to the plight of marginalised rural youth, especially in coastal areas, who turned increasingly to the one reliable source of regular pay: the armed forces. By 1963, they were strong enough to bring the Arab Socialist Ba'th Party into power and, by 1970, had fully consolidated their authority. The Ba'th party succeeded where other parties failed not only because it had attracted many influential army officers, but also because it was particularly attractive to members of marginalised groups.

Indeed, under the Ba'th, rural areas received far more attention than they had in the past. In addition to land reforms, the Government invested heavily in bringing electricity, roads, and schools to areas that had been neglected previously. At the same time, however, all forms of genuine political dissent were crushed, often ruthlessly, and important segments of the population felt that their values were being deliberately undermined. That sense of dissatisfaction eventually culminated in the Muslim Brotherhood insurgency and the tragic events of 1982 in Hama, where thousands of civilians were killed as the Government retook control of the city. Society was by now deeply divided, and no one seemed to have the vision required to escape the trap of interacting on the basis of sect, class or ethnicity. What primarily mattered to the Government was authority and control, and as long as those societal divides did not constitute a serious challenge, they were ignored. Indeed, the more the legacy of the past was ignored, the more it became part of the present.

When Bashar al-Asad was sworn in as Syria's president on 17 July 2000, the violence of the 1980s seemed a distant memory. However, a serious wound had yet to be healed. More than political, administrative, and economic reform, Syria was in dire need of a courageous attempt to acknowledge the sectarian and ethnic injustices and violence of its recent past. At the very least, steps should have been taken to address the grievances of those with missing family members, or whose property had been confiscated or damaged. Policymakers failed to see that a country in which segments of the population believe they had been gravely mistreated will prove vulnerable when dramatic events occur.

In March 2011, Syria was confronted by the one challenge it was not prepared to face: a spontaneous civilian demand to dismantle the authoritarian political strata that had been in place since at least 1963. On every other level, although with shortcomings and in need of reforms, Syria could not seriously have been described as vulnerable. Yet, the house that was Syria was built on soft sand. It was unable to withstand the earthquake of 2011. That Syria still has elements of a working economy and a currency that has not entirely collapsed shows how solid certain aspects of the Syrian State were in early 2011. Sadly, however, it was unprepared and indeed unwilling to change where it mattered most.

Chapter I

The Imady Family: Obscure, Distinguished, and Irrelevant (1530–1930)

HISTORY AS IDENTITY

History, as Mahmoud El-Kati, my professor at Macalester College, once taught me, is primarily concerned with the manufacturing of an identity.[1] In his mind, all the talk one hears and reads about history being useful for learning lessons from the past – for avoiding the repetition of past mistakes and identifying how and why things turned out the way they did – is flawed. History is a factory of identity; the art of using past events to legitimize a specific narrative. The Nation of Islam, for example, as El-Kati would explain, succeeded in attracting followers not because it provided them with a factual history. It succeeded, rather, because it provided African Americans with a historical narrative that empowered them with an alternate identity; an identity they could be proud of, an identity that made the experience of slavery a catalyst rather than a burden.

To grow up in the family of al-ʿImadi (henceforth Imady) was to know that it had its own version of history, and, in turn, a distinct sense of identity. Stories upon stories of who my ancestors were and all the values they allegedly upheld were shared with me throughout my childhood, often for no apparent reason. And whether it was my elderly aunt who was sharing these stories in her organic, fluid manner, or my father who had a far more sophisticated and formal way of articulating them, the impact on me was the same: because of all this, I was different, my father was different, in fact, all Imadys were different. We carried this distinct sense of identity with us everywhere.

Our Friday trips to Zabadani, a summer resort town around forty kilometres from Damascus, could not take place without pointing out pieces of land or even an entire village that the Imady family allegedly once owned; a gift from an Ottoman sultan to one of the Imady religious scholars or part of a trust that had found its way through marriages and inheritance into our family. A visit to a mosque could easily unleash stories of Imady grand muftis, all forty of them (I would later learn there were, in actuality, only seven). And a random encounter with a Damascene woman could remind my aunt of the fact that this woman's family were once recipients of the Imady family's charitable gift to Damascus: Waqf al-Qadi Muhibb al-Din al-'Imadi, the charitable trust of Judge Muhibb al-Din Imady. And while some of these stories had no basis in actual history, there was, in fact, a solid historical foundation for the Imady sense of identity; a foundation which was as old as the Ottoman conquest of Damascus.

The main outline of the Imady family history is not difficult to identify. Who were the main players? When were they primarily active? When and why did they become less prominent? All these questions are fairly easy to answer. What is difficult is trying to go beyond what was obvious, and, later, trying to solve the 'glitches', or historical anomalies, that even now remain resistant to my extensive attempts to unravel them. But as El-Kati would remind me, what you know and what you don't know about your past are both equally important when it comes to how your sense of identity is ultimately shaped.

ELUSIVE ORIGINS

One of the most peculiar aspects of the Imady family history is the dichotomy between how overwhelmingly easy it is to document its prominent members from early Ottoman Damascus until the present, and how overwhelmingly difficult, if not impossible, it is to find reliable information on its members in Damascus, or anywhere else for that matter, prior to the Ottoman conquest. Where were the Imadys prior to Sultan Selim's conquest of Damascus in 1516? Where exactly do they come from? Were they Arabs? Turks? Persians? Kurds?

These are the types of questions one stumbles upon when attempting to go back earlier than the man known as 'Imad al-Din al-Hanafi, the earliest documented ancestor of the Imady family, and the person after whom the Imady family is named.

'Imad al-Din was born in Damascus in 1530 and died in 1578 at the young age of forty-eight. The problem is that his ancestry, and the way in which it is treated by various sources, in contrast to the clarity with which his descendants' lives are documented, provides all the necessary ingredients for a fascinating historical thriller.

PROFILE: 'IMAD AL-DIN AL-HANAFI[2]

Based on early sources, 'Imad al-Din may have originally been from Samarqand, more specifically Boysun in modern day southern Uzbekistan, or alternatively descended from a Circassian knight named Kasbay, or even from a family that once lived in the Buqa' Valley in Lebanon.

Uzbekistan?

One of the most important biographical works of early Ottoman Damascus is *Tarajim al-A'yan min Abna' al-Zaman* (Biographies of the Notables from the People of the Time) by al-Hasan al-Burini (1556–1615), a Galilean historian whose family moved and settled in Damascus when he was ten years old. In this biographical work, which al-Burini kept editing and reworking until shortly before his death, we find a collection of approximately 205 biographical entries (the number varies from one manuscript to another) of notable religious scholars, rulers, and artisans.[3] Three Imadys are included: 'Imad al-Din al-Hanafi, Ibrahim ibn Kasbay (the cousin of 'Imad al-Din), and 'Abd al-Rahman (the son of 'Imad al-Din). Of these three, al-Burini's primary focus is on 'Imad al-Din, whom he regards as being his teacher and mentor.

The biography of 'Imad al-Din spans around nine pages, five of which are devoted to excerpts of his poetry. The remaining four provide various types of information on 'Imad al-Din, including how al-Burini met him and became his student. But hardly anything is shared about 'Imad al-Din's family origins. The ambiguity is apparent instantly from the way in which the biography begins: 'Imad al-Din al-Hanafi. "Imad al-Din', or Pillar of Faith, is, in fact, his title. His actual name, which we know from other sources to be Muhammad, is omitted. And even though biographical dictionaries from the Mamluk and Ottoman period would ordinarily include a person's given name, father's name, title, city of birth, city in which they settled and died, and (in the case of religious scholars) the specific guild of law to which they belonged (e.g. Hanafi, Shafi'i, Maliki, and Hanbali), all we have here is the title, ʻImad al-Din, and the guild of law, Hanafi. In the paragraph that follows his name, we are told: ʻHe is our teacher… al-ʻImad the son of al-ʻImad al-Hanafi…'[4] This only serves to inform us that his father, or one of his ancestors, also had the title of ʻImad al-Din. The only additional information al-Burini provides is that ʻHe is a Damascene, who was born in Damascus'.[5] Everything else he shares relates exclusively to ʻImad al-Din's scholarly life and contributions, and eventual sudden death at the age of forty-eight. All this ambiguity can so far be explained by al-Burini's style of biographical writing. Though he does generally provide far more detailed information in other biographies, it is true that he does not consistently provide the type of details found in other sources. However, when it comes to ʻImad al-Din, al-Burini does something else which defies this ʻinnocent' explanation. Throughout his work, and outside of the actual biography of ʻImad al-Din, al-Burini makes numerous references to ʻImad al-Din that are far more informative and, indeed, at times even peculiar. Why he would choose to omit these details from the actual biography of ʻImad al-Din is puzzling to the extent that one's initial impulse is to dismiss these details as involving another person who also had the title of ʻImad al-Din. This possibility, however, is aborted by al-Burini himself, who makes sure to state that this ʻImad al-Din, of whom he is sharing these details, is indeed the one whose biography is found in the section of the letter ʻayn (the first letter of the word ʻImad). And since all the extant manuscripts of *Tarajim al-A'yan min Abna' al-Zaman* include only one ʻImad al-Din it thus follows that all of these details relate to the life and origins of the ancestor of the Imady family.

Because we know al-Burini modified his work several times before his death, we are left with the suspicion that the main entry on ʻImad al-Din must have been censored over time. Why else would the main entry be so lacking? One reason for such censoring would have been to make it easier for the son of ʻImad al-Din, ʻAbd al-Rahman, who was a disciple of al-Burini, to rise up through the ranks of the scholars of Damascus. It is possible that al-Burini omitted aspects of ʻImad al-Din's life over the years that he saw as potentially incompatible with ʻAbd al-Rahman's ambition to become a grand mufti of Damascus, as he indeed would eventually become. It seems that al-Burini would have either forgotten to delete other references to ʻImad al-Din that are found throughout his work or chose to keep them for reasons that are unclear.

So, what exactly does al-Burini include on ‘Imad al-Din in other parts of his work? The most important perhaps is the far longer version of his name: "‘Imad al-Din al-Hanafi al-Samarqandi al-Bayasuni, who will be covered, God willing, in this work in the section of ‘Ayn...’[6] Here, al-Burini informs us that ‘Imad al-Din is from Samarqand, and, more specifically, from Boysun, in modern day southern Uzbekistan. This dual geographic characterization is repeated several times. Why al-Burini omits this information from his biographical entry of ‘Imad al-Din, and chose instead to only speak of him as a ‘Damascene, who was born in Damascus...’ is intriguing, but less so than the other interesting information which al-Burini omits from the biographical entry. First, we have ‘Imad al-Din's close relationship with Sokulluzade Hasan Pasha (d. 1602) who was thrice the governor of Damascus. ‘Imad al-Din is described as close enough to Sokulluzade Hasan Pasha to have had a chamber in the governor's palace. Second, is ‘Imad al-Din's occasional opium consumption which is explained by his ‘Aristotelian’ conviction of its therapeutic value. Third, is his strong grounding in logic and philosophy – strong enough to endow him with the epithet *Fadil al-Sharq*, or the Righteous Man of the East (the ‘east’ being regarded at the time as the heartland of philosophy and rational sciences).

The idea that the Imady family originates from southern Uzbekistan is also ascribed to an important Imady scholar of the seventeenth century, Hamid Imady. Hamid is quoted as having said that the Imady family originated in Bukhara, also in southern Uzbekistan (but not Samarqand), and that one of the Imady ancestors in Bukhara, ‘Abd al-Rahim ibn Abu Bakr ibn Burhan al-Din (d. 1253), is the author of a work entitled *Al-Fusul al-‘Imadiyyah*. The ascription of this quote to Hamid, however, is very problematic, since Hamid himself left behind a thorough treatise on the famous grandfather of this scholar and yet makes no mention of being related to him. Had Hamid actually been related to ‘Abd al-Rahim he would certainly have noted it due to the prestige such a family connection would have carried. Contrary to the quotes ascribed to him, in his own writings Hamid does not address the origins of the Imady family at all.

Lebanon?

Several early sources describe ‘Imad al-Din as ‘al-Buqa’i’,[7] or one whose family originated from the Buqa‘ Valley, which is located in modern day Lebanon, around thirty kilometres from Beirut. This designation, however, is almost certainly a result of an early copyist error. Instead of writing 'al-Salihi', or the one who is from al-Salihiyyah, a suburb of Old Damascus, it appears that a copyist mistakenly wrote al-Buqa'i, and the error was henceforth replicated:

البقاعي X - الصالحي ✓

Because extant manuscripts of these sources were often copied over several years, and at times decades after their original date of authorship, it is difficult to identify who first made this error.

A likely suspect is the copyist of a work by Sharaf al-Din ibn Ayyub al-Ansari (d. 1592). Al-Ansari's *Al-Rawd al-'Atir fi-ma Tayassara min Akhbar al-Qarn al-Sabi' ila Khitam al-Qarn al-'Ashir* (The Perfumed Garden of Assembled Notices of the People of the Seventh to the End of the Tenth Century) includes a biographical entry on 'Imad al-Din. It reads as follows:

> 'Imad al-Din, the son of al-Shaikh Muhibb al-Din al-Hanafi, al-Buqa'i al-'Annabi, who was born in Damascus…[8]

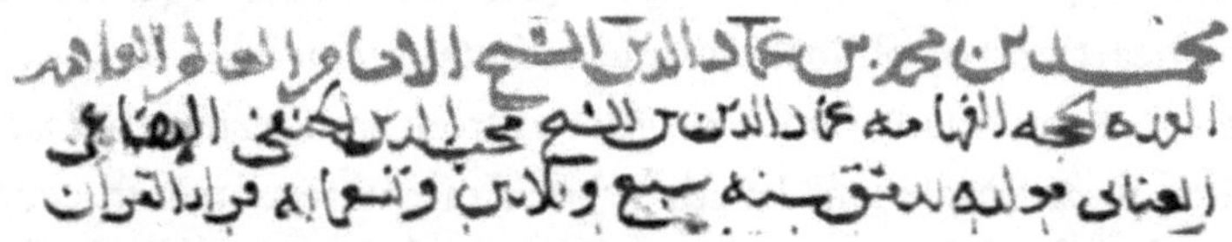

'Imad al-Din is here described as al-Buqa'i or from the Buqa' Valley, and (subsequently) as al-'Annabi, or from a suburb of Old Damascus known as 'Annabah (which is now the site of the neighbourhood of Bab Tuma). But, as is clear from the image of the manuscript page above, the word al-Buqa'i appears to be smudged. A word beneath it appears to have been erased and replaced by this term.

The Buqa'i designation was repeated by several later sources, until a Syrian historian, Muhammad Khalil al-Muradi (d. 1791), informed us that al-Buqa'i was indeed a copyist error, which he assumes is a corruption of the word al-'Annabi.[9] But the fact that both words exist in early sources (i.e. al-Buqa'i and al-'Annabi) means that al-Buqa'i must have been a corruption of another word. Another extant manuscript of an early source uses 'al-Salihi' instead of 'al-Buqa'i',[10] thereby potentially resolving this anomaly. Rather than providing any hint at his origins, however, all this erroneous 'Buqa'i' reference serves to inform us is that 'Imad al-Din lived in al-Salihiyyah prior to moving to al-'Annabah, and since both are suburbs of Old Damascus, this entire reference is, sadly, nothing more than a red herring.

UNDER THE MICROSCOPE: THE ENIGMA OF KASBAY[11]

Another important omission by al-Burini from 'Imad al-Din's entry is found in the biography of a man described as the paternal cousin of 'Imad al-Din: Ibrahim ibn Kasbay, a Qur'an scholar. Ibrahim is described by al-Burini to have been descended from a man named Kasbay, who served in the army during the age of the Mamluks. But if Ibrahim is the paternal cousin of 'Imad al-Din, then Kasbay is one of the grandfathers of both 'Imad al-Din and Ibrahim. This is, in fact, confirmed by a later source which also specifies Kasbay as the earliest (known) paternal ancestor of the Imady family.

The fact that 'Imad al-Din is descended from Kasbay is also attested to by a well-informed Ottoman scholar and historian, Muhammad Zahid al-Kawthari (1879–1952), who appears to have had access to documents on the history of the Imady family. According to al-Kawthari, Kasbay was the sixth ancestor of 'Imad al-Din:

1. Kasbay
2. 'Imad al-Din Isma'il Abu al-Fida'
3. Shams al-Din Muhammad Abu 'Abd Allah
4. Kamal al-Din Muhammad
5. Muhibb al-Din Muhammad
6. Shams al-Din Muhammad
7. 'Imad al-Din (1530–1578)

Of these, the only one we have information about is Shams al-Din Muhammad Abu 'Abd Allah who, according to al-Kawthari, was a student of Badr al-Din al-'Ayni (1361–1451).[12] To identify when Kasbay is likely to have been born, an average of thirty years separating the birth of each figure is calculated. According to this equation, Kasbay would have been born in approximately 1350. A generous lifespan of seventy years would place his death at around 1420. Using a more conservative estimate of twenty-five years between each birth would provide us with

1450 as Kasbay's possible death date, thus giving us a range of 1420 to 1450 for his death.

There are several figures in late Mamluk history who were known as Kasbay, each potentially being the Imady ancestor who travelled to Cairo or Damascus as a Mamluk slave soldier from either the Caucasus or (less likely) south Uzbekistan. The Mamluks were ethnically non-Arabs who were originally of Turkic roots from the Eurasian Steppe. Subsequently, this class expanded to include soldiers from Circassian, Abkhazian, Georgian roots, and various other peoples of the Caucasus as well as Albanians, Greeks, and South Slavs – all of whom were employed as military and administrative officers in Muslim Arab dynasties. The Mamluks would eventually become an isolated military aristocracy with de facto authority, irrespective of the de jure authority invested in the Abbasid rulers of Baghdad, and later of Cairo.

It is certain that some of the Mamluk soldiers did indeed originate in Uzbekistan, though a specific reference to Boysun is not found in historical sources. The problem, however, is that Kasbay is a very Circassian name, and there were no Circassians in southern Uzbekistan at the time. In fact, Circassians didn't arrive in Uzbekistan until the nineteenth century, and even then, only in very small numbers. Reconciling the idea that 'Imad al-Din is from Boysun in Uzbekistan, and at the same time descended from a man named Kasbay who was in the army of the Mamluks is therefore very difficult.

Another important thread that appears to be related to Kasbay is the existence of a fifteenth century manuscript belonging to the Imady family which contains an illustration of the Prophet Muhammad's family tree.

In one of the corners of this document it is stated that this Prophetic family tree was drawn and gifted by Prince Yashbak min Mahdi, an important Mamluk commander who was killed during a battle in 1480.[13] Yashbak was a prominent Mamluk figure who was initially owned by a man named Mahdi. This connection to Yashbak is consistent with the hypothesis that the Imady family descends from a Mamluk knight, since it is easy to visualise the exchange of such a gift taking place between two military figures of the Mamluk army.

So, following this logic, we are in essence in search of a Kasbay who: died in the first half of the fifteenth century; knew or was connected to Yashbak min Mahdi; and, at least at one point in his life, had lived in Damascus.

An exhaustive search in the works on late Mamluk history resulted in the identification of the following figures by the name of Kasbay:

1. Kasbay, the wife of a prince named Qarabgha who, along with her husband, died of the plague in 1348,
2. Kasbay al-Nawruzi (d. 1439),
3. Kasbay al-Shamshani al-Nasiri Faraj al-Mu'ayyadi Sayf al-Din ibn 'Abd Allah (d. 1465),
4. Kasbay Samz (the Fat) al-Zayni al-Mu'ayyadi (d. 1471),
5. Kasbay min Qansuh (d. 1473/1474),
6. Kasbay min Wali al-Din al-Zahiri Khushqadam (d. 1477),
7. Kasbay al-Ashrafi (d. 1488),
8. Kasbay min Uzbek al-Saqi (d. 1495),
9. Kasbay al-Salhadar (d. 1498).

While the possibility of the Imady family being descended from a woman named Kasbay is fascinating, the fact that al-Burini specifies that Kasbay was a soldier negates this possibility. Also easily excluded are those who died after 1470. It is simply impossible to have a sixth great grandfather who died only sixty years before 'Imad al-Din was born. This leaves us with two possibilities: Kasbay al-Nawruzi, and Kasbay al-Shamshani.

Kasbay al-Nawruzi was known by this title because he was initially owned by Nawruz al-Hafizi, the Mamluk governor of Damascus (1406–1411) who was killed after his rebellious stand against the Mamluk Sultan, al-Mu'ayyad Shaykh. Kasbay al-Nawruzi is described as having been a 'Prince of Ten' – a military rank in the Mamluk army denoting one who had ten knights under his command – and before his death he was promoted to one of the princes of the *tablakhanah*, or the military band division. He was based in Damascus, and he died there in 1439. The fact that al-Nawruzi died in Damascus, as well as the date of his death, makes it possible that he was indeed the ancestor of the Imady family. Furthermore, he was not a very prominent Mamluk military commander, as the majority of other figures named Kasbay were. This makes him, on one level, more likely to have been the ancestor of the Imady family, since if he had been an important military commander, his descendants are likely to have identified him in their lineage. Unless, of course, there was a deliberate and systematic attempt to conceal this connection.

The second possible candidate is Kasbay al-Shamshani who was born in 1375, or 155 years prior to the birth of 'Imad al-Din. This time difference amounts to an average of 25.8 years between each birth, which is within the range of the plausible. Al-Shamshani was initially, like al-Nawruzi, one of the commanders of the *tablakhanah* or the military band division. He was also an instructor of spear throwing. He was promoted to the position of *khaskiya*, or courtier of the sultan, one of the most trusted royal Mamluks who functioned as the Sultan's bodyguards, and subsequently to a *dawadar*, or holder of the Sultan's ink bottle, during the reign of Sayf al-Din Jaqmaq (r. 1438–1453). It was during the reign of Jaqmaq that Kasbay was exiled several times to *al-Diyyar al-Shamiyyah*, or the lands of Syria. This would have definitely included Damascus, but we also have records of his presence in Safad, and Tripoli (in modern day northern Lebanon). In 1448, Kasbay al-Shamshani was permitted to return to Cairo. He died in 1465, at the age of ninety and was buried at a desert cemetery outside of Cairo. His funeral was attended by the Sultan, Sayf al-Din Khushqadam. Interestingly, he was known for his pursuit of religious knowledge, not a typical interest of a Mamluk knight, and was praised for his generosity, humility and his righteous character; attributes rarely used by sources to describe military figures.

The important point here is that not only did this Kasbay have connections to Damascus, he also must have been very familiar with, and was possibly a friend of Yashbak min Mahdi who was already an important Mamluk commander in Egypt during Kasbay al-Shamshani's life, though not as important as he would later become.

But why would this significant connection to Kasbay al-Shamshani not be celebrated and made known by later Imadys? There are two possible explanations. The first is that by the time 'Imad al-Din was an active scholar in Damascus, a full century would have passed since the death of Kasbay al-Shamshani, enough to possibly make this connection with a knight who died in Cairo a distant memory.

The second explanation is more consistent with what appears to be a deliberate attempt by 'Imad al-Din to conceal or disguise his origins. Mindful of the fact that he was operating in an Ottoman age, 'Imad al-Din would not have wanted to be associated with a military Mamluk figure, and this concern would have applied to both Kasbay al-Nawruzi and Kasbay al-Shamshani. The Ottomans, after all, had only just fought and defeated the Mamluks and ended their rule in Damascus and elsewhere. This would have especially been the case if 'Imad al-Din was trying, as we indeed know he had been, to befriend an important Ottoman official, Sokulluzade Hasan Pasha. It would have been far wiser for 'Imad al-Din to present himself as a scholar who originated from south Uzbekistan, as al-Burini presents him, than to assert he was descended from a notable Mamluk knight, especially if he could get away with it, and the passing of an entire century could have made this possible.

'Imad al-Din's cousin, Ibrahim, on the other hand, identified himself as 'Ibn Kasbay',[14] or the descendant of Kasbay, though he would prove to be the only one from this family to do so. After his death, all the descendants of 'Imad al-Din would be known as Imady, or of 'Imad al-Din. The name Kasbay would disappear, and none of the many scholars descended from 'Imad al-Din would make reference to it. Nor would they make reference in their numerous scholarly works to their relative, the Quran scholar, Ibrahim ibn Kasbay. Like 'Imad al-Din, they all opted to distance themselves from this connection.

It is fitting to end this discussion of the elusive origins of the Imady family by introducing the far more recent contribution of DNA testing. As a male member of the Imady family, my DNA results[15] provide important insights that are not found in any historical sources.

Two aspects of these results in particular are illuminating. The first comes in the form of autosomal DNA results, which seek to identify and verify ancestral genealogical relationships. As shown in the map below, the results of my DNA tests, though far from error proof, include Anatolia, the Caucasus region, and Iran. Tellingly, however, Uzbekistan is not included. This result would seem to favour the Circassian ancestry theory of the Imady family origins.

Another, far more reliable test, involves the identification of Y-DNA or the haplogroup that designates paternal lineage. The result for the Imady family was J2 (with the confirmed subclade of By22506). In modern Syria, the haplogroup J1, which is primarily associated with Arabian Peninsula ancestry, accounts for 33.6 per cent of Syrians.[16] J2, on the other hand accounts for 20.8 per cent of Syrians. J2 is also known to be the fourth most frequent Y-DNA haplogroup in the Caucasus (21 per cent).[17] This appears to give further credence to the theory that the Imady family did indeed originate in the Caucasus.

What, then, is the conclusion of all this evidence? The likely story seems to be thus: A Circassian knight by the name of Kasbay migrated to Cairo or Damascus in the fourteenth century, his descendants settled in Damascus and became scholars of the Hanafi school of Islamic jurisprudence. For reasons that appear to be strategic in nature, these scholars chose not to present themselves as descendants of a Circassian Mamluk knight, and opted instead to emphasise an Uzbek ancestry, or, to remain silent on the question of their ancestry altogether, describing themselves only as Damascenes. Historians of the period, at least some of them, appear to have been complicit in this attempt to reframe the Imady family's ancestral lineage.

This finagling of family origins, incidentally, appears to be an ancestral trait; a modern, almost surreal mirroring of the denial of early Imady family connections is often currently found in the reverse. Numerous, unrelated families known as al-'Imadi, spread across the Middle East from Yemen to Turkey, are often deliberately treated as though they all constitute branches of the same tree. One striking example of this relates to the natives of the town of al-'Imadiyyah in Iraqi Kurdistan (also spelled 'Amadiya') named after 'Imad al-Din al-Zingi. These communities who migrated to Damascus in the nineteenth century assumed the surname al-'Imadi upon arrival in Syria. Despite their foreign and entirely unrelated origins, and despite the fact that they themselves do not constitute one family, they are often described by Damascene Imadys as being one of the many lost tribes of the Imady line. This assumption of affiliation even found its way into my father's own lifetime. During an official visit to Turkey, his host took him to visit the tomb of Ebussuud Efendi (1490–1547), one of the most prominent scholars of the Ottoman period. He also happened to be known as El-İmâdî, since his family originated from the village of Imad, near Iskilip. My father, strategically or diplomatically, did not deny the connection.

AN OTTOMAN LEGACY

As difficult as it may be to unearth the Imady family's pre-Ottoman origins, it is infinitely easier to shed light on its Ottoman legacy. All the guesswork and historical ambiguity is replaced by a line of celebrated religious scholars. From not knowing enough, we now move to knowing almost too much!

Though several aspects of the life of 'Imad al-Din al-Hanafi were enshrouded in a layer of mystery, there are facts about his life of which we are certain. We know, for example, that he was born in Damascus in 1530, and that he is the author of several works, many of which are presently found in the Arabic manuscripts collection of the State Library of Berlin. These include a treatise on the history and virtues of the Grand Mosque of Damascus, and a treatise entitled: *Ten Essays on Ten Subjects*, which he dedicates to the Judge of Damascus Hasan Bey (not to be confused with the Governor of Damascus Sokulluzade Hasan Pasha, mentioned in the previous chapter) who was first appointed to this position in 1552.[18] 'Imad al-Din was also a poet, and many of his poems are collected in early sources, including verses he wrote in defence of drinking coffee during the heated sixteenth century debate in Damascus on whether or not it was *halal*, or permissible, to consume it. When 'Imad al-Din suddenly died, seemingly from a heart attack, he left behind four children. 'Abd al-Rahman Imady (1570–1641) was the eldest and was seven when his father passed away. There was also his younger brother, Ahmad, who would die before reaching twenty, and two daughters of which we know very little.

'Abd al-Rahman began studying religious sciences at an early age. During his pilgrimage to Mecca, he met an Indian Sufi shaikh, Sibghat Allah, and was initiated into the Naqshbandi order. Upon his return to Damascus, he began teaching at several religious schools, including al-Shibliyyah, al-Salmiyyah, and al-Sulaymaniyyah. And in 1621, at the age of fifty-one, he was designated by the Ottoman Sultan as the grand mufti of Damascus, or the highest religious jurist, a position he would retain until his death at the age of seventy. 'Abd al-Rahman left behind several works, including works of exegesis of Quranic verses, several manuals on how to perform various acts of worship, and a treatise on the town of Darayya, southwest of Damascus, upon which the Syrian regime would, centuries later, drop over 7000 barrel bombs.[19] His *fatawa*, or legal decisions, are also collected both separately and as parts of larger collections.

One legal decision in particular proved to have implications far beyond the immediate context within which it was made. 'Abd al-Rahman was once asked for his opinion on sects regarded as heretical, including the Druze, Isma'ilis, and Alawites. His response constituted a legal verdict given his position as the grand mufti of Damascus.[20] It was void of any semblance of tolerance. Consistent with traditional Sunni Muslim positions on these sects at the time, 'Abd al-Rahman, in essence, advocated that all these heterodox communities be forcibly converted to orthodox Islam.

Centuries later, the tenth great grandson of 'Abd al-Rahman, Muhammad Imady, was approached by an Alawite colleague during a meeting at the Prime Minister's office: 'Dr Imady, are you aware of the fact that one of your ancestors spoke strongly against us?' Muhammad Imady smiled and, in his ever-accessible diplomatic demeanour, responded: 'Had he met you, and seen for himself the values and principles you hold dear, he would have realised how wrong his position was.'[21]

'Abd al-Rahman had three sons, 'Imad al-Din, Shihab al-Din, and Ibrahim, all religious scholars, and poets like their father. With the exception of Ibrahim, his sons would also become grand muftis of

Damascus. Henceforth, all biographical works would include long entries on Imady scholars, though none ever make reference to where the family originated.

The line of muftis continued through Ibrahim's sons, 'Ali and Muhammad, both of whom would also become grand muftis. Both sons of 'Ali – Hamid and Muhammad – would become grand muftis too. A total of seven muftis in one family; no other Damascene family could claim this achievement.

Of all these muftis, Hamid Imady (1692–1758) was by far the most prominent, the most prolific, and the one who is most remembered from amongst the Imady religious scholarly line. Hamid Imady served as a mufti for over thirty-four years and his legal decisions are compiled in two large volumes, many of which are surprisingly progressive in their advocacy of women's rights. A collection of his treatises is found at Princeton, and his historical scholarly lineage is listed in a work found at Harvard.

Despite the scholarly prominence of Hamid Imady, he, and other members of the Imady family, were not detached from the daily events of Damascene society. A rare extant diary by Ibn Kinan al-Salihi shares daily events in Damascus which took place during the first half of the eighteenth century (1699–1740). Al-Salihi includes numerous references to 'Ali Imady, and his two sons, Muhammad and Hamid, documenting their involvement in various social events which convey their proximity to Damascene popular culture. When Muhammad Imady dies in 1722, al-Salihi writes of him: '… there was none more magnificent to behold than he.'[22]

By the late eighteenth century, the Imady family's scholarly contributions receded. Their descendants became wealthy landowners who were regarded as notables of Damascus. But slowly they disappear from the works on important scholars. A notable exception was 'Abd Allah Afandi Imady (d. 1891) who has been recorded by several sources as having played an important role in protecting Christian families in his own home, shielding them from the mobs during the Damascus massacre of 1860. Even as late as the 1960s, a Damascene Christian doctor refused to be paid after making a house call to check on my sick grandmother. 'We don't charge a descendant of 'Abd Allah Imady' was his rationale.

The late nineteenth/early twentieth century would signify the age of the Imady family's decline. A work from this period would even lament what had become of this once vibrant scholarly family: 'No family in Damascus produced more muftis, and scholars of such prominence and wealth. And now all that is left of this are descendants who harvest the lands once bequeathed to them.'[23]

No record exists of the Imady family participating, directly or indirectly, in the Great Arab Revolt which evicted the Ottomans from Damascus in 1918. It is clear, however, that the family was indeed in favour of the arrival of the Arab Hashemite army. Jawdat Imady, my grandfather, who was only twenty-six at the time and the eldest male member of the family (his father had died in 1906), was so happy at the news of the arrival of Prince Faisal in Damascus that he chose to present him with his most valuable Arab horse as a token of his loyalty.

There are also no records documenting the Imady family's involvement in the Battle of Maysalun (24 July 1920) between the vastly outnumbered army of the Arab Kingdom of Syria and the French Army of the Levant. Nor do we have records of their involvement in the resistance that was predominantly based in the Ghuta, or the green orchards to the east of Damascus. Only one story survives of Jawdat Imady providing wheat to the rebels in the Ghuta.[24] Even the family's wealth had largely dissipated by the early twentieth century. Because none of the Imadys had income-generating jobs, all their wealth had to come from what they already owned. As family records confirm, this period is marked by legal disputes over modest rent payments, and the occasional selling of land that was owned by several family members.

By 1930, when Muhammad Imady was born, the Imady family were in many ways impoverished aristocrats. And because the framework that had made them an elitist family – the Ottoman empire – was by then dead and buried, even their aristocratic past was now more of a liability than an advantage. The Imadys were at once prominent, yet irrelevant; proud, yet impecunious; and rooted in history, yet with no prospects of future branches. It is into these contradictory dynamics that Muhammad Imady was born, and it is precisely these dynamics that explain how he came to understand his life, and his mission.

POST-UPRISING INTROSPECTIONS: MINOR & CARDINAL SINS

Growing up in Syria, I quickly learned exactly what constituted a political sin, or an error in one's political reasoning. These were not only sins in the eyes of official Syria, they were equally sins in the eyes of popular culture, including my high school friends, all born, like me, in post-1963 Syria where Ba'thist indoctrination was ubiquitous. I knew I had committed a sin not only as a result of the looks I would instantly receive – the wide eyes staring at me with disbelief – but also because of the lecture that was certain to follow. I also learned that there were sins that could be forgiven, provided certain acts of atonement were carried out, and sins that branded you forever as suspicious and almost certainly an 'agent' of a hostile power.

Categories of Sins

Being an urban notable – *minor sin*: Urban notables are simply not very trustworthy. They are either wealthy or had been wealthy in the not-too-distant past. Either way, their wealth was acquired from oppressing peasants. Where else could it have possibly come from? Educated urban notables, especially Western-educated, are, needless to say, the most problematic. So, if you happen to belong to one of these families, you should try to avoid the subject. The worst thing you can do is to demonstrate pride in your legacy. If you happen to commit a sin of such sorts, first listen politely to the lecture that will follow, then atone for your sin by denouncing all such families as inevitably corrupt and historically of no value.

Hashemite admiration – *minor with cardinal potential*: A more advanced version of the 'urban notables' sin is the sin of regarding the Hashemites as in any sense worthy of admiration. The Great Arab Revolt should never have happened because the Ottomans, Sultan 'Abd al-Hamid in particular, were anti-Zionist. The British played the Hashemites then turned against them – end of story! Any attempt to cast them in a favourable light is a sin; a sin, I confess, I proved capable of repeatedly committing, irrespective of the reactions it generated. The problem was that I grew up in a home that was fiercely pro-everything the Hashemite revolt attempted to achieve. Even my elderly aunt would describe with pride the Syrian National Congress (1919–1920) and the enlightened constitution that it produced. And so, when I would share stories of Prince Faisal's battle cry, 'Death, in the cause of freedom, is sweet, O Arabs', when I spoke with pride about the Arab state Sharif Hussein strived to create, I was quickly silenced. A long lecture would follow, as the heads of onlookers shook with contempt.

Respect for the Peace Makers – *minor with serious cardinal potential*: I was eleven when the late Egyptian president, Anwar Sadat, visited Israel; twelve, when the Camp David Accords were signed; and twenty-eight when the Israeli-Jordanian peace deal was signed in 1994. As I watched these events, I always had a feeling of satisfaction. Not because I felt the treaties restored all of the 'rights' that should have been restored, nor because I felt they succeeded in correcting all the 'wrongs' that had been committed. I was satisfied, rather, because peace to me was intuitively superior to war, and hence all peace makers were worthy of respect, at the very least for the courage this required. I hated how Sadat was vilified in Syria after 1977, but I was wise enough not to share my feelings even with close family members. Later, when I was nearly thirty-four, I watched with sadness and disbelief as the Asad-Clinton meeting in Geneva (March 2000) failed to achieve peace. The sin here is to imply that compromise and peace are superior to pride and war. My eighth-grade teacher of *Al-Tarbiyah al-Wataniyyah* (National Upbringing) would constantly reiterate to me that in matters of national pride, only cowards compromise. My words were a sin of ignorance, but if I repeated them they would become something much worse. To share examples of any such 'compromise', regardless of who had enacted it, from the Prophet's Treaty of Hudaybiyyah to Saladin's Treaty of Ramla, was to share stories of loss and defeat. All such treaties are wrong and should be rejected on principle. My teacher and others seemed so addicted to the idea of war and conflict that I often wondered if they could digest a peace treaty, even if entirely on their terms!

Freemasonry – *cardinal*: Arab nationalists, and subsequently Islamists, have made the conscious, or unconscious, decision to adopt the entire Nazi approach to freemasonry, which in turn had been adopted from earlier European anti-Semitic propaganda. Update and embellish, and you arrive at how most Syrians, even my teenage friends, regarded freemasonry – a global secret society created with the sole purpose of advancing the Zionist project in Palestine. As such, to be called a freemason was to be stigmatized as treacherous. Do not waste your time pointing out that the zealot of all zealots, Jamal al-Din al-Afghani (or Asadabadi), had joined freemasonry along with his disciple Muhammad 'Abduh, or that even 'Abd al-Qadir al-Jaza'iri, and numerous other Syrian notables, were masons. At best, you will have them all cast as traitors and proto-Zionists. Mind you, your mere attempt to rationalize this idea is to evict you entirely from the realm of the patriots with no possible path to atonement. Hence, despite its appeal and powerful potential as a hallmark of European and general liberal Enlightenment, do not expect to find any Syrian reformers – Damascene or others – dabbling in freemasonry.

Impugning Our Glorious Past – *cardinal*: Syria was once a perfect country. Do not ask when exactly this was the case. Dates are not relevant here. The point is Syria was perfect before it was 'messed up' by foreign hostile powers. In fact, the entire Arab nation (do not attempt to define this in geographic terms or – again – try to designate a date for it) was in a glorious state before foreign powers conspired against it (see below for more details). It is a sin to imply that our past is anything short of glorious, and a very serious sin to imply that it was problematic because of what we did, rather than because of what others had done. In a recent conversation, I dared to point out that the Alawite community in Syria suffered from severe poverty in the 1950s (an indisputable fact) and that post-independence governments should have done much more to reach out to this community. My Syrian friends, Sunni and Damascene, made it clear to me that it was a serious sin to imply that our past was not perfect. The Alawites were treated fairly, and everything that transpired in Syria in the 1960s and beyond was only because of foreign conspiracies that turned the Alawites against the rest of the country, rather than an expression of a historic injustice.

Questioning the Ancient Conspiracy – *cardinal*: You might think that the Syrian regime's talk of a cosmic conspiracy against it is a fascinating new product of a Machiavellian mind. Not in the least! The Syrian regime simply adopted an ancient tradition, one that I remember well from my teenage years in Damascus. A grand conspiracy of cosmic proportions is responsible for the break-up of the Ottoman empire, the borders dividing the Arabs, the regimes that rule above them, their scientific and economic backwardness and, last but not least, Israel and everything related to it. To be ignorant of this conspiracy is a sin that can be forgiven. Denying it, on the other hand, or daring to point out that even a fragment of it may not hold up to critical analysis, is a cardinal sin for which no atonement is possible. After all, what exactly would you be proposing? That we, Syrians and Arabs, are responsible for these tragic realities? Or that we are capable of changing them, yet choose otherwise?

What is perhaps the most unfortunate aspect of all of this is just how popular these ideas remain in contemporary Syria. They successfully transform most political discussions into a minefield. At any minute, your voice will be overwhelmed by emotional outbursts, and various types of proclamations. In my case, I am quickly dismissed as an extension of my American mother. What else could possibly explain my stubborn inclination to sin? The words of my late Sufi teacher, Bashir al-Bani (1911–2008) come back to me, 'Tread carefully my son, God forgives all sins, but Syrians do not.'

Chaper II

The Sculpting of a Reformist Mind (1930–1960)

FORMATIVE YEARS

When Muhammad Imady was born on the 31 August 1930, his father, Jawdat Imady, was forty-eight, and his mother, Yusra al-Hawasili, was thirty-two. His mother had had eight prior pregnancies, of which only five daughters survived. Muhammad was the anticipated son, and was named after his great grandfather, Muhammad Imady (d. 1861). He was born in a house that belonged to his wealthy maternal grandfather, Adib Agha al-Hawasili, which was located in the Damascene neighbourhood of Bahsa, northwest of the citadel, and was one of the earliest settlements to be built outside of the Old City's walls. In the 1930s, Bahsa still retained much of its Ottoman character, but by the 1980s, historic Bahsa had been entirely demolished and replaced by characterless concrete structures. Prior to living in Bahsa, Jawdat, along with his mother, six sisters and younger brother, had lived in a large luxurious compound in Salihiyyah, northwest of the old walled city of Damascus on the lower slopes of Mount Qasiyoun. The compound was in the same vicinity as the house in which Sir Richard Burton and his wife lived during their stay in Damascus. Sadly, neither of these houses have survived. In 1926, Jawdat took the decision to move out of this comfortable dwelling after a fallout with his younger brother. The Bahsa home was meant to be a temporary residence, but it would be five years before a new home was actually purchased. In August 1931, Jawdat and his family finally moved into their new house in Muhajirin on Mount Qasiyoun overlooking Damascus. Muhammad was one year old. The district of Muhajirin, which translates as 'Immigrants', was so called because it was initially settled by Muslims fleeing Greece in the late nineteenth century. The traditional house Jawdat bought in Muhajirin would eventually be torn down in the 1940s and rebuilt as a modern four-story apartment building – three floors for the family, and one to rent out.

In 1942, at the age of twelve, Muhammad Imady graduated from his primary school, Tariq ibn Ziyad, and enrolled in Tajhiz al-Ula, later named the Jawdat al-Hashimi school, which was founded in 1936 as the first formal secondary school in Damascus. It graduated many of Syria's important thinkers and politicians, and its teaching staff included many figures destined to play an important role in Syria's history, including Michel Aflaq and Salah al-Din Bitar, the future founders of the Ba'th party.

At the age of nineteen, Muhamad was enrolled in the Faculty of Law at the University of Damascus. His father hoped his son would one day become a judge, reminiscent of his notable ancestors, but instead the few courses in economics he enrolled in captured Muhammad's imagination, and economics quickly became his lifelong passion. In 1953, he graduated first in his class and then took the civil service exam for the Ministry of Finance. He served as a government employee at the Ministry for only seven months before being called into the army to perform his mandatory 18-months service. A year into his military duties, Muhammad was seriously injured when an anti-aircraft gun was accidently lowered on his head by a fellow officer, and he spent the last six months of his service recovering and performing only desk jobs. Though he fully recovered, he would continue to suffer from regular headaches throughout his life.

After completing his army service, Muhammad was sent by the Minister of Finance, 'Abd al-Wahhab Hawmad, an old family friend, on a government scholarship to study economics at New York University. He arrived in November 1955, and by August 1956, he was married to Mildred Elaine Rippey, known as Elaine, whom he met in a reading room in NYU. In July of 1957, his first daughter, Susan Sahar, was born.

Though he was initially sent to obtain only a master's, Muhammad was able to convince the officials in Damascus to extend his stay so he could complete a PhD. By January 1960, he had obtained his doctorate and, in recognition of his distinguished academic record, he received the Founders Day Award of New York University for having achieved 'a place in the highest bracket of scholastic preferment recognized by the University'.[1]

Having completed his academic mission, Muhammad, as stipulated by his scholarship, now had to return to his country and serve the government for a minimum of eight years. Because Elaine was not fond of the idea of flying, Muhammad and his new family decided they would travel to Syria by boat. On 7 February 1960, they boarded the Hellenic Sailor. After a three-week trip across the Atlantic and the Mediterranean, Muhammad, Elaine, and their daughter Susan arrived in Beirut on 1 March 1960, and travelled to Damascus by taxi. Nearly five years earlier, Muhammad had left his home in Muhajirin as a single man who had never travelled outside of the country. He returned with an American wife, a daughter, a PhD in Economics, and, perhaps most importantly, a dramatically changed sensibility and outlook.

All the major building blocks of Muhammad Imady's reformist mind can be traced back to this formative period, which ended with his arrival back in Damascus, and the impact four specific individuals had on him: his father, his mother, his mentor, 'Abd al-Wahhab Hawmad, and his wife, Mildred Elaine Rippey.

A DAMASCENE ETHIC & A PALISADIAN SENSIBILITY

Families, like countries, move from one phase to another. Through wealth and prominence, to difficult times and irrelevance. At times, a family can experience a rebirth, though this, as is the case with countries, is not a common occurrence. A golden age is, more often than not, a singular event that is seldom replicated. By the early twentieth century, members of the Imady family could still pretend to be notables, though in actuality they were living in an age that was largely indifferent to their prominent past. What is even more important is the fact that the income they earned from the land they still owned had reached a point when it could no longer maintain the lifestyle of a family that needed no other source of income.

Jawdat Imady had all the eccentric characteristics one would associate with a notable, including an aversion to the idea of being employed or managed by anyone, an unwillingness to compromise anything for anyone, and an overall indifference to how others, including close family members, regarded him. Already the father of five surviving children, by the time Muhammad was born, Jawdat was entirely established in his ways. Jawdat was the archetypical embodiment of the patriarchal head of the family, whose rules could not be questioned and who was seldom willing to engage in an intimate conversation. His children learned of him from the stories their mother would share, and by observing from a distance how he interacted, or chose not to interact, with various people and events. One story in particular captures Jawdat's sense of himself. Through his wife's family connections, Jawdat was appointed at a government department to collect taxes from peasants and oversee the selling of their agricultural produce. Only a few hours after he had left for his job on his first day, however, Jawdat returned home markedly upset. When his wife inquired about what had taken place, his response was that someone had dared to ask him, an Imady notable, to carry out a task!

Another important story concerns the reason Jawdat had chosen to leave his mother, six sisters, and young brother, and move into a different home. Jawdat felt his younger brother had been behaving in a manner that was not morally consistent with the family's heritage, and when his mother and sisters sided with his brother, Jawdat simply walked out. Eventually, he would purchase his own house, but his unwillingness to compromise despite the financial burden entailed in his decision is the important point here. His children, Muhammad in particular, would see in such stories not the triumph of an idealist, but rather the self-destructive nature of excessive idealism. As a young man, and as an adult, there were few things Muhammad Imady hated more than intransigence.

Jawdat's impact on his son, ironically, was to instil in him an awareness of what he did not want to be. In contrast to his father, Muhammad Imady would grow up keen to have a job, at peace with being supervised and managed, and eager to dedicate himself completely to what he regarded as his professional mission. It was as though he had acquired a Damascene version of the Protestant ethic: a commitment to work that placed a spiritual value on the capacity to work hard, daily and consistently, irrespective of conditions, and regardless of odds. For the vast majority of his life, Muhammad would work for a minimum of twelve hours a day, with no annual vacations of any type. He was so eager to work, so eager to disassociate from his father's example, that at the age of seventeen he got a summer job in Nawa, a village in southern Syria that required, at the time, a three-hour bus ride from Damascus. Even at the age of ninety, he would still refuse to fully retire; opting instead to preside over the board of the Arab International University, attend regular meetings and take part in the board's major decision making.

Furthermore, as a direct result of his father's example, Muhammad Imady came to regard the willingness to compromise as the critical foundation of any meaningful act of reform. Rewording the famous quote ascribed to Otto Von Bismarck, Muhammad would repeat, 'Reform is the art of the possible.' Hence, those who insist on the impossible are operating outside of the realm of reform.

Muhammad, however, did not disregard the entirety of his father's example. He identified himself with what might be called the essential traits of an heir of the Imady religious scholarly line. This included performing the five daily prayers, fasting in Ramadan, charity, pilgrimage, and refraining from drinking alcohol. To this, Muhammad would also add smoking simply because he hated the idea of an addiction.

In lieu of his father's model, Muhammad found alternative inspiration – by chance or deliberate design – in his very home. In 1947, when Muhammad was only seventeen, his father let out an apartment in the newly rebuilt Imady building to 'Abd al-Wahhab Hawmad, a lawyer from Aleppo who had been elected to parliament that year. Hawmad had several qualities that Muhammad would quickly come to appreciate and adopt as his own. Hawmad was well educated, with a doctorate in criminal justice from the University of Paris. He was dedicated to a strong work ethic, having had several jobs, including working as a lawyer and a university professor.

The only aspect of Hawmad that was not readily accessible to Muhammad's young mind was his involvement in politics. This, even at a young age, was seen by Muhammad as distracting and ultimately futile. What he highly admired was the educated, hardworking man who would eventually become a minister of finance (1955–1956) in perfect time to send the newly graduated Muhammad on a scholarship to NYU. Hawmad is, in fact, remembered as having launched one of Syria's largest foreign scholarship programs which sent over 300 students to various universities in the US and Europe.

It was Adib al-Shishakli's coup in December 1949, however, that cemented Muhammad Imady's approach to politics. Two of his future brothers-in-law were arrested and imprisoned after the coup. And in November 1951, Hawmad himself was also briefly imprisoned. Al-Shishakli regarded all those who supported union between Syria and Hashemite Iraq as enemies, and Hawmad was at the time a firm believer in the dream of a Hashemite Greater Syria, though he would later become a Nasserite. After the Ba'thist coup of March 1963, Hawmad was also imprisoned for five months, this time because the Ba'thists, though officially pro-unification with Egypt, were very suspicious of pro-Nasserite figures.

Reflecting on the suffering his close ones endured, and more importantly, the lack of any tangible achievement that resulted from their ordeal, Muhammad concluded that to be involved in politics in Syria was to be willing to be participate in a dangerous gamble that had repercussions even for family members and friends. Membership of a political party was the gateway to becoming involved in this dangerous gamble, and hence, Muhammad vowed never to become a member of any party. Even decades later, when serving as a minister in a Ba'th-led government, when he was encouraged to become a member of the Ba'th party, he still regarded this as contrary to his principles and, politely, declined.

But to stop here would not fully capture Muhammad Imady's interaction with the world of politics. In addition to his aversion to politics, he was also averse to all things revolutionary in nature. Even when it came to causes he fully supported, like Syrian independence, he believed that the price of revolutionary activities was too high and the practices often far too volatile in nature. During his school years, Muhammad had often participated in demonstrations against the French Mandate. However, although he willingly participated in these demonstrations, he remembers how during the last such protest prior to the French withdrawal from Syria, his schoolmates made a bonfire of their French textbooks. He, however, discreetly chose to keep his books unharmed. He simply did not regard such acts of protest as meaningful or helpful.

There can be no doubt that Syria's nationalists and rebels played a significant role in securing Syria's independence in 1947. However, it is equally true that had it not been for the direct military intervention of British forces in 1945, in what came to be known as the Levant Crisis, the French occupation would have continued far longer and Syrian casualties would have been far higher. This was even recognized by President Shukri Quwatli who granted General Sir Bernard Paget, leader of the British forces, the status of honorary citizen of Damascus and presented him with a Damascene sword, now preserved at the Imperial War Museum, as a token of appreciation for the important role the British carried out in curbing French ambitions in Syria. The road to independence was a winding one and had not been paved solely by revolutionaries. None of this went unnoticed by the observant Muhammad Imady.

Though the Damascene ethic Muhammad Imady possessed was uncommon, the sensibility he acquired over time was far scarcer. It was a sensibility that was first implanted in him by his mother, Yusra al-Hawasili. Once, as she was watching an Egyptian war documentary that showed Israeli soldiers being killed, her eyes teared up even as others in the room cheered. When her children inquired why she seemed so sad, her response was: 'But they [the Israeli soldiers] have mothers, too.'[2] Anyone who has lived in Syria would recognize that empathy for those regarded as having committed injustices towards Syrians or Arabs is not a common attribute.

Against this background, one comes to understand that Yusra al-Hawasili was articulating a sentiment that could easily have branded her, outside of the small circle of her own home, as harbouring traitorous inclinations. Among all her children, none was closer to Yusra's sensibility than her son, Muhammad. And as was the case with his encounter with 'Abd al-Wahhab Hawmad, it was either by chance or deliberate design that Muhammad would meet someone who would reinforce what his mother had planted and transform it over time into a spiritual, human-centred approach to people and events.

PROFILE: MILDRED ELAINE RIPPEY[3]

Mildred Elaine Rippey was born in April 1934 in New York. Until she met and married Muhammad Imady in 1956, Elaine, as she was known, lived with her mother and two sisters at their home in Palisades, a hamlet in the town of Orangetown in Rockland County, where her maternal Dutch Presbyterian ancestors had lived since their forebear Jacob Post bought a farm of ninety acres in 1765. Through her direct maternal line, she goes back, ten great grandmothers earlier, to Christina Jans van Westerhaut who was born in The Hague in 1637.

There was a time when the Posts owned most of the houses in Palisades. But they either moved elsewhere or died out until, by the mid-twentieth century, only one Post family remained, Mildred Lawrence Post Rippey, and her three daughters. Her husband, my grandfather,

Harold Garst Rippey was an educated man, who once worked as a book salesman before succumbing to alcoholism and moving out of his family's home. He wasn't the first Rippey to have trouble with alcohol. In fact, the Rippeys, who were originally Huguenots from southern France, had only found peace in Clark County, Kentucky where they owned land and prospered. From the moment William David Rippey, my great great grandfather, decided to move to Pueblo Colorado, he and his family were met with one ordeal after another. America's industrial cities of the late nineteenth/early twentieth century were not kind to the Rippeys.

The wife Harold left, but never divorced, Mildred Lawrence Post Rippey, was a strong woman, who wrote poetry and worked at the Palisades library. She loved Roosevelt, Kennedy, and later corresponded with Jimmy Carter. She was a pure liberal democrat who was ecumenical to the extent of not hesitating to call herself in later life a 'Muslim Presbyterian'. It was in her home that Muhammad's future wife, Mildred Elaine Rippey, would grow up, with an even stronger identification with liberal values. Elaine didn't hesitate to express her opposition to America's foreign policy long before she met Muhammad. In her very conservative high school, she remembers standing up and voicing her opposition to America's covert role in overthrowing the popular Iranian Prime Minister, Mohammed Mossadegh. During the infamous McCarthy investigations, Elaine had been a student at NYU studying English literature. To express her opposition to what she regarded as a witch-hunt, she became part of an organization called 'Students for Academic Freedom' and protested the firing of three NYU professors for invoking their right to take the Fifth Amendment. Some family acquaintances in Palisades even referred to her as 'Red Mildred' because of her leftist political positions. And though she did attend Sunday service with her mother and sisters at Palisades' Presbyterian chapel, by the time she was an NYU student she regarded herself as a disillusioned Christian.

Soon after Elaine met Muhammad, she converted to Islam. The concept of God in Islam, or at least how Muhammad presented it, seemed far more consistent with her own sensibility. Initially, her conversion only meant fasting during the month of Ramadan, and not drinking alcohol or eating pork, though decades later she would perform the daily prayers and go on pilgrimage to Mecca. Islam's prohibition of alcohol left a particularly favourable impression on Elaine, the daughter of a man she had always felt would have been so much more had it not been for his alcoholism. But nothing was more striking to her than Muhammad's innate spirituality, his mother's gift, which saw no conflict between his adamant desire to visit Elaine's family at her home in Palisades, and asking her mother, after dinner, in which room he could perform his night prayer.

But while Elaine would convert to the religion of Muhammad, he would likewise embrace her distinct sensibility, a Palisadian sensibility which was thirsty and curious about the meaningful and the authentic and withdrawn from and disinterested in the shallow and the artificial. It was a sensibility that regarded all humans, irrespective of race or creed, as having spiritual worth, and entitled to live free of political dehumanisation and economic marginalisation; an outlook on society that seemed far more akin to Scandinavia than the America of the late 1950s. And just as Elaine's Islam would separate her from her world, Muhammad's Palisadian sensibility would, upon his return to Damascus, serve to separate him from his. Mindful of how hostile his friends, and even relatives, would be to this sensibility, Muhammad kept his lenses, the way he perceived things, largely to himself. His sense of alienation from how most of his acquaintances understood their realities would often make him confide in his wife that he felt like he had been born on a different planet.

POST-UPRISING INTROSPECTIONS: ALL THE SYRIANS YOU WILL MEET

I begin with the Syrians I met in 'the wilderness of North America', an evocative term once used by Malcom X.[4]

Jude is a Syrian woman who was born in Damascus. She is a Presbyterian Christian who taught at one of the prestigious international schools in Damascus. Around mid-2011, Jude realized that something very ugly had happened to her country. The regime wanted her to believe a certain narrative: that her Sunni Muslim friends whom she had known for decades constituted an existential threat against her. It was a narrative that she felt was being pushed on her daily and systematically. This was long before ISIS, and even long before the FSA (Free Syrian Army) was heard of.

> We were still in the phase of peaceful protests, we were still in the phase when Muslims and Christians were marching together, and they wanted me to believe that only the regime can guarantee my safety and the safety of my family.

By 2013, Jude and her family had resettled in California. Today, when Syria is brought up, she says in a lowered voice, almost by reflex though she is well aware that no one in Anahiem cares about her political views on Syria:

> History will record that the worse thing this regime did wasn't using force; everyone when cornered uses force. The worse thing this regime did was the way it purposely turned us against each other. It will take a century for Syria to recover from these wounds.

An entirely different perspective is shared by none other than Jude's sister, Lara. Lara, in fact, tries to interrupt Jude several times. Her point is simple:

> Sunnis can't be trusted. They did all the things the government said they did and more! And had the government not crushed them, they would have returned Syria to the dark ages.

I remind Lara that the regime doesn't use the term 'Sunnis' to describe the opposition. This time Jude interrupts,

> They may not use the term, but we all know who they mean.

Let's move on to Europe.

Ahmad lives (or perhaps lived, I have lost contact with him for some time) in Germany. He was twenty when he arrived in Berlin – one of the Syrians who arrived in Lesbos, a Greek island, by boat, and then later made his way northwest into Germany. Ahmad would speak beautifully about all the academic and professional dreams he wanted to accomplish, about how much he respected the West, how much he admired Germany which he felt had treated him exceptionally well. But when Syria would come up, a different Ahmad would start to speak, an Ahmad determined for revenge. He would say such things to me as:

> I will never forgive what this regime has done. Even if I am 80, and I have an opportunity to get my revenge from this regime, I will not hesitate.

As Ahmad spoke, I would recall stories of how an angry Syrian followed Adib al-Shishakli, once president of Syria, all the way to Ceres, a small municipality in the Brazilian highlands.[5] Nawaf Ghazali [often incorrectly spelled Ghazaleh], who had lost his mother and sister as a result of Shishakli's bombardment of Jabal al-Druz, approached the ex-president as he crossed a bridge between Ceres and Rialma, and shot him five times.[6] Just how many Nawafs have been produced since 2011, only God knows!

But perhaps the most peculiar Syrian I have met is Imad, who lives in Manchester. To Imad, everything that has transpired in Syria since the Uprising is the result of an American-Israeli conspiracy. The regime, and in particular its army, are fighting for Syria's unity and integrity against those funded by Saudi Arabia and the Gulf. The irony is that Imad left Syria even before 2011 because he couldn't stand the corruption. He had the option to leave because he had a British passport. Another Syrian who happens to be sitting with us reminds him that it was against corruption that his fellow Syrians started protesting in March 2011. But Imad is relentless: 'They were nothing other than American agents and Wahhabis.'

The kindest way Imad is willing to describe them is as 'simpletons who were deceived by a grand "cosmic conspiracy".' A few minutes later in the conversation, Imad finds it perfectly appropriate to talk about how regime checkpoints are blackmailing the population, how nothing can be done in Syria without paying bribes to officials. At no point is the irony captured by him, just as much as at no point is it lost on me.

In London, I met Sami, an older Syrian who reminded me somewhat of my father. He spoke of how none of this was necessary, of how it could all have been avoided, of how tragic it all was. He sees the opposition as mostly to blame because 'they kept provoking the beast until it came after them.'

But regardless of what he would share with me, he always seemed to return to one particular point, his fear of where Syria is headed:

> No one seems to understand how close we are to being irreversibly broken as a country. Some say we have already seen the worst. I don't believe this to be true. I believe that unless a miracle takes place, the worst is yet to come.

Hasan met me in Paris over coffee not too long ago. Hasan is an Alawite from the beautiful town of Draikish. He appears to have studied history because he was constantly making historical references.

> You [he referred to me as somehow representative of all of Syria's Sunnis] have been ruling us and oppressing us since the Fatimids were overthrown in 1170. That's 800 years, my friend. And if you think we are willing to let go of Syria to be oppressed all over again, you are as wrong as an Omar in Qom.[7]

My attempt to remind him that even 'Ali, the Prophet's cousin, named one of his sons Omar is easily dismissed.

> You mean 'Umar al-Atraf, well he wasn't the type of son that any father would be proud of, nor an Omar you should bring up!'[8]

Had I known then about 'Umar al-Ashraf, the son of 'Ali, Zayn al-'Abidin, I would have brought him up since he is regarded very highly by Sunnis and Shi'is alike,[9] but all of this is clearly a digression. The point isn't how much Hasan didn't like my name, the point rather is that he was also very angry.

Syrians are angry, and their anger is based on fear. Fear of each other, fear of the regime, fear of the opposition, fear of what is, and fear of what will be. This fear is manifested in various ways, at times subtle, at times forthright, at times rationalized, and at times barely coherent. But it is there, and it has become the trademark of Syrians post-2011.

Though concerned with a very different geography, and indeed cosmic conspiracy, George Lucas, ironically, captures this process best:

> Fear is the path to the Dark Side. Fear leads to anger, anger leads to hate, hate leads to suffering.[10]

Chapter III

The Rites of Passage (1960–1972)

TURBULENT YEARS

When Muhammad Imady arrived in Damascus in March 1960, he had already acquired all the ingredients necessary to embark on a career of an apolitical technocrat; a man of expertise who is willing to work under any regime as long as it allows him to contribute meaningfully to his country and people. The distinct qualities he exemplified were unusual, even amongst those Syrians who had, like him, studied in the West and married a foreigner. His relentless work ethic, his intrinsic inclination towards diplomacy, his spiritual religiosity, and the home he built for himself inside his wife's world – all these were the distinct pillars of his reformist mind. In addition, Muhammad Imady was one of those very uncommon reformers who would operate from within. It was one thing to be a reformer at a school, a mosque or a private law practice. Imady was destined to carry the standard of reform, literally and metaphorically, inside the very lion's den.

The Syria Imady had left in late 1955 was not the Syria he returned to in 1960. The critical year was 1958. It was the year his father died a few months after a stroke, and the year Syria had transformed from a largely democratic political system to the United Arab Republic (UAR), an absolute presidency ruled from Cairo in which all political parties were disbanded. Muhammad had actually left New York for a brief trip to Cairo in March 1959 to attend an Arab students conference. During this meeting, he was introduced to Jamal 'Abd al-Nasir, and pictures were taken of the UAR's president surrounded by proud Arab students. Unlike his younger brother who would have a bust made of Nasir to place in his home, Muhammad Imady had mixed feelings toward the president. He was, of course, in favour of many of the ideals with which Nasir identified, including the creation of a unified, developed, and strong Arab state. He was also in favour of empowering the poor and providing them with economic opportunities. But the methods Nasir used to advance his objectives, and the revolutionary discourse he often employed were all inconsistent with Imady's sensibility, though he would confide these thoughts only to his wife.

Before Hafiz al-Asad took power in November 1970, Imady would work within three markedly different political contexts: the UAR, from his arrival in March 1960 and until 28 September 1961; the Separatist Era, a turbulent democratic framework which lasted from 29 September 1961 until 7 March 1963; and, finally, the neo-Ba'thist regime, which lasted from 8 March 1963 until 13 November 1970 when Hafiz al-Asad carried out a coup, which came to be known as the Corrective Movement. What is ironic, and instructive, is that throughout all of these changes, each of these distinct periods, Muhammad Imady was regarded as a valuable economist who had no political affiliation that classified him as suspicious or potentially untrustworthy.

In each of these periods, Imady's expertise was recognised by an important official, who would subsequently proceed to take Imady under his wing. This form of political patronage was extremely important throughout these periods, as it continues to be today in Syria. An official is primarily defined by the patron with whom he or she is identified. Without this form of definition, the risks of being marginalised, neutralised or even eliminated are multiplied.

In the first phase, and in addition to becoming a professor of economics at the University of Damascus (a position he would retain until 1996), Imady was adopted by Nur al-Din Kahhalah, Minister of Planning and Vice President of the UAR. Upon his return to Syria, Imady was expected to work at the Ministry of Finance, since it was through this ministry that he had been sent on scholarship to America. 'Abd al-Wahhab Hawmad, the Minister of Finance, had signed Imady's scholarship to the US in late 1955. In March 1960, Imady wanted Hawmad to sign his transfer to the Ministry of Planning. Because his PhD was in economic planning, a new field at the time, Imady felt that working at the Ministry of Planning would provide him with the ideal opportunity to apply his new expertise. Hawmad agreed, and when Imady met the Minister of Planning, Nur al-Din Kahhalah, who, like Imady, had been educated in the US, the transfer was immediately formalised. Along with Kahhalah,

Imady would play an instrumental role in preparing Syria's first Five Year Plan (1960–1965). And by January 1961, Imady had become Kahhalah's trusted advisor, accompanying him on many of his official trips.

During the brief period which has come to be known as the Separatist Era (29 September 1961–7 March 1963), the State Planning Commission where Imady worked ceased to be as important as it was during the UAR. Many of the new officials who took office during this period were not in favour of socialist policies or the type of economic planning associated with socialist economic systems. Furthermore, though Imady did not belong to a pro-Nasserite grouping of any kind and had, as previously noted, important reservations about the UAR, he was, nevertheless, known as being in support of the union with Egypt. Indeed, it wouldn't be difficult to argue that the majority of Syrians at the time were in favour of some type of unified Arab state. Still, the new officials who were appointed to the Ministry of Planning after the UAR came to an end found it difficult to place their trust in a man who had been the confidant of the UAR's Vice President. And yet, once again, Imady's expertise would be quickly recognised, this time by Husni al-Sawwaf, the Governor of the Central Bank, who asked Imady in 1962 to travel with him to Germany and to the US to secure various development loans for infrastructure projects.

Though the period between the Ba'th coup of 8 March 1963, and Hafiz al-Asad's coup of 13 November 1970, is usually regarded as constituting one era, in actuality it includes two major phases. The first lasted until 20 February 1966, when the Ba'th party's old guard and intellectuals dominated the government. The second began on 21 February 1966, when young Ba'th army officers took over and the majority of the old guard left the country.

During the first phase, Imady was held in high esteem by Major General Ghassan Haddad, the Minister of Planning from 13 April 1963 to 23 September 1965. Haddad reports in his memoirs that in April 1964 he asked Salah al-Din Bitar, the Prime Minister-designate, to appoint Imady as Minister of Planning. Instead, Bitar chose to reinstate Haddad as minister. Yet, during his tenure, Haddad's reliance on Imady was significant, and it was during this period that the second Five Year Plan (1965–1970) was prepared. As was the case with the first, Imady was one of the key figures who prepared this important document.

Under the Microscope: The Snowdon Spy Ring[1]

In 1965, several spy rings were discovered in Damascus. The first involved a Syrian man named Farhan Atasi who had lived in New York and married an American. He returned to Syria in 1959 with his wife, Joan Ganim (Atasi). At some point in 1964, Atasi was afflicted with Bell's Palsy, from which Imady had also suffered in July 1963. This shared physical ailment was the reason Imady was introduced to Atasi. An American woman who knew both Farhan's wife, Joan, and Imady's wife, Elaine, thought it would be a good idea to introduce Farhan, who was very depressed about his facial paralysis, to Muhammad who had by then recovered from the ailment. They met briefly, and Imady assured him that this would soon be behind him. Only a few months had passed when Imady and his wife would be shocked to watch on television the trial of Farhan Atasi for espionage. Atasi was accused of having been recruited by Walter S. Snowdon, the Second Secretary of the US Embassy, to gather information on a Soviet navy weapon. Farhan shared his mission with his cousin, Lieutenant Colonel 'Abd al-Mu'in al-Hakimi. Some initial information was obtained, and payments were made to the bank accounts of both Atasi and Hakimi. When Hakimi asked some of his army contacts to help in acquiring the information Snowdon was after, they informed the authorities and by December 1964 both Atasi and Hakimi were arrested. This took place approximately one month prior to the arrest of Eli Cohen, the famous Israeli spy, on 18 January 1965. Snowdon, and his secretary Martha Scherrer were expelled, and the trial of Atasi and Hakimi was aired on TV.

The climate was charged, and tolerance was low, and had Atasi mentioned that he had been visited only recently by Dr Muhammad Imady, an important official in the Ministry of Planning, this could have had a traumatic impact on Imady's life. In his televised trial, Atasi, still visibly under the effects of the torture he endured during his interrogation, did not digress and focused on his relationship with Snowdon and Hakimi. At one point during his trial, he stated that all his confessions had been obtained through electric torture, a charge the court dismissed. On 23 February 1965, Atasi was hanged and Hakimi was shot by a firing squad, only three months before Eli Cohen was to meet the same fate. The fact that Atasi had actually renounced his Syrian citizenship and was a naturalised American did not alleviate his sentence. His pregnant wife and two children left Syria shortly after.

TUTORING THE PRESIDENT

Situated on the western side of Mount Qasiyoun is the neighbourhood of Muhajirin (Arabic for 'immigrants'), given this name after the area was settled by refugees from the Balkans (1890), Greece (1896), and Crete (1900). Muhajirin is also the site of the old presidential palace, which was built by Nazem Pasha, the last Ottoman governor of Damascus. Damascene families began to move into Muhajirin in the early twentieth century after recognising it as an attractive suburb of the city. Before becoming a modern four-floor building, the Imady residence in Muhajirin was an Arab-styled house with a courtyard and a fountain. It was torn down in the late 1940s and rebuilt as a modern building, albeit with some very strange structural features including an inner courtyard that was overlooked by the bedroom windows of the higher apartments. Two unmarried sisters of Muhammad Imady lived on the first floor, Muhammad and his family lived on the second, and his unmarried brother lived on the third. The fourth floor was usually rented out.

In 1962, not too far from where Imady lived, Hafiz al-Asad rented an apartment further up the mountain in Muhajirin. At times, Imady and Asad would cross paths at the small local grocery store owned by a disabled man whom everyone referred to as Abu Tahsin. He didn't use a wheelchair, but he moved quickly on his two crutches. Years later, Abu Tahsin loved to share the story of how Asad once stopped his motorcade and instructed his guards to invite him into his car so he could give him a ride back home. In contrast to such stories that conveyed how loyal Asad was to his friends, there were other stories. These stories conveyed just how ruthless Asad could be, like the story of how a young man was shot because he accidentally crossed the street as the presidential motorcade drove by.

Though they lived for a while in the same neighbourhood, Imady's relationship with Asad remained distant and formal. A decade later, Muhammad Imady became Minister of State for Planning Affairs (March 1972) and, subsequently, Minister of Economy (December 1972). Imady was not qualified for this position, not according to the standards of Syria's Ba'th party at least. After all, Imady belonged to a family that didn't even regard itself as bourgeois. Indeed, the Imadys regarded themselves as noble aristocrats. And it didn't help that some of the Imady scholars of the Ottoman age had written *fatawa* (religious legal positions) against the Alawite sect. Nor did it help that he had a PhD in Economics from New York University and had committed the treacherous act (from the perspective of most Ba'thists) of marrying an 'imperialist' American from Palisades, New York. As though this was not enough, Imady regularly prayed and was not embarrassed to walk on a weekly basis to Al-Murabit Mosque near his home to perform the Friday prayers. Even worse still, he had not found it existentially necessary to join the Ba'th party, or any other political party for that matter. In short, he embodied everything Ba'thists loved to hate. And yet in spite of all this, Hafiz al-Asad would choose this man to be his chief economic official from the time he became president until his death. There is, however, an explanation for this enigma, and it is found in a story that took place in the late 1960s.

In 1969, several Syrian generals, including Hafiz al-Asad, were enrolled in a programme of military sciences that was organised by a Russian academy. Most of the professors were brought in from the Soviet Union to teach this elite group of Syrian generals. When it came to the course on the economy of war, a decision was made to recruit a local economist to teach the course, and Imady, who taught part time at the University of Damascus, was selected. So it was that Muhammad Imady found himself teaching the intricate features of war economy to Hafiz al-Asad, Mustapha Tlas, Naji Jamil and other important generals of the time, thirty of them in total. Asad, who was far too proud than to ask questions in the presence of his military colleagues, would arrange to meet Imady privately to acquire a stronger command of the subject.

In March 1972, after Asad had settled in his new position as the undisputed ruler of Syria, he had his assistant phone the Imady household. The message was brief, yet life changing: 'Dr Imady, you have been chosen by the President to be Minister of Planning.' Ironically, the phone call came as Imady and his wife were about to leave Syria. Imady had been offered a position with the United Nations Development Programme (UNDP) in Libya and had promised to be in Tripoli on 1 April 1972. Rather than joining a UN agency, Imady instead found himself initiated into the circle of new cabinet ministers, who were, in their vast majority, hardcore party members with strong ideological convictions.

Hafiz al-Asad had clearly come to admire Imady, enough to make him a member of his inner circle, but the admiration was not one-sided. Imady, too, admired Asad and had many reasons to feel indebted to him. Asad, starting in 1969 and until his death in 2000, would repeatedly provide Imady with a layer of protection that often proved life-saving. The first such event took place in late 1969/early 1970 when an assistant of Imady's at the Ministry of Planning, a man named Badr al-Din al-Siba'i, accused Imady of sharing classified information without prior authorization. In the charged climate of the 1960s, this accusation would have entailed Imady being put on trial for treason.

PROFILE: BADR AL-DIN AL-SIBA'I[2]

Badr al-Din al-Siba'i was born in Homs in 1918. He studied law, and in 1938, he joined the Syrian Communist Party, which was first founded in 1924. He subsequently travelled to France and obtained a doctorate in law. Upon his return to Syria, he became a leading member of the party, and suffered, often along with his fellow party members, from the arbitrary arrests and restrictions imposed by the regime's security apparatus. In 1959, Siba'i left Syria again – this time with his wife, Najah Sa'ati, also a leading figure in the Syrian Communist Party – heading for Moscow where he would obtain a doctorate in economics. Siba'i returned to Syria in 1964 and joined the Ministry of Planning. By then, he was known as a prolific author and translator, and had established his own publishing house specialising in Marxist works. In short, Siba'i was an intellectual heavyweight and a political force, not a man to be easily dismissed.

Siba'i wanted to bring several of his fellow party members into the Ministry of Planning, possibly as part of a strategy pursued by the Syrian Communist Party to infiltrate key government institutions. He first attempted to pursue this goal via the Minister of Planning, Naji al-Darawshah. When the minister declined to entertain his request, Siba'i turned to Imady for help. Imady politely explained that he neither had the authority to hire these individuals, nor was it proper for him to pressure the minister into a matter that was essentially political in nature. In response, Siba'i accused Imady of sharing classified information relating to Syria's

GDP with the Planning Institute in Egypt. Since the minister had to have authorised this, Siba'i's accusation implied a conspiracy between Imady and the minister to share state secrets with another country. Perhaps, Siba'i's plan was to get rid of both individuals so as to be able to bring in his comrades whom the minister had declined to employ. Though Imady repeatedly explained that all the data shared was found in public UN reports, and that the purpose of sharing it with the Egyptian institute was to make use of their computerised processing unit, the inflamed words of Siba'i resonated in the charged political climate and eventually found welcome ears. Just when Imady was convinced that he was about to be put on trial for treason, he decided to turn to the general he had once tutored, Hafiz al-Asad. He sent a message via Mustapha Tlas, Asad's long-time friend and future Minister of Defence, in which he explained what had taken place with Siba'i. Asad's response was swift. Siba'i was transferred out of the Ministry of Planning to the Ministry of Industry, and the entire subject was abruptly dropped. As though by magic, it was no longer a topic of conversation. The dark cloud had been lifted.

When asked, decades later, what he had learned from this event, Imady responded: 'I learned that, in this setting, you are not eliminated because of what you do, you are eliminated because of what you don't do.'

POST-UPRISING INTROSPECTIONS: OF MICE AND MEN

Exploring Syria's political history in the 1960's can easily feel like reading sequels to John Steinbeck's novella, *Of Mice and Men*; unknown sequels that are often far more dramatic in their twists and turns than anything America's 1930s could have actually inspired. A recurrent theme of this period is how the year 1963 changed everything. Numerous are the 'men' who built themselves winter homes – homes that appeared safe and secure – only for these to be suddenly razed. The forces of destruction were unleashed by a system that was incrementally and systematically after raw power. By 1970, this process of crowning and eliminating was complete, and those who found themselves homeless, the 'mice' of Steinbeck's story, are the exiled, imprisoned or killed in Syria's story.

Regardless of your background and motive, participating in Syria's post-1963 politics amounted to engaging in high-stakes gambling. This metaphor helps one come to terms with how these stories ended. All the figures involved must have known that to be engaged in Syria's army or politics (or both) was a very dangerous game with potentially very serious consequences. Even the 'technocrats', like Muhammad Imady, who worked along with these politicians, were treading on dangerous ground. What is fascinating is to focus on what happened in the moments in which it became clear that they didn't have a winning hand.

First, there are those who simply opted to 'exit'. Suicide was not an uncommon ending in Syria's post-1963 political world. Yes, there are many who firmly believe that these suicides were actually disguised assassinations. Yet, since I am inherently allergic to conspiracy theories, given the overwhelming lack of evidence confirming them, in my mind these were simply men who committed suicide after realising that they had been (or were very close to being) eliminated. 'Abd al-Karim al-Jundi (1932–1969), from the north-western town of al-Salamiyyah, is reported to have committed suicide while on the phone with 'Ali Zaza. His final words being, 'Tell Hafiz [al-Asad] I am leaving Syria for him.'[3] One wonders if the memory of this event came back to Asad when he was informed that Mahmud al-Zu'bi (1935–2000), the man who had served as his prime minister for nearly thirteen years, had also taken his own life. It was clearly impossible to predict who would lose his calm and why. Ghazi Kan'an (1942–2005), the man who was once feared by the strongest figures in Lebanon, the man one phone call from whom could change the lives of hundreds, decided one Wednesday afternoon that to press the eject button himself was far more dignified than what the forces of elimination had planned for him.

It is almost eerily tragic how the exits of these men would frequently be followed by the exit of a close relative. Jundi's suicide was followed by the suicide of his wife; Zu'bi's by the death of his son Humam, allegedly by an overdose; and, nearly a year after Ka'an's suicide, his brother, too, took his own life, or for those who can't possibly accept this, was found dead on some train tracks.

Then there are those who blinked – who, at the very last second, froze rather than make the decision to depart with 'dignity'. This is a much larger list that includes figures like Salah Jadid (1926–1993), the idealist from the beautiful mountainous village of Duwayr Ba'bdah where on clear days even the sea is visible. On this list, too, were Nur al-Din al-

Atasi (1929–1992), Ibrahim Makhus (1925–2013), and Yusuf Zuʿayyin (1931–2016) – the three 'doctors' of the Baʿth leadership who were all, like Jadid, unable to bring themselves to the clarity that Hafiz al-Asad had; specifically, that this was an existential battle that would not show respect for friendship (all had known each other for decades), communal allegiance (both Jadid and Makhus were Alawites like Asad), or to ideological convictions (all were firm believers in the principles of the Baʿth). On 16 November 1970, Asad sent the head of military police, 'Ali al-Madani, from the hardcore Sunni town of Hama, to arrest all three men. The list of those in this category is far longer than is mentioned in most books documenting this event. There were, of course, some who managed to escape, like Makhus to Algeria and, earlier, Muhammad 'Imran (1922–1972) to Lebanon. But in the end, even Jordanian members of the National Leadership, such as Hakim al-Fayez (1932–2013) and Dafi al-Jamʿani (1927–2020), figures whose only crime had been to vocalise their support for Atasi rather than Asad, found themselves in prison for at least twenty years. By the early nineties, when Asad decided to release these prisoners, some, like Jadid, had already died and others were very close.

There are always exceptions, no doubt, especially when fate seems to intervene in inexplicable ways. Yusuf Zuʿayyin was diagnosed in 1981 with a terminal brain tumour, and subsequently released only for him to be operated on in the UK. He went on to live in the shadows in Prague and later Stockholm until 2013.

We must also speak of those who ran away; those who realised that they were about to be killed or arrested, and so got in a car and headed for the border. Many would find out that departing Syria was by no means the end of the story. Some chose to live in Lebanon, where they were drugged and kidnapped, only to wake up in a prison in Mazzah. Others, like Muhammad 'Imran, were assassinated in Beirut, perhaps because kidnapping him proved too risky. The numerous figures who left Syria after 2011 must live in fear that the countries they chose to abide in – like Qatar, Jordan, or Kuwait – will one day restore their relations with the Syrian regime and send them on a one-way journey back to Damascus. Of these, Asʿad Mustafa comes to mind, a man, currently living in exile in Kuwait, whom I knew well as the Minister of Agriculture and Rural Development during the days I worked for UNDP and who was trying to launch a microfinance programme in rural Syria. During our meetings, I would consistently get the feeling that this man, like my father, did not quite fit in the system he was obligated to defend. Perhaps Mustafa felt this too when he finally decided to 'defect'. I find myself wondering if he and others like him regret their decision. But the only other viable option for Mustafa, and many others, was to remain silent and disappear into the shadows; a very difficult art mastered only by a few.

The option of 'living in the shadows' is by far the most intriguing to me, perhaps because it was chosen by some of the most interesting political figures Syria has produced in its recent past. Or perhaps because it reminds me of how my father lived after Hafiz al-Asad died. These figures rose to high prominence but never lost sight of the fact that in post-1963 Syria they were, in essence, metaphorical mice, the mice of Steinbeck's story, and hence when the forces of elimination came after them, they simply faded. Fading is an art that was mastered by figures like Naji Jamil (1932–2014), the head of the air force and Asad's right hand in the early 1970s. Suddenly, it became clear that Jamil had lost favour. For more than thirty years, Jamil became invisible – a true master of the art of fading. This was also the case with a far more prominent figure, an Alawite officer who stayed loyal to Hafiz al-Asad throughout all the major crises of the seventies and eighties. And yet, possibly because he vocalised his objection to Hafiz al-Asad's decision to groom his son rather than his comrades as his successor, 'Ali Haydar (b. 1932) suddenly lost favour. Today, the man who is approaching his nineties can, at times, be seen sipping tea at the Four Seasons coffee shop, his face barely visible behind the smoke clouds of cigars and waterpipes, too old to be considered a threat to the regime.

A more recent member of this category is Faruq al-Shar', Syria's vice-president since 2006, one of the few men who managed to remain as important to Asad the Son as he was to Asad the Father, until he faded away from the public eye in 2011 after daring to express his discomfort with the way in which the regime dealt with the early protests during that year. In an interview with *al-Hayat*, Lakhdar Brahimi mentioned that during one of the visits he made to Syria as the UN/Arab League envoy he asked repeatedly to see Shar', not only because he wanted to hear his views on what was taking place, but also because he regarded him as a friend. Finally, according to Brahimi, he received a phone call from Shar' in which he apologised for not being able to meet Brahimi in person.[4] Shar', like Haydar and Jamil before him, had no doubt understood all along that no matter how important his position had been, all of this, in the final analysis, could be stripped down to moments. A day had arrived when the very man who once negotiated with Clinton and Rabin in the White House was unable to leave his own house without permission. But here, too, history can be full of surprises. Those who 'fade well' can suddenly and unexpectedly come back to play a role at times far more significant than the role they played prior to their calculated disappearance. We saw this in Iraq where Adnan al-Pachachi, once a prominent civil servant in royal Hashemite Iraq, survived decades of ruthless coup d'états and Ba'th rule, only to suddenly find himself a member of the Iraqi Governing Council. Not in his wildest dreams could he have imagined that he would be offered the presidency of Iraq at the age of eighty, or that he would decline it. Regardless of where Syria's faded figures will end up, it is clear that what began in 1963 – this phase of raw and graphic power – has far from ended.

Chapter IV

The Age of Camelot (1972–1979)

GOLDEN YEARS

The seven years between March 1972, when he was appointed as Minister of Planning, and August 1979, when he left for Kuwait after he was elected as the new Director General and Chairman of the Board of Governors of the Arab Fund for Economic and Social Development would be remembered by Imady as the golden years of his career. Everything somehow felt more meaningful. It was a period when he and his wife, now the parents of three children (Susan (b. 1957), Muna (b. 1962), and Omar (b. 1966)) observed their bond bloom into something they couldn't have possibly imagined as students at NYU. The couple, who at their first New Year's celebration in 1957 couldn't afford to buy a cake, were now invited as VIP guests to dine with presidents and royalty. There was also a sense of pride after the 1973 war, followed by an atmosphere of openness and a promise of prosperity. Perhaps most importantly, this was the period before Hama, and before the Hindawi Affair and the dark implications about the Syrian regime these events inescapably confirmed. It was also before Asad withdrew after his heart attack in 1983, and posters of him smiling and reaching out to his people were replaced by posters of an angry, fierce, and disappointed man. There were several key events in this period, and in their totality, they constituted the milestones along the navigational route which Muhammad Imady, the Damascene reformer, pursued towards his goals of meaningful change.

* * *

In the Syria Hafiz al-Asad created, every important official had to be balanced or neutralised by another important official who would be naturally inclined to act against him. A liberal minister of economy, for example, always had to be balanced by a leftist minister of finance; the minister of agriculture by the head of the Peasants Union, the minister of interior by the head of a security branch, and so on. Furthermore, every important official was to be overseen by one of the many security branches. There were, however, exceptions to this rule, and Imady was one of a very small group of officials who were classified as belonging to the category of 'the President's men'. In practical terms, this status translated into the following: (i) Imady was not expected to regularly visit the head of a security branch and report events and developments at the ministry to him; (ii) Imady was not expected to write reports to the head of a security branch, as many other ministers were required to do; (iii) Imady could not expect to be immune to the harassment of other officials, but could count on being protected if the harassment evolved into a direct plot against him; and (iv) if it was established that Imady had betrayed the President's special trust, his punishment would be far more severe than those who had never been granted his trust in the first place.

Many events illustrated all of this. Once, for example, a high-ranking government official had decided he had no reason whatsoever to tolerate Imady, who was, after all, a Sunni, non-Ba'thist, western-educated nobody. Usually, these events would last a week or so and then fade away. Not this time. This particular foe seemed determined to persist in his opposition. It was not until a foreign dignitary arrived in Syria, a prince from one of the Gulf States, that Imady was unexpectedly granted redress. As was usually the case, Hafiz al-Asad and his entire cabinet arrived at the airport to receive the guest. As they gathered inside the VIP room awaiting the arrival of the prince, Asad abruptly and entirely out of context turned to this official and said, pointedly: 'Those who do not know that it was I who chose Imady for his post clearly don't know anything about how the country is run.' Asad, in other words, was making it clear that in attacking Imady, this individual was attacking his judgement, and this (rather than the harassment of Imady in itself) was a very serious offence that could easily warrant this official's dismissal from the government.

Asad trusted Imady to the extent of including him in a very small group of officials who were aware that a decision to attack Israel had been made and that it would take place during the autumn of 1973. One of the main responsibilities of Imady, in so far as the war preparations were concerned, was to ensure that Syria had enough food stockpiles. Imady would often relate how, when he first arrived at the secret bunker where Asad was overseeing the war, he found many members of the Syrian government, in his words, 'literally terrified'. But what about Asad, Imady would be asked? Imady would smile, the smile of a man who was clearly proud, at least in this instance, of the man he worked for. 'Asad was the mountain in that room.'

Imady understood well that as one of the President's men he was expected to occasionally act and make statements in a manner that was not entirely consistent with his own sensibility. There was nothing explicitly unethical that was ever expected, but Imady, unlike the regime he represented, was not a revolutionary. He regarded himself as a reformer and his deepest traits all converged into this sense of identity. Imady was also a believer in peace, and regarded extreme revolutionary rhetoric and behaviour vis-à-vis Israel as reckless, and of no real value in so far as the alleviation of the plight of the Palestinians was concerned. It was the expectations of his position as one of the President's men that explains why, in 1976, during the annual meeting of the Board of Governors of the International Monetary Fund (IMF) and the World Bank (WB), Imady acted in a manner that was consistent with his regime's expectations, yet so contrary to his own sensibility.

The IMF/WB annual meetings are chaired by a Governor of the World Bank and the IMF, with the chairmanship rotating annually among member states. In 1976, it was Syria's turn. The meeting was held in Manila, at the newly built Philippine International Convention Center, designed by Leandro Locsin. The opening address was given by President Ferdinand Marcos and it was followed by the Chairman of the Board of Governors, Dr Muhammad Imady. Imady's speech was the perfect combination of the technical, insightful, and the diplomatic:

> 'The activities of the International Monetary Fund and the World Bank – under the imaginative leadership of Mr. Witteveen and Mr. McNamara – have contributed significantly to improving the well-being of the world community.'

He ended his speech with an invitation to alter perceptions:

> 'Two hundred years ago, Adam Smith wrote of the wealth of nations. Since then, that wealth has multiplied to a level unimaginable in 1776. The question before our international community is not one of sharing the wealth a few nations possess today. Our goal instead must be the creation of a new order that will put today's wealth to its most productive uses, to join in a cooperative effort to invest in a more prosperous future for all nations.'[1]

Imady was complimented on his speech by many, especially Robert McNamara, President of the World Bank Group (1968–1981), who was clearly having difficulty processing the idea that the Syrian Minister of Economy had a PhD from NYU and was accompanied by his American wife. But it wasn't Imady's speech, or conversations over dinner, that would be regarded by McNamara and other western delegates as unbecoming of the Chairman of the Board of Governors. It was, rather, what took place during the fifth joint session when Moshe Sanbar, the Governor for Israel approached the podium to deliver his speech. Imady and Sadiq Ayyubi, the Syrian Minister of Finance, both stood up and walked out of the conference hall. A number of representatives of Arab and Muslim states followed suit. It would have been one thing for someone sitting in a back row to leave the hall, but it was something entirely different for Imady, who was sitting at the main central table facing the audience, to stand and leave. It was meant as a statement, and it was seen as such. The next day, local newspapers blasted the move as sabotage, but the deed was done. The *New York Times* took a less judgemental tone:

> 'MANILA, Oct. 6 (AP) – In the first overtly political moves at the International Monetary Fund meeting, Arabs and some Africans walked out today before a speech by an Israeli … Mohammed Imady, also left the podium before Mr. Sanbar's speech and returned after he finished.'[2]

Upon his return to Damascus, Hafiz al-Asad met Imady and made reference to the event. He told Imady that he had 'whitened our faces', a Syrian expression which translates into 'you have made us proud'. The irony was that Asad was complimenting him for an act that Imady himself would not have undertaken had it not been for his realization that remaining in the room as an Israeli official gave a speech would have been regarded by Asad and his regime as bordering on treason. In his own mind, Imady felt that there was far more strength in communication than in walking out of a room, that Syria's positions could be eloquently defended, and that he had already demonstrated this in the way he had interacted with heavyweights like Robert McNamara. But Imady kept all of this to himself; his wife is probably the only one who heard him clearly speak of such frustrations.

Though Asad was fond of revolutionary gestures, he was intelligent enough to realize that his minister of economy could serve as a bridge between his regime and an otherwise distant and suspicious West. Asad first noticed this shortly after the Arab-Israeli war of 1973 when Kissinger, and subsequently, Nixon visited Damascus. The US graduate, married to a New Yorker, left an instant and distinct impression on these American officials, and made it difficult for them to approach the Asad regime as entirely alien to them, as they would have otherwise done so. Asad encouraged Imady to establish a relationship with the American Ambassador, Richard William Murphy, and a friendship was born between them and their families that was nurtured through regular visits to the Ambassador's residence in Damascus. As the wives and children watched seventies movies like *Jesus Christ Superstar* and *Lost Horizon* projected on a large screen (in an age where these movies would not have been available anywhere else in Syria) Murphy would engage in deep discussion with Imady about Syria and the Arab world.

Interviewed in 2017 by Charles Stuart Kennedy, Ambassador Murphy recollected his days as ambassador to Syria (1974–1978):

> 'There were three principle players with whom I dealt at the senior level: the president, the foreign minister, Abdul-Halim Khaddam, and the Minister of National Economy, Dr Mohammad Al Imady, an English-speaking NYU graduate. He was the one most familiar with economic principles and comfortable with market economy thinking. The many strong-willed Baathi doctrinaires in the government knew Imady was there because of the president's support but did their best to outmanoeuvre him.'[3]

Though willing to fulfil the role Asad envisioned for him, Imady was far more interested in translating this relationship with Ambassador Murphy into something that had a tangible impact on the lives of ordinary Syrians. This was achieved in March 1977, when a detailed agreement on the improvement of the agricultural infrastructure of Syria was signed by Murphy and Imady. There was much more Imady would have liked to secure for Syria, but the inflamed anti-American politics that dominated these years made any type of sustainable cooperation virtually impossible.

Finally, it was also during this phase that Mohammad Imady was elected as a member of parliament. In 1977, during the second legislative session under Hafiz al-Asad (1977–1981), Imady received the highest number of votes as an independent non-party member for the City of Damascus. Since Imady was also the Minister of Economy during this period who attended parliamentary sessions as a member of the cabinet, his position as a member of parliament was largely symbolic, and also short-lived since he would leave for Kuwait in 1979. It was clear, however, that Asad wanted the 'People's Council' to include members with whom non-politicized Syrians could identify, and Imady, the Sunni, non-Ba'thist Damascene, was an ideal choice for such a role.

A SUNNI ALLIANCE

It wasn't only American and foreign dignitaries with whom Asad encouraged Imady to communicate. Imady, from Asad's perspective, had the potential to become a cornerstone in a very important local network of support, a Sunni alliance, which Asad regarded as critically important to his regime's survival. This was a network of Damascene religious scholars and merchants. And Imady, given aspects of his background and character, was selected by Asad to be his special envoy to this network.

PROFILES: AHMAD KAFTARU & MUNIRA AL-QUBAISI[4]

Sunni Islam in post-independence Syria, in sharp contrast to how it is regarded today by many observers of the Syrian Uprising, was articulated, spread, and organised by two Muslim scholars who strongly believed in an enlightened, spiritual, and ecumenical Islam: Shaikh Ahmad Kaftaru and Shaikha Munira al-Qubaisi. Ahmad Kaftaru was born in 1918 to a Kurdish family that had recently migrated from the north of Syria to Damascus. His father, Shaikh Amin Kaftaru (1877–1938), is a largely unknown figure, even though it was his distinct reformist vision of Sunni Islam that was destined to spread throughout Syria's urban centres from the 1960s onwards. Shaikh Amin's message was simple, yet profound in its implications: Sunni Islam had become overly consumed with matters that are entirely irrelevant to the modern age. Rather than cling, in an extreme fashion, to the rules of various Sunni schools of law, the time had come for Sunni scholars to embrace the scientific progress of the modern period and to adapt Sunni jurisprudence to the requirements of the twentieth century. Not only did Shaikh Amin want to reform the legal framework of Sunni Islam, but he also wanted Sufism to move beyond the various orders and complex rituals that permeated Damascus and other urban centres in the late nineteenth and early twentieth centuries to a spirituality that was not *tariqah* (spiritual order) defined, and that emphasised only silent meditation as its unifying ritual. He also wanted his followers to show genuine respect towards members of other sects and religions. It was this message that was instilled in the young Shaikh Ahmad Kaftaru. It was also the message that many young educated men and women in Damascus found extremely courageous and captivating. When Shaikh Amin died in 1938, his son Shaikh Ahmad became the leader of this small movement and he proceeded, with his well-known charisma, to preach this reformist message in several mosques in Damascus. By the late 1940s, his close followers had absorbed the message enough to begin preaching in many mosques both in Damascus and other urban centres.

In the early 1950s, a young woman with a degree in sciences began attending Shaikh Kaftaru's lessons in the Abu al-Nur mosque in the neighbourhood of Rukn al-Din, and by the mid-1950s, she made the strategic decision to begin to share this message of a reformist Sunni Sufi Islam with the educated young women of Damascus. This was Shaikha Munira al-Qubaisi (b. 1933), the woman destined to become the leader of an all-female movement with an estimated following of over seventy-five thousand students worldwide and considered by the Royal Islamic Strategic Studies Centre to be the 24th most influential Muslim in the world.

There was, of course, another reformist vision of Islam being preached in Syria's mosques at the time. This was the message of the Muslim Brotherhood, a movement founded in the 1920s by Hasan al-Banna (1906–1949), an Egyptian scholar who came from a strong Sufi

Sunni background. Al-Banna also reached the conclusion that a reform movement was needed, but he decided to detach his vision of reform from Sufism and to infuse it with more emphasis on political activism. In Syria, a branch of the Muslim Brotherhood, led initially by Mustafa al-Siba'i (1915–1964), was established in 1937, and membership swelled, especially in conservative cities like Hama. And so, from the 1960s onwards, two major visions of Sunni Islam competed to attract Muslims in Syria who wanted to maintain and assert their religious identity vis-à-vis the secular and leftist visions circulating at the time.

The massive Arab defeat of 1967 provided religious movements throughout the Arab world with a strong sense of momentum. The defeat was regarded as a failure of Arab nationalism and leftist ideologies. The late 1960s are also the time when Hafiz al-Asad began his rise to power. His attempts to survey Damascene society for possible future allies began during this period. Asad, as Minister of Defence, would always make a point of resolving whatever problem a religious scholar may present to him. In the late 1960s, it was very common for religious scholars in Syria to be treated with contempt by important officials. Even on a societal level, many members of elitist families regarded religious scholars in a similar fashion. Numerous popular movies, mostly Egyptian, had reinforced the image of the shaikh as an ignorant man who was either superstitious or manipulative. It was in this context that many religious scholars came to appreciate Hafiz al-Asad, though an Alawite and a socialist, who would not only receive them in his office in a very welcoming manner but did his best to solve the various types of difficulties they brought to his attention. In one phone call, he could release a relative from prison, reassign a son performing military service to a base closer to Damascus, or even secure a passport for a person who had been on a no travel list. Asad was willing to help even when their requests involved people he knew were hostile to his regime.

It was during this period when Hafiz al-Asad and Shaikh Ahmad Kaftaru first met. In private sessions with his close disciples, Shaikh Kaftaru described meeting Asad and how and why his alliance with him began:

> It was clear to me that this man was going to be Syria's president. Even as the Minister of Defence he already controlled the most critical

> components of the army and, unlike those he was competing with, he had an acute understanding of the fact that to truly rule Syria, you must show an understanding of and respect for its Sunni heritage. And so, as Salah Jadid and his followers considered us as the ignorant layer of Syria that needed to be eradicated, Asad approached us and emphasised his desire to create an informal alliance with us. Most of my colleagues, the religious scholars, rejected Asad's initiative on the grounds that he belonged to a heretical sect and it was forbidden to be aligned with a man who stood for the principles of the socialist Ba'th party. My perspective on the other hand was that if we don't embrace him, not only will others who oppose us do so, but we will lose the opportunity to influence his policies as well as our freedom to spread our message in society.[5]

Kaftaru's decision to align himself with Asad was extremely significant given the fact that Kaftaru had become the Grand Mufti of Syria in 1964. And so, regardless of all the scholars who opposed embracing Asad, Kaftaru stuck to his decision, and by November 1970 when Asad overthrew Nur al-Din al-Atasi and Salah Jadid, it appeared as though Kaftaru had been vindicated, for a time at least.

The religious scholars were not the only segment of Damascene society to which Asad reached out. Even before he took over, it was clear that Asad was not as radical as the Salah Jadid faction of the Ba'th when it came to how he regarded the private sector and its role in the Syria that he intended to rule. The key figure in this domain was Badr al-Din al-Shallah who, like Kaftaru, regarded Asad's rise to power as inevitable and, given the existing alternatives, highly preferable.

And so, we come to fully understand how the Alawite Ba'thist Asad could have as his chief economic officer a Sunni, non-Ba'thist. Not only was Imady ideally suited to liaise with both of these groups – the private sector, by virtue of his Western economic training, and with the religious group by virtue of the fact that he belonged to the Imady scholarly family and was known to regularly attend Friday prayers – he was also seen as representing yet a third important group: the Western-educated technocrats of Syria. This group included doctors, like Sami Kabbani, the renowned cardiologist who was destined to become Asad's private physician, Mufid Jukhadar, also a cardiologist, and Hisham Bakdash, a neurologist and professor of neurosurgery; engineers like Burhan Tayyara, and Muhammad Asami; scholars, like Fu'ad Sha'ban; and economists such as 'Adnan Mardini and Bashar Kabbara. All, like Imady, had studied in the West and were married to Americans. And all, like Imady, were trying to make a meaningful contribution to Syria.

Imady was not the only Sunni official in Asad's inner circle. There were, in fact, many Sunnis in far more important positions ('Abd al-Halim Khaddam, Hikmat Shihabi, Mustapha Tlas, to name but a few). But Imady was the only one amongst them who was not only a non-Ba'thist, but who openly expressed his sense of religiosity. It was unthinkable to see any other Syrian official regularly attending Friday prayers in Syria of the 1970s. Yet, respected and admired as he may have been in the eyes of the Kaftaru and Qubaisi groups, Imady would not have been regarded by them as someone they could fully trust or who truly identified with the reforms they were seeking to achieve. This was all to change in 1974. It was in September of that year when Imady's eldest daughter, Susan, who was seventeen at the time, made the decision during the month of Ramadan to commit herself to the Qubaisi movement. Her decision immediately translated into a dramatic change of public attire; she donned a white headscarf and a dark blue coat, key identifiers of the movement. She also became very active in charity work in poor Damascene neighbourhoods and engaged fully in the culture of religious lessons and spiritual rituals that the Qubaisis upheld. Susan's decision to join the Qubaisis had significant implications on how Imady was perceived by others. He was exposed to various critical remarks by his colleagues, the strongest of which came from secular Sunni officials. But he was also seen by technocrats, many of whom were also married to foreign wives, as having allowed his daughter to cross an important line. This group of Western-educated doctors and engineers had no problem with Imady attending Friday prayers, in fact many of them did so as well. But wearing a headscarf was associated with a far more serious religious sensibility than the one with which they liked to identify. Regardless of how much Imady and his wife would emphasise that their daughter had done this entirely of her own will and despite their clear disagreement with her, it was difficult for many to accept that a seventeen-year-old girl would make such a decision had it not been for her father's encouragement or, at the very least, his consent.

In the eyes of the Kaftaru and Qubaisi movements, on the other hand, Susan's decision was regarded as evidence that Asad's minister of economy was an official whom they could now claim as their own. This perception was signed and sealed, as it were, in December 1976 when Susan married Dr Owais Tarakji, the son of Dr Muhammad 'Arif Tarakji, who was known as one of Kaftaru's closest and most loyal disciples, and who was also the nephew of Shaikh Muhammad Bashir al-Bani, Shaikh Kaftaru's right hand and the Orator of the Grand Mosque of Damascus. Susan's *kitab* (the celebration of the religious marriage ceremony) was attended not only by Imady's colleagues from the Syrian government, including Prime Minister Mahmud al-Ayyubi (1932–2013), but also by Badr al-Din al-Shallah, and the Grand Mufti of Syria, Ahmad Kaftaru. With the exception of the Eid celebrations at the Grand Mosque of Damascus, the representatives of these various groups were rarely seen in public together.

The Imady-Shallah-Kaftaru alliance was not disliked by Asad. Had he been uncomfortable with it, Imady could have been easily removed in the very next cabinet change. Not only did Asad trust these three individuals, but he was also not alarmed by what they were trying to achieve. Kaftaru, Shallah, and Imady were all very conscious of this fact and all mastered the art of using segments of Asad's speeches, however out of context, to cover the initiatives they sought to advance. Kaftaru emphasised Asad's repeated assertions of his Islamic identity, and Imady and Shallah used his emphasis on encouraging all productive forces in society, including the private sector, to contribute to Syria's economy.

And so it came to be that by the mid-1970s, Asad felt that he ruled over a population which was largely loyal; most through sheer fear, others by virtue of the power and wealth they acquired during his reign and, to an important segment of urban Syria (the religious scholars, merchants, and technocrats), by virtue of the fact that they believed that not only was Hafiz al-Asad the best of other possible alternatives, but also that he genuinely supported them, as long as they did not become politically motivated. And yet, this state of affairs was not to last. Everything was to change on that infamous day in June 1979 when eighty-three Alawite officers were killed by a faction of the Muslim Brotherhood at the Aleppo Artillery School, an attack which, according to most analysts, was carried out without the approval of the more modern leadership of the Brotherhood but which nevertheless represented the culmination of the feud between the Muslim Brotherhood and the Ba'th regime. A new phase had begun, and the age of Camelot was officially over.

POST-UPRISING INTROSPECTIONS: THE DAMASCENE REFORMER

Damascene reformers are men and women who have mastered that impossible equation of trying to do something meaningful in a country where no change can be introduced without the prior approval of the security apparatus. Lawyers, western-educated doctors, religious scholars, economists, engineers, and teachers; I have memory upon memory of listening to them, observing them and, above all, noticing over time the changes, subtle yet significant, that they were remarkably able to introduce.

In the minds of Damascene reformers, the map was always clear. There were four possible paths that could be pursued in Syria, and only one of them promised a meaningful harvest. The first option was to become one of those Syrians who were willing to do anything that would result in wealth, power, and status. The second was to become a member of the opposition, and since all opposition was treated as criminal and treacherous, it was a willingness that had to take into account the repercussions, not only for the individuals who choose this path, but also those associated with them. The third path was, in essence, to survive – to do nothing other than those aspects of daily life that didn't mean anything to anyone.

And then, finally, there was the fourth path. The path of those adamant about introducing meaningful changes to what appeared to be a meaningless setup. The path of allaying the regime's security fears and then proceeding to work quietly in the shadows. The path of signing an agreement, as it were, with the security pillars of the regime:

> We will not work against you. We will say those things you like us to say in public. We will even allow others to regard us as your supporters. But in return, you will allow us to truly work for this country in a manner that reflects our own values and moral sensibility. And you will allow us to do so outside the framework of your politicised institutions. Furthermore, we will accept that we will be regularly harassed, especially when our achievements become too noticeable. You will harass us, yes, but you will not eliminate us.

This, in essence, was the operational philosophy of Damascene reformers and their counterparts in Aleppo, Homs, Latakia and other Syrian urban centres. It explained the choices they made, and it provided the rationale for those choices.

Ask a random group of Syrian revolutionaries today how they feel about those Damascenes who chose the fourth path described above and the majority will respond by saying that this was the path of cowards; the path of those who provided the regime with legitimacy, and who taught Syrians to appease their oppressors. Not only were they cowards for choosing this path, but they were also cowards for having not spoken out in categorical terms against the regime.

With every day that passes, not only is Syria further polarised between the revolutionaries and regime loyalists, but also between the reformers and the revolutionaries. It is the latter divide that troubles me the most. My mind is cluttered with noise from both sides. I can hear the revolutionaries scream: 'How dare you be silent when children are being killed?' And I can hear the reformers respond: 'If only screaming helped. You have been screaming for years, and this tragedy has only become worse.'

The revolutionaries reflect the duality of their perception, the black and white worldview that energises them. The reformers reflect their complex lenses; it's not just about what should be done, it's equally about when it must be done and how it must be done. Stories come back to me; stories I heard over and over again about respecting the principle of time, about the price of harvesting a field that isn't ready, about the danger of unleashing a beast without having the power to effectively subdue it. But these reformist principles, wise and insightful as they felt at the time, cannot change the fact that it must be extremely difficult to be a Damascene reformer today.

To be a Damascene reformer is to watch over forty years of planting – of development, education, and infrastructure – burn within the flames of TNT bombs and mortar shells.

To be a Damascene reformer is to watch a war glorified by both sides that has killed hundreds of thousands, and created wounds in Syrian society that may take decades to heal.

To be a Damascene reformer is to watch the enlightened, spiritual, moderate Islam, so carefully sculpted since Syria gained independence, handed over to those who regard beheading as the grand symbol of their medieval cult.

And finally, to be a Damascene reformer is to stand for the very first time stripped of the capacity to even contemplate reform; watching the country being torn at its seams, and waiting for the day when the last of the reformers will finally be eliminated for daring to believe that reform was ever possible.

Chapter V

Sheltered in the Desert (1979–1985)

THE ARAB REFORMER

It was in the spring of 1979 when Hafiz Al-Asad gave his permission for Imady to be nominated officially for the chairmanship of the Arab Fund for Social and Economic Development. Asad's approval was crucial because candidates needed to have their government's official backing. Following his nomination, Imady had to be elected by the Board of Governors, which consisted of the ministers of economy and finance of all Arab countries. Because he was supported by both Saudi Arabia and Kuwait, the two primary contributors to the Fund, Imady was, in effect, the strongest candidate. Asad's only condition was that Imady had to be unanimously elected. Otherwise, he was asked to refuse the post and remain in his position as Minister of Economy in Syria. The meeting of governors was held in Kuwait in April 1979, and Imady was indeed elected unanimously. Years later, when Imady was once again appointed as Minister of Economy and asked to return to Syria, Hafiz al-Asad, during one of those very rare occasions in the 1980s when Imady had the opportunity to meet him, bluntly proclaimed that, against the background of the economic difficulty Syria was experiencing, his decision to allow him to leave Syria in 1979 had in fact been a mistake.

Early in the summer of that year, as the Imady family prepared to relocate to Kuwait, stories of arrests, bombings and assassinations overtook Damascus. The attacks of the Muslim Brotherhood on the regime first began in 1976, but it wasn't until mid-1979 when the confrontation fully exploded. Significantly, most Damascenes couldn't relate to either side of the conflict and were primarily focused on identifying who was more worthy of their fear; the members of the Muslim Brotherhood who were being described by official media as eager to kill anyone associated with the regime, including innocent civilians, or security officers described by the Brotherhood as willing to torture teenagers and rape wives in the presence of their husbands.

Ironically, the very characteristics which one would have expected would protect Imady from the fury of the Brotherhood made him a far more likely target of their assassination attempts. His reputation as one of the few officials who were not corrupt, as someone who regularly prayed, and whose daughter even wore a headscarf, all of this, in the eyes of the Brotherhood, made it more difficult for its propaganda to portray the regime as fiercely Alawite and secular, and hostile to all manifestations of Sunni religiosity. Imady, in short, was seen as a Sunni traitor who whitewashed the regime by his very willingness to work with it. In June 1979, a bomb, hidden in the trash across the road from the building where Imady's office was located, exploded. The bomb was comparatively small, and did not cause much damage. It was probably meant only as a warning. That the Muslim Brotherhood did, at the very least, contemplate assassinating Imady appears certain, though it is also likely that the decision to carry out the attempt was not easy, and encountered opposition from some members of the group. Years later, a man would visit Imady's office in Kuwait and ask for a favour. He was a Syrian member of the Brotherhood living in exile in Kuwait. When Imady hesitated, the man confided, 'You are indebted to me. I was one of those who objected to including your name in our assassination lists.'[1]

Not surprisingly, Imady and his family were eager to escape all this and begin a new life in Kuwait. Imady had informed his family that even though he had been elected for his new position, and was meant to depart Syria in late August, he could not actually leave before Asad, yet again, approved his departure. The phone rang in the Imady residence, as it had once done back in 1972. But this time, Asad was authorizing Imady to leave rather than asking him to stay. Days later, wary that Asad may still change his mind, Imady left Syria. On 30 August 1979, the Imadys' new life in Kuwait began.

In retrospect, and especially after the Hama massacre of 1982 when the regime destroyed the city and killed thousands of civilians in an attempt to supress the Muslim Brotherhood insurrection which began in 1979 after the Aleppo Artillery School massacre, Imady would regard his departure to Kuwait as a form of divine protection; a separation from a regime right before it unleashed its overwhelming violence against the

Muslim Brotherhood, and anyone who was regarded as sympathetic to their cause. This was not a regime with which Imady wanted to be associated, and though he was not the type of person who would have resigned had the opportunity to depart to Kuwait not arisen, he felt blessed that he could credibly state, primarily to himself, that he was not directly associated with the regime that carried out the Hama Massacre in February 1982. Imady, like Kaftaru, Shallah, and many others, did not regard these events as reflecting Hafiz al-Asad as much as they regarded them as reflecting a regime capable under certain circumstances of unleashing uninhibited fury. This distinction, though impossible to document, is perhaps what made it possible for those who shared Imady's sensibilities to continue to work either as officials, or as technocrats affiliated with the regime.

Unlike Imady, who was fortunate enough to be outside of Syria during this period, Ahmad Kaftaru, the Grand Mufti of Syria, and Badr al-Din al-Shallah, the head of the Damascus Chamber of Commerce, not only remained in Syria, but played an instrumental role during this critical period. As previously emphasised, both Kaftaru and Shallah regarded Asad as the best of the possible alternatives, and by 1979 they also regarded the Muslim Brotherhood as capable of bringing about significant damage to everything they had been trying to build. At the same time, the Brotherhood was entirely incapable – regardless of whether or not merchants and religious scholars supported them – of bringing down the regime. Kaftaru and Shallah had an acute understanding of the fact that this regime, though eager to be regarded as legitimate both within Syria and in the larger Arab and international spheres, was ultimately capable of surviving the loss of all of this. Even then, long before the Syrian Uprising of 2011, the critical foundation of the regime was its capacity to use a loyal, armed and dedicated force against anyone who dared to confront it. Everything else was almost decorative; helpful but not critical.

The story of Shallah preventing the fall of Damascus to the Muslim Brotherhood by mobilising the merchants to ignore the calls for a general strike is one that highly overstates the impact which such a strike would have had over the power foundations of the regime.[2] At worst, armed gangs would have been sent out to forcibly open the closed shops. It was certainly far more comfortable for Asad to not have to worry about the merchants of Damascus rising against his regime, but he had reliable and tested means to suppress such actions if they were to have taken place.

Though far more significant, the role of Kaftaru in supporting Asad in the 1980s could also be described in similar terms. Again, the regime was no doubt capable of surviving even if Kaftaru himself had spoken out against it. In February 1979, Zahir Kaftaru, the eldest son of the Grand Mufti, and the one he relied on the most to advance his reformist project, was killed near the Ghuta town of Mlayhah, allegedly over a land dispute with farmers from the area. It was never made clear who exactly was responsible for his death. The close followers of Kaftaru would consistently repeat their conviction that it was members of the *Mukhabarat*, or the security apparatus, who were responsible for the murder of Zahir Kaftaru, and that the intention behind this was to encourage the Grand Mufti to side with the Muslim Brotherhood, and in turn provide the regime with the excuse to turn against him and his followers. Others believed it was the Brotherhood who killed him because of his father's support of the regime. Either way, Kaftaru was aware of this trap, and hence, did not allow his angry followers to attend his son's funeral. He wanted a small and quiet event, and he consistently asked all those who were loyal to him to simply be silent about what had taken place. But if Kaftaru preferred silence regarding the death of his son, he was not at all silent regarding his reasons for not siding with the Muslim Brotherhood. In his mind, none of this was necessary. What sense did it make to provoke the regime?

> They insisted on unleashing the beast. They would send me private messengers asking me to join them and I would tell them: go back to your leaders and inform them that they would be responsible for unleashing this beast. Wisdom, my children, is to do what needs to be done in the way it should be done, and in the time it should be done.[3]

Even more than this, Kaftaru regarded Asad as genuinely not inclined to use force against his opponents. He was certainly willing to use that option, but it was not the one he preferred. Kaftaru regarded the events of 1982 as a product of Asad unleashing forces in his regime that in fact had wanted to use ruthless methods far earlier. Asad kept hoping the insurrection would be put down without the need for an outright confrontation, especially amidst a civilian population like Hama. When the confrontation finally took place, Asad, and the country he ruled over irreversibly changed.

POST-UPRISING INTROSPECTIONS: AFTER THE PIGEONS DEPARTED

In August 2013, the Marwan Hadid Brigades declared responsibility for the firing of six rockets into Lebanon (Hermel region) in retaliation for Hizbullah's involvement in Syria.[4] Marwan Hadid, who died in 1976, is a figure most Syrians have forgotten and of whom only a few historians of modern Syria are aware. He belongs to what might be termed the prelude to the Muslim Brotherhood revolt of the 1980s. Born in Hama in 1934, Hadid grew up in a politically active family. His older brother was a prominent member of *al-Hizb al-'Arabi al-Ishtiraki* (the Arab Socialist Party), which would subsequently merge with the Ba'th Party. After graduating from high school, he moved to Egypt where he studied agriculture at the University of 'Ayn Shams in Cairo. It was during these years that he was introduced to the Muslim Brotherhood and was fully converted to their ideology. Unlike the more scholarly orientation of the Brotherhood which was manifested in such figures as Mustafa al-Siba'i, the founder of the Brotherhood in Syria, Hadid represented the more militant and activist side of the Brotherhood. In 1963, Hadid returned to Syria, shortly after Ba'th supporters in the Syrian army had seized power. In April 1964, Hadid took part in the first major stand against the new Ba'thist government when he organised a sit-in at the Sultan Mosque in Hama. To the dismay of Hama residents, Prime Minister Amin al-Hafiz and General Salah Jadid ordered an armed force to shell the mosque. Hadid, along with others, was arrested. When he was subsequently released, he made a decision, not fully sanctioned by the leadership of the Muslim Brotherhood, to organize violent attacks against the government. Hadid continued his underground activity until June 1975 when he was arrested again. A year later, he died in prison due to health complications resulting from the torture he had suffered.

In the 1960s, few Syrians sympathized with Hadid's cause and even fewer were willing to adopt his path. Today, Syria is home to thousands who believe, as Hadid once did, in armed resistance as the only possible means to bring down the Syrian government. The story of Hadid is one of the many fascinating, yet invariably tragic connections between figures and events in Syria's modern history and the Syrian Uprising. The relevance of Hadid's legacy cannot be fully appreciated without an understanding of a very different religious legacy that dominated Syria until 2011: the legacy of Ahmad Kaftaru, the Grand Mufti of Syria. Kaftaru constituted the antithesis of Hadid's approach to Ba'th rule. Hadid wanted the government overthrown, whereas Kaftaru wanted society reformed.

The green belt encircling Damascus, known as the Ghuta, is one of the principal strongholds of the rebels currently fighting to topple the Syrian government. The Ghuta that I came to know after I completed my studies in the US and returned to Damascus in late 1993 was not only where Kaftaru lived, but also where the majority of his followers originated. Ahmad Kaftaru came up with the idea of opening the Asad Institutes for the Memorization of the Qur'an. Under the cover of these institutes, almost every mosque in Damascus – and subsequently in other Syrian cities – could suddenly host various forms of religious instruction which had previously been banned. Despite the spread of these institutes, Kaftaru's primary focus remained on Damascus, and, more specifically, on the towns and villages of the Ghuta.

Each Friday morning, Kaftaru would give a lesson at the Abu al-Nur mosque which was attended by a large number of the inhabitants of Ghuta towns and villages. Kaftaru appealed to these rural Damascenes and made sure that he often attended their weddings and funerals. Due to his very busy schedule, at times he would ask Bashir al-Bani, a Damascene scholar and the Orator of the Grand Mosque of Damascus, to attend these events on his behalf. Al-Bani was a close relative of mine whom I highly admired on account of his spiritual and ecumenical views. Because he knew that I enjoyed listening to him, he would often invite me to drive him to these events. With time, I fell in love with the Ghuta and decided to buy a piece of land a few kilometres from where Kaftaru lived, mid-way between the villages of Shab'ah and Deir al-'Asafir.

After Kaftaru's death in 2004, Ghuta residents continued to visit the Abu al-Nur mosque on Fridays. The morning lessons were now given by Bashir al-Bani and this continued until his death in 2008. Buses carrying his followers from 'Irbin, Saqba, Hammuriyyah, Mlayhah, and other towns in the Ghuta would arrive early and block the narrow streets around the mosque. They would come as families, often carrying along sandwiches and tea flasks as though heading to their weekly picnic.

By the eve of the Syrian Uprising, numerous families in the Ghuta had deeply absorbed Kaftaru's approach to Islam and reform. The Uprising however, would quickly change everything. The brutal repression of protesters in Dar'a, which became overwhelmingly clear in April 2011, coincided with the first peaceful demonstrations to be held in the Ghuta. But by January 2012, most of the towns and villages I had once visited with Shaikh Bashir al-Bani were under the control of armed rebels. In late January, the government hit back with a large offensive. Over 2,000 soldiers and fifty tanks stormed into the walnut orchards of the Ghuta. The rebels withdrew from the towns, but the army failed to retake the area completely. The way in which the Syrian regime opted to interact with the Syrian Uprising had succeeded in undermining the logic of Kaftaru's reformist approach. Suddenly, Marwan Hadid was being cloned all over the Ghuta, and the path of reform became the path of cowards and traitors.

Kaftaru's home in the Ghuta was once a place where the representatives of various sects and denominations, from both Syria and other countries, would meet and have warm and friendly conversations in the presence of the Grand Mufti. At times, Bashir al-Bani would take me along to attend some of the fascinating events that would take place at Kaftaru's home, from lunch with Cardinal Martini, to dinner with Robert Schuller, and spiritual meditation at dawn with Muhammad 'Ali. It was quite natural to see Alawite religious figures visit Kaftaru, often with their children, as one would visit an old friend. Attracted by the serenity of the place, pigeons, in surprising numbers, would sit on the terrace and the grass outside of the house. It all seemed as though it would never change. Nine years after his death, and not too far from where his home once stood, chemical weapons were used against innocent civilians. Children died during their sleep. The pigeons had long departed.

POST-UPRISING INTROSPECTIONS: A SATIRICAL HISTORY OF THE GHUTA

Don't be fooled by the headlines:

> UN calls for end to 'hell on earth' violence in eastern Ghuta[5]

You see, the Ghuta has a history, secret and dark, that these journalists are not sharing with you. The Ghuta's inhabitants, let's call them the Ghutans, have long been infected by an incurable love for freedom. And as if this is not enough for people in the region, the Ghutans have a version of this virus that comes with hideous courage and pathetic idealism. The first, in recent history, to encounter this type of disease were the Ottomans. On 6 May 1916, deep within the Ghuta, and at a house that belonged to the Bakri family, Prince Faisal was told that the Ottoman governor of Syria, Jamal Pasha, had executed twenty-one Arabs simultaneously in Damascus and Beirut for alleged anti-Ottoman activities. Prince Faisal, with too much Ghuta air in his lungs, cried out: 'O Arabs, death (in the path of freedom) is sweet'; a battle cry destined to haunt the Turkish armies until their departure from Syria.

But it was the French who had the most close and personal encounters with the Ghutans. They, too, had to use aerial bombardment, and artillery fire to subdue the 'terrorists' of their time. Villages were destroyed and at certain points, the entire population of the Ghuta were treated as a hostile enemy worthy of ruthless punishment. Passages from Philip Khoury's *Syria and the French Mandate* and Elizabeth P. MacCallum's *The Nationalist Crusade in Syria* sound eerily similar to the type of coverage we encounter today:

> 'The sweeping operations of four columns composed of 5000 troops, supported by tanks, armored cars, field artillery, and airplanes encountered some resistance and the number of rebels actually swelled owing to the severity of French repression. On 23 April, the French authorities warned village leaders in the Ghutah that after five days all villages in which rebels were being harbored would be burned without further notice. Over three quarters of those killed were said to have been non-combatant peasants ...'[6]

Of course, what Khoury and MacCallum aren't sharing with you is the fact that the Ghutans clearly deserved this. After all, the French Mandate was a progressive secular authority with noble objectives. Like all mandates, the French had no objective other than to govern Syria on the principle that 'the well-being and development of such [...] peoples not yet able to stand by themselves under the strenuous conditions of the modern world [...] form a sacred trust of civilization.'[7] But you could count on the Ghutans to ruin this experience. After all, what concern do they have for progress when their feverish love for freedom is willing to make them continue to fight even after water was cut off to their villages?

And in the same manner that the Ghutans spoiled everything the French wanted to do for Syria, so too would they ruin everything the Ba'th regime was trying to do. Here we had another secular and progressive experience, with a plan to take Syrians to a democratic future in around fifty years,[8] shattered by rural hard-headed peasants with no appreciation for a concert hall erected on the western borders of their overcrowded ugly towns.[9]

Perhaps it all started with Elijah. Yes, the Biblical Elijah. Perhaps he is responsible for infecting the Ghutans with all of this. Of all the places to anoint Hazael to be king over Syria,[10] why choose the 'Wilderness of Damascus'? Or perhaps it was the Prophet of Islam, why choose the Ghuta as the site where the righteous would fight till the very end?[11] Whatever the cause, it is clearly too late to fix any of this. The Ghutans have to be stopped before they ruin everything.

A MINISTER FOR ALL ARABS

Away from the madness in Syria, Imady focused on what he loved most, contributing in a meaningful way to the lives of ordinary people. Through his position at the Arab Fund, he could now do this not just in Syria, but in all twenty-two Arab countries. On the day he left Syria for Kuwait, an editorial proclaimed: 'Dr Imady has left his position as the Minister of Economy of Syria to become the Minister of Economy of the Arab world.'[12]

Over a period of six years, Imady would travel constantly, focusing on the countries that were most in need of development assistance. His visits to Sudan, Somalia, and Mauritania, and the loan agreements that

The Arab Fund for Economic and Social Development (The Arab Fund)[1]

The Arab Fund for Economic and Social Development (the Arab Fund), based in the State of Kuwait, is an Arab regional financial institution focused on funding economic and social development by financing public and private investment projects and providing grants and expertise. The Arab Fund's activities are characterized by a number of important aspects that make it a model of cooperation and Arab economic integration, and a reflection of outstanding joint Arab action.

The loans provided by [the] Arab Fund to Member countries are characterized as being concessional; by providing easy financing conditions to assist these countries implement their development plans. In this context, the Arab Fund has paid close attention to improving the concessional nature of its loans by reducing interest rates to 2.0 per cent for low-income Arab countries and to 2.5 per cent for others. Furthermore, it has increased the grace period before loan repayments start to between four and six years and extended the loan term to between 22 and 30 years. In addition, the Arab Fund continues to provide non-refundable grants as a contribution to various fields of studies, institutional support and training, as well as support for emergency situations and circumstances faced by some Member countries.

Achieving Arab integration and consolidating cooperation among the Member countries is the main objective of the Arab Fund. Priority is therefore given to financing joint Arab projects of particular importance and specifically to those projects that increase the interdependence of Arab countries. Hence the emphasis on contributing to projects involving the interconnection of electrical power, transportation and communications. The Arab Fund also pays close attention to social development and reducing poverty by financing projects covering health care, education, drinking water, rural development, and social welfare.

were signed by the Fund with these countries were described in detail by Imady in his book, *Equitable Development – My Experience at the Arab Fund for Economic and Social Development*.[13] In this work, we learn that Imady participated in the first Arab meeting that discussed the creation of the Arab Fund. The meeting was held in Baghdad, in August 1967, and was part of a series of meetings that took place after the 1967 war to identify mechanisms that could address the ramifications of the massive Arab defeat. The loss of the Golan Heights, the West Bank, the Gaza Strip and Sinai Peninsula to Israeli occupation, and the deaths of nearly 20,000 – all this was regarded as overwhelming proof that unless Arab countries invested seriously in economic development and integrated their economies, their reliance on military expenditure and the purchase of arms would be of no real value. And though the initial agreement for the establishment of the Fund was signed in April 1968, the creation of the Fund's capital and the initiation of its activities did not begin until July 1973 when the Fund's first chairman, Dr Saeb Jaroudi (1929–2014), a Lebanese economist, was elected.

Upon Imady's arrival in Kuwait, several employees complained of the Fund's lack of morale. For over a year, loan provision had been suspended, and important managers had already resigned or were contemplating terminating their relationship with the organisation. Past loans exceeded available resources, and some managers felt the entire institution was about to collapse. As one senior official put it: 'We are not cowards, and this is the only reason why we didn't escape this sinking ship.'[14]

But Imady was adamant that this ship would not sink on his watch. After settling in his new home, a villa in Bneid al-Gar, behind the American embassy compound, Imady's first move was to actively encourage donor countries to increase the Fund's budget. The idea was simple, yet with the potential to cause a significant change in perception. The most powerful way to convey the intention of becoming very active in funding development projects is by significantly increasing the budget allocated for such a purpose. A large budget would translate into an active and expanding loan portfolio, which in turn would reinvigorate morale and reaffirm the vision and mission of the Fund. By April 1982, the Fund was operating on a budget of KWD 800 million (approximately $2.656 billion) compared to its previous limit of KWD 400 million (approximately $1.328 billion).

Imady succeeded in dramatically increasing the Fund's involvement in development projects throughout the Arab world. Projects differed in size and focus. Some concentrated on road restoration, others on rural development. Numerous studies were funded on such topics as earthquakes in Arab countries, food security, and monetary integration. An Arabic adaptation of the children's show *Sesame Street*, renamed *Open Sesame*, was sponsored, as well as many literacy campaigns throughout the Arab world. When he was not travelling, Imady was likely to be organizing a conference in Kuwait on various themes of economic development. His leadership and vision were respected even by those whose governments had a hostile position against Syria at the time, such as Iraq.

When Imady's first term ended in April 1984, he was unanimously elected for a second five-year term (1984–1989); though only one year would pass of this second term before he was again appointed as Syrian Minister of Economy and asked to return. There were several attempts to convince the Syrian government, Hafiz al-Asad in particular, to allow Imady to stay in Kuwait, but the copious correspondence, phone calls, and pleas failed to change the Syrian president's mind. He wanted Imady back in Syria, and he was not willing to entertain any compromise on this matter. The last report on the Fund's activities before Imady's departure (The Annual Report of 1984) indicated that the lending activities of the Fund consisted of 26 loans with a value of $279 million extended to 14 Arab states.

Imady's intensive interaction with government representatives of Arab countries, and his frequent visits to various project locations from Morocco in the northwest to Yemen in the southeast served to refine his views and perceptions of Arab identity and politics. In the vast majority of cases, he only shared these views with a small circle of people whom he trusted.

He generally regarded working with representatives of Arab countries ruled by monarchies as far easier because they were less inclined to use revolutionary rhetoric and were not keen on politicising everything that crossed their path. They were no less democratic than Arab republics since no Arab governments during this period allowed for genuine political participation nor freedom of expression. Arab monarchies were simply less politically charged, and when it came to the realm of economic development, Imady would learn that politics has a way of undermining politicians' capacity to interact on the basis of rational and sound economic principles.

Another important insight into the Arab psyche which Imady would acquire during this period was the existence of a stark distinction between those who were addicted to discussing the past glories of Arab civilisation and those, far fewer in number, who were forward-thinking and were interested in identifying solutions to the problems and challenges their countries were currently facing. Those who were past-focused were likely to be confrontational when invited to focus on the present. They were also far more likely to regard their failure to overcome poverty, illiteracy, and unemployment in their countries as manifestations of a Western and/or Israeli conspiracy against them.

There was also a deep divide between poor and wealthy Arab countries, with those belonging to the former frequently resentful of those belonging to the latter. After a few years in Kuwait, Imady would share his conclusion, with those he trusted, that the way in which Arabs who lived in Kuwait regarded the wealth of Kuwaitis provided significant insights into their value system. There were those, for example, who felt Kuwaitis didn't deserve this wealth because, according to their logic, they were uncultured and not genuinely supportive of Arab causes. This category was far more likely to be insecure, and lacking in a strong sense of identity, whereas those who were not intimidated by the wealth of the Kuwaitis, or any other Gulf country for that matter, were more likely to have a strong sense of who they were and a neutral, if not positive, attitude towards the resources enjoyed by others. In Imady's mind, these were character flaws disguised as political positions, just as the over-glorification of the past and the conspiracy mind-set were flaws in reasoning disguised as religious or political views.

Finally, there were Arabs who understood the value of time; the value of acting now to address the challenges their countries were facing. These stood in contrast to those Arabs who seemed to take pleasure in indefinitely discussing, reflecting and pondering over the challenges they were encountering. Imady felt strongly that time was not on the side of Arab countries; that far too much time had been wasted already. Rational planning was important, but planning was meant as a prelude to action, rather than as an objective in and of itself.

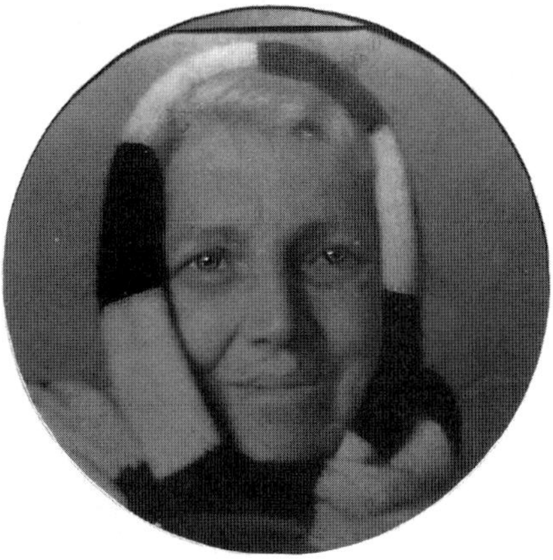

Muhammad Imady's mother, Yusra al-Hawasili (b.1898, d.1969) who instilled in him a spiritual, human-centred sensibility.

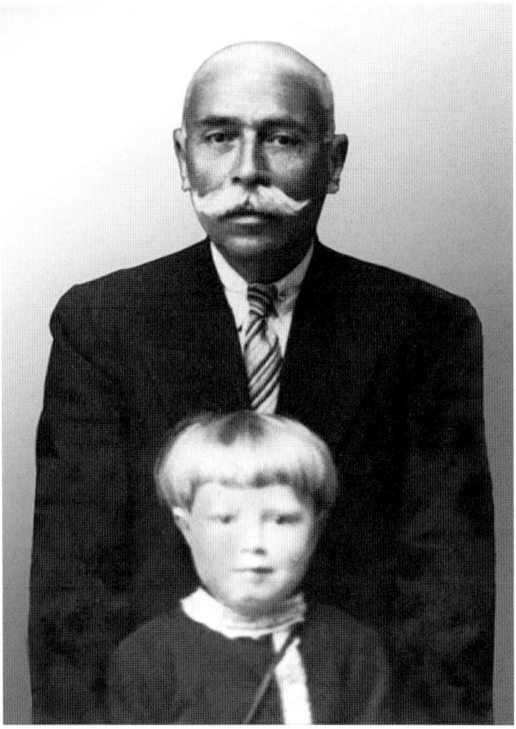

Muhammad Imady as a young boy with his father, Jawdat (b.1882, d.1958), circa 1935.

Muhammad Imady Graduating from the Faculty of Law, 1953.

Muhammad Imady with 'Abd al-Wahhab Hawmad (Syrian Minister of Education and later Finance), the man who first inspired Imady to join public service, circa 1955.

Muhammad Imady with President Gamal Abdel Nasser at the Arab Students Conference in Cairo 1959.

Muhammad Imady presenting Hafiz al-Asad with a copy his book on the Syrian economy, March 1971.

Muhammad Imady with Omar Imady, 1971.

Muhammad Imady with his wife, Elaine, meeting US Secretary of State Henry Kissinger and the American Ambassador to Syria, Richard Murphy, at a reception held in Damascus in 1974.

Muhammad Imady with President Hafiz al-Asad receiving President Richard Nixon upon his arrival in Damascus, June 15th 1974.

Muhammad Imady meeting with King Faisal of Saudi Arabia, circa 1974.

Muhammad Imady presenting the opening address at the Annual Meeting of the World Bank held in Manila in October 1976.

Muhammad Imady with Hafiz al-Asad on pilgrimage in Mecca, Saudi Arabia, in 1977.

Muhammad Imady greeting Mustafa Tlas, Syrian Minister of Defence, circa 1977.

Muhammad Imady with Sheikh Zayed bin Sultan Al Nahyan of UAE, the first President of the United Arab Emirates, in 1979.

Muhammad Imady's first meeting with President Hafiz al-Asad upon his return from Kuwait in April 1985.

Muhammad Imady and his wife, Mildred Elaine Rippey, in 1990.

Muhammad Imady being sworn in to the Second Cabinet of Prime Minister Mahmud al-Zu'bi in June 1992.

Muhammad Imady with his wife Elaine on the Hajj pilgrimage to Mecca, 1997.

Muhammad Imady's last meeting with Hafiz al-Asad in April 2000 prior to the president's death in June.

Muhammad Imady with Shaikh Bashir al-Bani, Orator of the Grand Mosque of Damascus, along with Imady's grandson, in the prayer hall of the Grand Mosque in 2002.

Omar Imady with his father during their last meeting in June 2017 at a small family reunion in Beirut. Given the political situation in Syria, they have not been able to see each other since.

It was with this expanded vision that Imady returned to Syria. On 8 April 1985, the new cabinet was sworn in. With his name categorically announced as one of the ministers of this cabinet, Imady flew to Damascus on 11 April, and was rushed from the airport to the presidential palace where, in the presence of the Prime Minister, 'Abd al-Ra'uf al-Kasm, he was sworn in. During this event, Hafiz al-Asad shared with Imady his views on the current status of Syria's economy, and on how it should be revived, and ended his brief talk by stating: 'One of the few mistakes I have made was to agree to you leaving for Kuwait.'

Chapter VI

Ideologues & Terrorists (1985–1991)

A TWITCH UPON A THREAD

Imady was acutely aware that the Syria of 1985 was not the Syria he had left in 1979. During the 1970s, high rates of economic growth had been achieved, and Syria's economy had shifted from a largely traditional agrarian economy to one with a strong base in the service, industrial, and commercial sectors. This trend was reversed in the 1980s, and prosperity was replaced by austerity. Several internal and external factors contributed to this economic decline, including the Muslim Brotherhood insurrection (1979–1983); Syria's costly military involvement in Lebanon, the dramatic decline in Arab aid as a result of Syria's support for Iran during the Iran-Iraq War (1980–88); the political rivalry between Hafiz al-Asad and his brother, Rif'at, which culminated in Rif'at's attempted coup in 1983; and agricultural devastation due to severe drought. All of this was exacerbated by the economic policies adopted by Syria's then prime minister, the man destined to become Imady's chief adversary.

PROFILE: 'ABD AL-RA'UF AL-KASM[1]

'Abd al-Ra'uf al-Kasm was born in 1932 to a prominent religious Damascene family. Unlike the Imadys who had not boasted an important religious scholar since the eighteenth century, Kasm's father, 'Ata Allah al-Kasm, was an important religious figure who was appointed by Syria's King Faisal as a grand mufti in 1919, and he remained in this position until his death in 1938. 'Ata Allah's sons, however, all of whom he had at a very old age, would move away from this legacy and become strong proponents of secular Arab nationalist ideologies. His eldest son, Badi' al-Kasm, was one of the founders of the Ba'th party and is considered by some to be a major competitor of Michel Aflaq over the intellectual leadership of the Ba'th party. His younger brother, 'Abd al-Ra'uf al-Kasm, joined the Ba'th party in 1949, less than two years after it was founded and was very active in student politics until 1954 when he left Syria for Turkey, and subsequently went on to Switzerland to complete his education. He obtained a doctorate in architecture from the University of Geneva, married a Swiss woman, and remained in Switzerland until 1963, returning to Damascus a few weeks after the Ba'th coup of 8 March. Upon his return, Kasm started teaching at the University of Damascus, and held several academic positions, including Dean of the Faculty of Fine Arts in 1964, Chairman of the School of the Department of Architecture in 1970, and Deputy President of the University of Damascus in 1977. His political career began in 1979 when he was appointed Governor of Damascus. Less than one year later, Hafiz al-Asad appointed him as Syria's 60th prime minister.

At first glance, there was much in common between Imady and Kasm. Both came from notable Damascene families, both had studied in the West and married foreign wives, and both had a strong academic grounding in their respective fields – economics and architecture. And yet, despite these commonalities, it was widely known in the mid-80s amongst average Syrians that these two men were worlds apart. While Imady was seen as an independent technocrat who was trying to revive Syria's economy despite a regime that was opposed to him ideologically, Kasm was seen as a regime insider who was adamant at defending the Ba'th's leftist approach to economic laws and practices. Afterall, Kasm had been a Ba'th party member since he was seventeen, and his brother was one of the founders of the movement.

Very quickly after Imady's arrival in Damascus did the conflict between him and his prime minister become apparent. Most Damascenes regarded Kasm as an official who was not in touch with either their political sensibilities or economic concerns. That he was a Damascene himself, and that he belonged to a prominent religious family was seen as evidence against him, since he was not perceived to be acting in a manner that was consistent with this legacy. Imady, on the other hand, was regarded as having been willing to sacrifice his lucrative position in Kuwait (though as aforenoted, he had little choice in this) and to be genuinely trying to liberalise the economy and improve the standard of living. The very presence of Imady in his cabinet was problematising to Kasm. He had been prime minister since 1979, and Asad's decision to bring back Imady in 1985 was understood to mean that Kasm's economic policies had failed and what was required now was a different approach to the economy, an approach to which Kasm was ideologically opposed. From 8 April 1985 and until 1 October 1987, nearly two-and-a-half years, the conflict between Imady and Kasm flared, reaching a moment where Kasm threatened Imady with putting him on trial for violating Article 13 of the constitution which clearly states that Syria's economy is a socialist planned economy.

By 1987, Imady felt severely depressed and helpless. He had been placed in an impossible position. He had been abruptly called back, only to find himself at war with his direct supervisor. How was he to succeed in reviving Syria's economy when every policy change he proposed was vetoed by Kasm? Imady's predicament was intensified by the fact that, unlike the 1970s when he could ask at any time to speak directly with Asad, the Asad of the 1980s had become largely inaccessible, concealed by officials who constantly warned Imady not to attempt to share news or information with the president that may upset him since he had only recently recovered from a heart attack. In Imady's mind, this amounted to a catch-22, a problem for which the only possible solution is denied by a circumstance inherent in the problem. It was only a matter of time before he would be framed as having failed in his mission. He knew he had to do something. This 'something' took the form of an event in honour of the visit of a foreign dignitary that brought him in direct contact with Asad for the first time since he had been sworn in. Imady knew that this may be his last chance, and so he decided to take the gamble and speak his mind:

> 'Your excellency, you have honoured me with your trust and asked me to become minister of economy, And I have, over the last two years, done everything I can to promote policies which I believe can improve economic growth and the standard of living. But every time I propose something, I am told this is not what the president expects from me. If I had misunderstood what your expectations are, I humbly ask for your clarification and guidance.'

Asad seemed caught by surprise. He nodded, as though to convey that he had understood what Imady meant. It was clear to Imady that this was the cutting point. He had succeeded in forcing his president to arbitrate in his conflict with Kasm and now a decision was bound to be made; a decision which would either send Imady into obscurity or finally provide him with the opportunity to implement his reformist economic vision. A few weeks later, Kasm resigned and Mahmud al-Zu'bi was asked to form the new cabinet.

UNDER THE MICROSCOPE: THE HINDAWI AFFAIR[2]

It was during Kasm's tenure that an incident occurred, later to be known as the Hindawi affair, which contributed significantly to Imady's sense of alienation from the political setting in which he was operating. Imady could suspend, with difficulty, his awareness of what had taken place prior to his return to Syria – the February 1982 massacre of Hama. He could at least credibly claim to himself that he had not been a member of the regime when this took place. But the Hindawi affair happened while he was Minister of Economy, and the more information that media outlets shared about this incident, the more Imady felt like there was an uninhibited criminal element to the regime with which he was associated.

To contextualise the Hindawi affair from the perspective of the Syrian regime, one must begin with an event that took place two months earlier. On 4 February 1986, Israeli planes intercepted a Libyan executive jet over the Mediterranean near Cyprus and forced it to land in Ramat David air force base, near Haifa. Israel claimed that its aim was to capture a Palestinian terrorist, but it released the plane after it discovered that the only passengers aboard were seven Syrian politicians and two low-ranking, pro-Syrian Lebanese militia officials, in addition to a three-man crew. One of the Syrian officials was 'Abd Allah al-Ahmar, the man Asad had trusted with the position of Assistant Secretary-General of the Ba'th Party's National Command, the same position his fierce enemy, Salah Jadid, had once held prior to being imprisoned in November 1970. Following this incident, Syrian newspapers promised revenge, and, according to Hindawi's own confessions (which he would later recant), it was indeed immediately after this incident that the serious planning by Syrian intelligence for the bombing of an Israeli airplane would begin.

Nizar al-Hindawi, a Jordanian of Palestinian descent, was born in 1954 in Baqura, a village to the east of the Jordan river. Hindawi had been a teenager during the civil war between Jordanian forces and the Palestine Liberation Organisation (PLO), one of several factors which contributed to his radicalization and hostility towards the Hashemites. Hindawi eventually left Jordan for Iraq where he appears to have studied journalism, and later to Lebanon, where he worked as a journalist, publishing articles in leftist nationalist newspapers. In 1980, he departed for London, where his father and one of his brothers had settled earlier. In London, he continued to publish articles in various Arab newspapers, and enrolled in English language courses. It was in one of these English courses that he met Barbara Litwiniec, a Polish student, whom he would marry in December of the same year, and with whom he had a daughter two years later. Barbara was required to return to Poland in 1984, though Hindawi would continue to visit her there and would send her postcards from the various places he travelled to.

In the same year that Barbara left for Poland, Nizar was introduced to Anne-Marie Murphy. Born into a conservative Catholic family in Sallynoggin, a working-class area in South Dublin, Anne had been working as a chambermaid at the Park Lane Hilton Hotel in London. She had left school at fourteen, and had moved to London in 1984 in search of employment, having been out of work for five years. The twenty-nine-year-old, the fifth of ten children, met Nizar through a friend, Theresa Leonard, who was the girlfriend of Nizar's flat mate at the time. By December 1984, Anne was pregnant with Nizar's child. By the time she had discovered her pregnancy, Nizar had already disappeared. His recurrent and unexplained disappearances became a trademark of their relationship. By the time he reappeared, Anne had suffered a miscarriage. After a second reappearance in November 1985, Anne informed Hindawi that she was again pregnant with his child. Unhappy with this news, Nizar asked her to end the pregnancy, which she refused to do.

Ideologically motivated and in search of a sponsor for what he called the Jordanian Revolutionary Movement, an organization whose membership never grew beyond himself, his brother Ahmad, and a few other sympathisers, Hindawi appears to have travelled from the UK to Libya and Syria in the hope of convincing Arab security officials to adopt his movement. Eventually, through an introduction made by the UK's

Syrian Ambassador, Dr Lutf Allah Haydar, in Damascus in early 1986, Hindawi met with Brigadier General Muhammad al-Khuli, head of Syrian Airforce Intelligence, and his deputy, Lieutenant Colonel Haytham Sa'id. This was later confirmed by communications intercepted by the British. This meeting marked the beginning of Hindawi's recruitment, and under the banner of his movement, he was instructed to carry out various terrorist attacks.

The first of these took place in Germany. On 29 March 1986, Ahmad, one of Nizar's brothers, using their original family surname 'Hasi', along with an accomplice, Farouk Salameh, carried out the bombing of the German-Arab Friendship Society in Berlin, which was regarded as being in league with Israeli intelligence. Nine people were injured in the attack and Hasi would be subsequently convicted of the bombing. During his trial, Hasi would state that the act had been carried out in the name of the Jordanian Revolutionary Movement. As later confirmed by the prosecutor, Detlev Mehlis, ironically the same man who would be appointed in 2005 as the Commissioner of the UN International Independent Investigation Commission into the assassination of former Lebanese Prime Minister Rafik Hariri, there was no doubt that the planning for this Berlin bombing was carried out by Nizar Hindawi with the help of Syrian officials.

Although Hasi was found guilty of the bombing of the German-Arab Friendship Society, he denied any connection with the bombing of La Belle discotheque in Berlin carried out a week later which killed three people, including two American soldiers, and wounded 229 others, including 79 Americans. The United States subsequently blamed Libya for this particular act, and Reagan used this attack as justification for the bombing raid on Tripoli ten days later. The perpetrators of the discotheque bombing were eventually caught in 1996 and convicted in 2001. Neither Hasi nor Hindawi were implicated in this event.

Hindawi was, however, found guilty of enacting the revenge plot against the Israelis that Syria's officials had allegedly called for. Again, the Jordanian Revolutionary Movement he aspired to build acted as the perfect cover for Syrian intelligence. Hindawi was instructed to plant a bomb on an El Al flight from London to Tel Aviv using a woman to smuggle the device aboard. He received a new Syrian passport (issued under the name of 'Isam al-Shar') and the first payment of $12,000 which was given to him by Sa'id, who promised him $250,000 upon the successful completion of his assignment. Hindawi was informed that, if apprehended, he should hide any connection with the Syrian government, and that failure to do so would result in the killing of members of his family.

On 5 April, shortly after the Berlin attack, Hindawi landed in London using his false Syrian passport, posing as a Syrian Arab Airline employee. He spent two nights in a room at the Royal Garden Hotel in London which was paid for by the Syrian airline. On 6 April, at the Syrian Embassy in London, Hindawi was given the bomb intended for use in the upcoming attack on the El Al jet airplane. A day later, Nizar reappeared in Anne-Marie's life, proposing marriage. Now five months pregnant, she was relieved at his reappearance and proposal, since she had been against aborting the child, but was daunted by the prospect of raising it alone. Nizar told her that he had planned a wedding for them in Jordan and that they would travel there via the Holy Land. They had to travel separately, he informed her, because his employers had purchased a ticket for him on a different flight. He paid for the reissuing of Anne's passport, new clothes, and gave her a brand-new suitcase which, unbeknownst to her, contained three-and-a-quarter pounds of Semtex in the hidden compartment of a false bottom. This was undetectable by the x-ray technology of the time.

On 17 April, Hindawi inserted a detonator into the suitcase bomb, hidden in a calculator. He had explained to Anne that this device was to help her calculate how much local currency she would need upon arrival in Israel. He dropped his pregnant 'fiancée' off at the airport, telling her that his plane left from a different terminal. He then returned to the Royal Garden Hotel with a plan to travel back to Syria via Syrian Arab Airlines at 2pm that same afternoon. Anne's flight, the New York-London-Tel Aviv route, was intended to explode at 39,000 feet over the Alps. There were 395 passengers and crew on board. Anne passed through all the security checks completely unaware of her deadly cargo. It was not until she reached the departure gate at 9am that she aroused the suspicions of the Israeli security staff, when she informed them that she would be staying at the Hilton in Tel Aviv despite not having enough money to cover her stay. She also informed them that she had not packed her suitcase herself. Hearing this, the security staff searched her luggage, and discovered the explosives attached to the timer device.

In the meantime, Hindawi had boarded the Syrian Arab Airlines bus back to the airport in order to catch his flight to Damascus, posing as an airline employee. He was sitting on the bus waiting to depart when news of the attempted El Al bombing spread from Heathrow. Hearing this news, he quickly disembarked before the bus had a chance to leave the station. He was directed by his intelligence contact to head to the Syrian Embassy and hand a sealed envelope to the Syrian Ambassador. Upon reading its content, the Ambassador sent him to a safehouse in West Kensington where he spent the night. There, his hair was cut and dyed in an attempt to change his appearance. The next morning, however, panicking and believing, as a result of the foiled plot, that he was about to be killed by Syrian intelligence who were en route to collect him, Hindawi fled the hotel and surrendered himself to British police.

Upon handing himself in, Hindawi was arrested and interrogated. During his interrogation, Hindawi shared multiple stories. His first version of events was that he had believed the suitcase contained drugs which were to be sold in Israel. After being deprived of sleep, however, Hindawi confessed to having been recruited by Syrian intelligence to carry out the bombing plot. This confession formed the basis of the case for the prosecution. During the trial, however, he retracted his statements, claiming he was the victim of a conspiracy by Israeli agents, and that the police had deprived him of sleep and forced him to sign his confession without his having read it. His defence tried to argue that he had been manipulated by Israeli intelligence with the aim of damaging and embarrassing the Syrian government. The jury were not convinced, and thirty-two-year-old Hindawi was found guilty and handed a 45-year prison sentence on 24 October 1986, the longest sentence issued in British criminal history up until that date. Following his conviction, the British government severed its diplomatic relations with Syria. The UK-Syrian Ambassador was sent back to Damascus, and the United States and Canada also recalled their ambassadors. Minor sanctions were imposed on Syria by the European Community.

In staunch opposition to the narrative espoused by the British government, the Syrian regime, along with a number of unexpected voices, presented a counter-narrative. Their accounts attempted to recast the event as an Israeli intelligence (Mossad) plot that aimed to both embarrass and destabilise the Syrian regime. A number of variants to this narrative emerged. The first claimed that the bag Hindawi had given to Anne (which he believed had contained drugs, as he had claimed in one of his confessions) had been replaced with the one with explosives in order to frame him, and in the process implicate Syria. This theory, however, appears to have been disproved by the fact that one of Hindawi's hairs was found inside the suitcase containing the bomb. An alternative theory asserted that Mossad had been informed well in advance of the plot and had allowed it to proceed up until the point the bomb was discovered. According to yet another version, Syrian intelligence had been manipulated by one or more double agents who had instigated this plot, using Syrian intelligence officials to facilitate it. Rather than having been discovered by chance by a security guard at Heathrow, therefore, the bomb had actually been intended to be detected before it could be taken on board.

An unlikely supporter of the validity of a counter-narrative was found in Jacques Chirac, the French Prime Minister at the time. He asserted in an interview with the *Washington Times* that it was naive to think that this plot had been solely orchestrated by Syrian intelligence, and that he, along with the West German Chancellor and the Foreign Minister, believed that it was likely to have been manufactured by Mossad.[3] Asad himself confirmed this narrative in an interview with *Time* magazine.[4] Chirac further speculated that the plot may have also been the work of allies of the President's brother, Rif'at, who by then was on bad terms with Hafiz al-Asad, and would have wanted to discredit his brother's regime.

That the Hindawi affair was a case of infiltration and manipulation by Mossad via an insider is also supported by Patrick Seale, the famous biographer of Hafiz al-Asad. He states that Syrian intelligence officials had informed him personally that they had fallen victim to an Israeli trap. He further makes mention of one Mufid 'Akkur, a Syrian intelligence officer who was subsequently arrested in connection with the Hindawi affair on suspicion of having worked with the Israelis. The premise of all these narratives, whether advanced by Patrick Seale, Jacques Chirac or others, is that this plot was simply far too irrational, even strategically suicidal, for Asad to have endorsed or agreed to it. Had the bomb actually exploded, Israel would have certainly declared war against Syria, as Shimon Peres, the Israeli prime minister, confirmed.[5] Significantly, no one attempted to make the point that officials of Syria's security apparatus were ethically above such an act; but only, rather, that Asad was far too intelligent to have approved it.

It would take years following the Hindawi affair for relations between the UK and Syria to be normalised. Only when Imady was invited to attend an official event in London in 1994 was the shadow of this memory finally lifted.

ART OF THE POSSIBLE

Imady's recollections of his return to Syria in 1985 focus on a consistent theme – that of frustration. He stresses his conviction that nearly three crucial years of potential progress were lost due to the ideological intransigence of the prime minister, 'Abd al-Ra'uf al-Kasm, who blocked the majority of measures Imady wanted to introduce. From April 1985 until October 1987, Imady's energies were spent painstakingly navigating Kasm's socialist sensibilities, succeeding, as a result, in introducing only very modest reforms. What puzzled and vexed Imady the most was the extent to which Kasm and others could ignore the sheer severity of Syria's growing economic crisis.[6]

Beginning in the 1980s, the inflow of capital to the country had significantly decreased. A collapse in oil prices had caused a large fall in profits from oil exports and reduced the flow of payments from expatriate Syrians working in the Gulf. Agricultural output also dropped to record lows as a result of a three-year drought which wreaked havoc on the lives of rural communities. Between 1982 and 1985, annual growth fell to approximately 1 per cent, even as population growth soared to an average of 3.4 per cent per year. The year 1986, the same year the Hindawi affair gripped the international community, marked the nadir of the economic crisis with GNP decreasing by 5 per cent and official currency reserves plummeting to record lows. Though official figures placed inflation at approximately 60 per cent in 1986, real inflation was almost certainly above 100 per cent.

Imady understood well that there was an urgent need for change, but as long as Kasm remained in office, the majority of his proposed reforms had to be postponed. There were two prominent exceptions in this arid landscape of economic change: the Decision of the Supreme Council for Tourism No. 186 (July 1985), and the Agricultural Law No. 10 (February 1986).

The Decision of the Supreme Council for Tourism No. 186 – which exempted investors in the tourism infrastructure from a package of taxes and currency restrictions – marked Imady's first successful initiative. It was a very modest step, and almost symbolic in nature, but it was important because it was the first economic measure since 1979 that aimed at relaxing, rather than restricting, private investment. Although it was only focused on tourism and tourism-related establishments, in accordance with this decree, Syrian investors were allowed to open foreign currency accounts with the Central Bank to finance their imports, and the companies they owned could keep up to 75 per cent of their foreign currency earnings to finance imports.

Seven months later, Imady's second initiative was born, the 1986 Agricultural Law No. 10, which provided for the establishment of stock corporations in the agricultural sector with a minimum 25 per cent stake held by the state. New corporations with private capital and management were empowered to fast track the development of the entire agricultural sector, which accounted for approximately 30 per cent of Syria's economy. Though the law did not challenge the authority of the state's hold on the economy, new corporations were granted exceptional conditions, including: total freedom of decision and action in all matters of production; freedom from the restrictions of five-year plans; freedom to regulate and set wages, freedom to import needed equipment; freedom to transfer capital; and freedom from all tax relating to proceeds and capital for seven years, starting from the first year in which profits are earned. Eleven stock corporations were established by the autumn of 1989 with a share-capital ranging from 25 million Syrian pounds to 500 million. All proved highly successful in economic terms. By the late 1980s, joint stock farms had become leading suppliers of fruits and vegetables to the Arab Gulf states. Indeed, Syria's agricultural sector had experienced a U-turn, with record crops and harvests. The positive change to which the passing of the Law No. 10 and the ensuing establishment of stock corporations clearly contributed, was also boosted significantly by the end of Syria's severe drought.

All of this was achieved despite the fierce resistance Imady faced. Anything beyond these modest reforms would require, at the very least, a prime minister who was not ideologically against the types of reforms Imady was eager to introduce, and of which the economy was in dire need.

POST-UPRISING INTROSPECTIONS: THE PRICE OF LIFE

Case:	Colvin et al. v. Syrian Arab Republic
Civil Action No:	2016–1423
Judge:	Amy Berman Jackson
Decision:	1 February 2019
Funeral expenses:	$11,836
Solatium Damages:	$2.5 million
Punitive Damages:	$300,000 million
Total:	$302,511,836

Marie Catherine Colvin was born in Astoria, in the New York borough of Queens. She died in Baba 'Amr, Homs. On 1 February 2019, Amy Berman Jackson, a District Judge for the District of Columbia, ruled that '… the Syrian Arab Republic engaged in an act of extrajudicial killing of a United States national by planning and executing an attack on the Baba 'Amr Media Center, and is liable to plaintiffs for the resulting injuries.'[7] Marie Colvin's family were awarded a total of $302,511,836.[8]

I read carefully document number 59, constituting 'the redacted public second amended memorandum opinion' by Judge Jackson. Thirty-six pages that cover everything from the arrival of the Arab Spring in Syria to whether or not Marie had planned on retiring by age 65. Thirty-six pages that aimed at calculating the price of the most precious of all human experiences: life.

How does one go about calculating the price of life? How much would it take, for example, to compensate for the loss of Ghiath Matar? Ghiath, only twenty-six and a father-to-be, was known for giving out flowers and water to soldiers who were attacking peaceful protesters in early 2011. Do we have a figure for Mohamed Abyad, the Syrian doctor working for Doctors Without Borders who was only twenty-eight when he was abducted and killed? Or perhaps we have one for Razan Zaitouneh, the human rights lawyer and civil society activist and recipient of the International Women of Courage Award, who was abducted in 2013 and has not been seen since. Do we have special figures for children? Like Rua Ismail, an eleven-year-old girl who was killed by an explosion in Salamiyyah; or Hamza Al-Khateeb, the thirteen-year old who was tortured to death. Do we have figures for mass killings? Families killed in Zara'a, Houla, Aqrab, and Darayya? All of those killed had names, though we may only be able to document the identity of some. But all, like Marie, had family, friends, and loved ones. Some died reciting a prayer, others died suddenly and unexpectedly. Some died while being tortured, others drowned as they attempted to escape a country that had become a factory of death.

The attempt to document Syria's economic damage has become quite popular in recent months, but neither this approach nor its conclusions capture what I am after. It almost seems cold and out of touch to attempt to place a price tag on reconstructing a country which is yet to determine what exactly it has lost in terms of human life. Over 500,000 people have been killed since March 2011. How does one attempt to capture the price of these lives? How does one begin to reconstruct the lives of their families and loved ones? To follow the logic of Judge Jackson's decision is to award $302,511,836 to each of those killed in Syria since 2011. This would amount to approximately $151 trillion, or over three hundred times as much as the highest estimate for the cost to reconstruct Syria's economy.[9] But even this fails to fully capture the price we have paid; the price Syria has paid. Even $151 trillion does not seem sufficient to heal the wounds that have evolved over the last ten years into deep faults, time bombs buried deep within Syria's earth, waiting for the right, or wrong, moment to explode all over again.

And who exactly would be found liable for the killing of over 500,000 Syrians? Perhaps the most tragic aspect of all of this is the fact that in the vast majority of cases, those killed in Syria since 2011, were killed by Syrians. Loyalist fighters, opposition fighters, secularists, jihadists – they believed in different visions, and fought for different Syrias, but in the end, they killed Syrians. We have the tendency to use abstractions when it comes to identifying those responsible. Judge Jackson identified the 'Syrian government', and at times even 'Syria' as liable for the killing of Marie Colvin. We often speak of the Syrian regime as liable for most of the killing. Jihadist organizations are described as having had the will, but not the capacity, to kill as many as those killed by the regime, a regime with a long history of actual and alleged acts of violence against civilians.

But all of this is far too intangible. In the final analysis, Syrians were killed by Syrians. Barrel bombs were not dropped by abstract entities. They were dropped by Syrians. Mortar shells were not fired by organizations, they were fired by Syrians.

No doubt, thousands of foreign fighters contributed to Syria's tragedy and, needless to say, the role and actions of regional and international players were often destructive and at times even tantamount to war crimes. Yet, despite the strong tendency of my Syrian friends and family members to attribute responsibility to various conspiracy theories, it is clear, in my mind at least, that the primary authors of Syria's tragedy were Syrians.

At the heart of the logic of Judge Jackson's decision is the idea that significant financial penalties act as deterrents. Fine a company that sold harmful products millions of dollars, and you deter other companies from acting in a similar manner. Syria, however, seems immune to this logic. Severe economic sanctions, even 59 Tomahawk cruise missiles, have made little, if any difference. This is not a geography that has shown itself open to the logic of deterrence.

My search for the price of life in Syria usually ends with reaching out to *The Forgiveness Project: Stories for a Vengeful Age*, a book by Marina Cantacuzino, with a forward by Archbishop Emeritus Desmond Tutu. The book is, in essence, a compilation of stories, stories that provide a very different take on the price of life. Here 'life' is not something that can be numerically quantified. Life, rather, is measured by the extent to which the living are willing to protect it, to create a conducive climate for its sustainability; and, indeed, to act in a manner that is not consistent with the violence inflicted upon them. Cantacuzino draws our attention to the fact that, in the context of violence, no ingredient is more critical for the preservation of life than the capacity to forgive. Forgiveness is not an irrational act of kindness. Rather, it is a calculated act that aims at ending a cycle of violence that is immune to deterrence and only thrives when confronted with more violence.

My favourite story is that of Kemal Pervanic, a survivor of the notorious Omarska concentration camp, set up by Bosnian Serb forces. Kemal eloquently summarizes the price of life when he states:

> I didn't decide not to hate because I'm a good person. I decided not to hate because hating would have finished the job they'd started so successfully.[10]

Kemal had reached the conclusion that as long as we act in a manner consistent with the pain we suffered, we empower the narrative of those who have committed acts of violence against us. And yet, even Kemal could not have forgiven a person who stubbornly and arrogantly continues to degrade, wound and kill. Even Kemal required a genuine apology before his forgiveness could be extended.

In Syria, more than ten years after this tragedy began, no one is willing, or ready, to apologize.

POST-UPRISING INTROSPECTIONS: *THIS IS FOR SYRIA!*

On 6 June 2017, a man armed with a hammer was arrested after attacking a police officer in Paris.[11] As he carried out his attack, he shouted, 'This is for Syria!' This scene, along with other similar scenes from London Bridge to Saint Petersburg, converge like a surreal mosaic no scholar can succeed in interpreting.

How does killing an eight-year-old girl at a concert in Manchester help my wounded country heal?[12] How does it help the young women and men of Syria who marched for freedom and dignity attain these objectives? How does it help the displaced, the refugees, those dying in the basements of security offices, or those living in fear of being stoned? I visualize myself interviewing some of these men and women. Perhaps the three girls who attacked the nursery school worker in Hermon Hill in London in a seemingly random terrorist attack, have the answers.[13] Perhaps they can help me understand how stabbing an innocent woman who works for Little Diamonds nursery will help the families of the hundreds of thousands who were killed in Syria; or how will it stop the regime's barrel bombs or the indiscriminate shelling of those fighting the regime.

But of course, those carrying out these terror attacks in my country's name are not alone. The list of those convinced they are somehow contributing to my country's future is long and varied. One would have to start with all the well-intentioned neighbours in the region who have decided that the best thing they can do for Syria is to transform it into the primary field of their regional sectarian war. Zoom out a bit, and you would have to include those who believe Syria is best served by organically linking it to the attempt to end NATO's eastward expansion, missile systems, and last, but not least, Western sanctions against Russia over its annexation of the Crimea. Across the Atlantic, Syria has special friends too, who are adamant that nothing can serve Syria more than carrying out thousands of airstrikes. After all, we all know by now, as Afghanistan makes crystal clear, that airstrikes promise a quick end to terror bases and networks. With each smart bomb that falls, the chances are enhanced for Syria's infrastructure to be rebuilt, for its hospitals to become operational again, and for its roads to be safe again. Even collective international efforts are carried out in Syria's name. The UNSC resolutions are all for Syria. The votes in favour are for Syria, and the vetoes are equally for Syria. The reports documenting war crimes are for Syria, and the countries protesting the lack of adequate evidence do so for Syria. How popular my country has become!

Not since its independence in 1946 has Syria had more countries, organisations and individuals carrying out acts in its name. And yet, in over seventy years, never has a moment arrived when Syria, when its people, have been this alone.

Chapter VII

Till Death Do Us Part (1991–2000)

MAGNUM OPUS

Asad's intervention in 1987, which ushered in a new cabinet led by Zu'bi, allowed Imady to now shift his attention to a far more significant reform package. It would still take Imady three years of hard negotiations with the ideological pillars of the regime, and the frequent creative use of selections from Asad's speeches to support his arguments and deflect leftist attacks, to introduce his magnum opus, the 1991 Investment Law No. 10.[1] This law effectively opened up every sector of the Syrian economy to Syrian, Arab and foreign investors. From 1991 onwards, the socialist approach to Syria's economy, which had been in force since at least 1963, became increasingly irrelevant.

The law, passed by parliament in July 1991, constituted the most ambitious economic initiative to date. Its focus was to revitalise the economy by simultaneously boosting the private sector and encouraging foreign investment, as well as facilitating interactions between these two strands. This was achieved through the provision of a wide range of fiscal incentives, including:

- the extension of tax-holidays for investors;
- duty-free privileges on the importing of capital goods;
- access to the foreign exchange by the private sector;
- and assurances of the right to repatriate invested capital and profits.

The success of the law was substantial. By the end of the following year, 529 projects had been approved, and by the turn of the millennium, estimates held that this had increased to 1,500 projects, valued at $6.5 billion. Most of these centred on the pharmaceutical, textile, and food-processing industries, with the majority of the foreign component of this investment stemming from the Gulf states. In May 2000, Decree 7 was passed as an amendment to Law No. 10, extending these incentives further to attract yet more investment into the economy.

Prior to, during, and following the passing of Law No. 10, several important events took place. These, in their totality, created an ideal context for changing the course of Syria's economy. A number of favourable events served to amplify and enhance Syria's economic growth, thereby solidifying the perceived association between Imady's initiatives and prosperity. These included the end of Syria's severe drought, and the fact that newly discovered oil fields resulted in an increase in oil production from 160,000 barrels per day in 1984 to 480,000 in 1991. As a result, Syria's GDP grew throughout the late 1980s from around SP75 billion in 1983/1984 to approximately SP270 billion in 1990. In 1989, a balance of trade surplus of $1.192 billion was reached for the first time in decades; and while these positive official figures (best approached as general indicators rather than precise calculations) can be largely explained by the foreign exchange rate used to calculate transactions, the fact remains that the balance of trade had significantly improved during this period. Perhaps far more significantly, Imady's case for liberalizing the economy was aided by the fact that the Soviet Union and its European allies had collapsed in 1989, leaving Syria's hard-core socialists perplexed and wary of using arguments in defence of state-centralised economies that had been discredited on such a massive scale. Finally, Hafiz al-Asad's decision to join the coalition to liberate Kuwait in 1991 ended much of Syria's international isolation and reinvigorated the aid it received from Saudi Arabia and other Gulf states. Estimates of the amount of aid Syria received after the Gulf War are as high as $1 billion. Indeed, by 1991 when Law No. 10 was passed, Syria appeared to be finally back in from the cold. In retrospect, however, this year would, in fact, mark the beginning of the unravelling of Syria's economic fabric, and like all events of unravelling, this was both messy and largely unpredictable.

No sooner had Law No. 10 been passed than the business community began voicing its complaints, often inflammatory in tone but largely justified in content, against what it regarded as the dire contradictions between the new law and the stifling bureaucracy and corruption which permeated Syria's economy. Ironically, the investment law had served to draw attention to these contradictions in the same manner that a newly built house in a rundown neighbourhood suddenly draws attention to all the other houses that need to be repaired or entirely rebuilt. Some, for example, pointed to the fact that over 200 governmental decrees directly affecting Investment Law No. 10 were not found in the text presented to investors, despite having a direct bearing on their investment activities. Others asserted that without a genuine anti-corruption campaign, Investment Law No. 10 would only result in providing the corrupt with additional opportunities for their own personal enrichment. Imady was diplomatic and patient when confronted with such criticisms, which were often voiced in Syria's parliament and at various seminars organised to discuss Syria's economy. Privately, however, he would articulate his frustration with the logic underlying the attacks he confronted. Rather than acknowledging what he was able to introduce, critics blamed him for that over which he had no control – Syria's bureaucracy and corruption. In Imady's mind, reformers, like diplomats, engage in the art of the possible, whereas those who demand what is not possible are, in fact, only serving to undermine any process of reform. Imady was under no illusion regarding what had been achieved or how it was achieved. He understood well that the regime was focused on its own survival and would only permit what it regarded as conducive to this end. He further understood that regardless of how well-crafted any articulations of reform were, there would always be those who found ways of using them to promote their own contrary causes, especially those who enjoyed positions of untouchability given the services they provided to the regime. Whilst others may have recoiled from these unintended consequences, which became starkly apparent during the 1990s, Imady would stress that there was simply no other viable course of action that would have resulted in the substantial change he was able to achieve.

UNDER THE MICROSCOPE: RECEPTION AND ASSESSMENT OF IMADY'S REFORMS

For the most part, studies, articles, and reports that have analysed Imady's attempts at reforming the Syrian economy during the 1990s have been sympathetic towards his intentions and persistence, though not always towards the final outcomes of his efforts.

'... Muhammad Imady, a Western-educated, economically neoliberal, socially conservative, Damascene aristocrat and yet the longest serving Minister of Economy in Ba'thist Syria. He was the mastermind of a liberalisation process undertaken by a reluctant regime faced with no other viable option. As such, one can argue that he embodies the different trends that encompass contemporary Syria, rendering him the most eligible to narrate the story of economic development thought in Syria.'[2] – Ferdinand Arslanian

'The need to balance the interests of various and changing regime constituencies, and to avoid drastic measures, led President Hafiz al-Asad to give his conditional support to Muhammad al-'Imadi, the minister of economy and foreign trade and a major force behind liberalization. It was reported that Asad told the minister that support would be forthcoming in the face of intensified opposition to al-'Imadi's reforms. Asad noted, however, that the minister cannot expect blanket support for all his measures.'[3] – Hisham Melhem

'Muhammed Al-Imadi, the Minister of Economy and Foreign Trade, was the main driver of the liberalisation process during this period. Previously, he had been persuaded by President Hafiz Al-Assad to leave his work with the Kuwait Gulf Fund in order to lead Syria's economic liberalisation and was promised full authority to execute the needed economic reforms. However, Al-Imadi did not get the required power and had to work patiently and, sometimes, to struggle for his reforms.'[4] – Mahmoud Alajaty & John R. Anchor

'Although not a Ba'thist and once viewed in the party as a rightist, the support of the President has allowed Imadi to push for reform against the resistance of statists. In fact, Imadi was lured by Asad to return from his position with the Kuwait Gulf fund on the condition that he would be given real power over economic policy. But he has not had a free hand and has had to struggle for change... Imadi has worked patiently, in stages, to promote liberalisation. He first opened tourism and then agriculture to joint venture (private-state) enterprises in the 1970s and 1980s. The foreign investment law is his latest initiative... Imadi is, however, no neoliberal ideologue. Third

World countries, he argues, need economic intervention by a strong state on behalf of more equal distribution and to undertake investment in infrastructure and strategic industries. Private economic interests should not be allowed to dominate economic policy. But private property is a social good and the private sector should be given much greater scope… Imadi's middle position between vested interests suggests he can be seen as an autonomous technocrat looking out for the state's economically rational best interest, rather than, as some suggest, a representative of the bourgeoisie, who, in fact, do not see him as their man.'[5] – Raymond Hinnebusch

SCANDALS AND CLOSURES

When Imady reminisced about the latter part of the 1990s, his memories usually revolved around two events: the Airbus scandal which implicated Mahmud al-Zu'bi, the prime minister, Salim Yasin, the deputy prime minister for economic affairs, and Mufid 'Abd al-Karim, the minister of transportation; and the secret hard currency account he, along with a group of handpicked officials, created, incrementally enlarged with deposits over a period of fourteen years and kept a secret from everyone, including Prime Minister Zu'bi. While the former event belonged to a series of 'scandals' that shed light on the dynamics of transition from Hafiz al-Asad to his son Bashar, the latter belonged to a series of 'closures' that took place prior to the death of Hafiz al-Asad in June 2000. The recurrent figure involved in both the closures and the scandals was Prime Minister Zu'bi.

PROFILE: MAHMUD AL-ZU'BI[6]

Mahmud al-Zu'bi was born in Khirbet Ghazaleh, a village in the Dar'a governorate, near the Jordanian border. He joined the Ba'th party at a young age, and studied agricultural engineering at the University of Cairo. He returned to Syria, like Kasm once did, right after the 1963 Ba'th coup. Under the Ba'th, he held several important positions, including the Head of the Agricultural Office in Idlib, the Governor of Hama (1970), Secretary of the Peasant Bureau in Damascus (1972), Member of Parliament (1971), Director of Development of the Euphrates River

(1973), Director of the Peasants Bureau (1980), Speaker of Parliament (1981), and Prime Minister (1987–2000).

When Zu'bi was appointed to this last position on 1 October 1987, Imady was very relieved. He knew Zu'bi would have none of the ideological stances that obstructed the reforms he wanted to introduce. Zu'bi, too, understood that his mandate was to facilitate what Imady wanted to achieve. Alas, however, every setup comes with its own trials. Unlike Kasm, who was a hard core socialist and light years away from any form of corruption, Zu'bi defended whatever positions he believed Asad wanted him to defend, and his image was quickly mired in rumours of corrupt dealings. By way of example, no one in Damascus ever heard of the children of Kasm. Muflih, the eldest son of Mahmud al-Zu'bi, on the other hand, was infamous for conducting himself as a mafia don.

Zu'bi was savvy, though not intelligent. He had mastered the skills required to survive under the Ba'th, meticulously building a network of patronage, and including only a select few in his inner circle. Imady remembered how often Zu'bi, along with his deputy, Yasin, kept him out of the loop, even on decisions he felt he should have been involved in. Both regarded him as a 'President's man', or an official who answers directly to the president, and as such he was not to be trusted because he may also report things directly to the president. And yet, as careful as Zu'bi was, Imady also regarded him as reckless. One of the most important principles of working under the Ba'th regime had entirely eluded him. Corruption is the monopoly of those who have power. To those who do not, it is a game of Russian roulette. As historian Sami Moubayed eloquently notes, Zu'bi was both weak and corrupt, and thus, he lent himself to being a perfect candidate for focus the moment the Syrian regime decided to initiate an anti-corruption campaign.[7] Yes, it may decide not to, in which case Zu'bi would disappear into the shadows with his millions, or it may decide that the image of the regime required a 'clean up' campaign, in which case Zu'bi, or anyone else in the unfortunate position of being corrupt and weak, would suddenly realise that no record of service to the regime would be enough to save him, and his family, from Ba'th annihilation.

In Zu'bi's defence, Imady regarded him as having been willing to become part of corrupt dealings precisely because of his weakness, rather than greed. When powerful figures of the regime asked an official to authorise a project, it was almost impossible for such an official to refuse their requests. Imady, and a few others were an exception, because they had enough credibility in the eyes of the president to share such incidents with him. To inform Asad, for example, that one of his own relatives was demanding the authorization of a project that was not technically legal, as Imady at times did, is not the type of incident the majority of officials would be willing to convey to the president, even if they had a direct line of communication with him, as Zu'bi indeed did. The risk involved offending the president, alienating the powerful figure who would instantly become a sworn enemy, and (most problematic of all) obstructing a project that the president himself wanted approved via the relative who was pursuing it. The safer route, especially for a weak official, was to approve the project, gain the favour of this powerful figure, and, at times, receive a percentage of the profit. It was indeed the safer route, but it was also, at times, a suicidal one.

UNDER THE MICROSCOPE: THE AIRBUS SCANDAL[8]

In 1996, the Syrian government signed a contract with Airbus, the French airplane manufacturer. Airbus was to provide the Syrian government with six A-320 planes for a total price of $374 million. In May 2000, the Syrian regime turned against all the officials who were involved in this contract, alleging that the actual price of the six planes was $250 million, and that the additional $124 million had been distributed by Airbus as bribes to secure the deal with the Syrian government. Four figures were alleged to be the recipients of these bribes: the Prime Minister Mahmud al-Zu'bi; his deputy, Salim Yasin; the Minister of Transportation, Mufid 'Abd al-Karim; and Munir Abu Khudur, a Syrian residing in Spain who allegedly acted as an intermediary between Airbus and the Syrian officials.

There are two noteworthy aspects to this story, which, when identified, help to shed light on exactly what took place in the Airbus scandal. The first is that one of the three accused, Mufid 'Abd al-Karim, was an Alawite; and the second is that four years passed before Asad, or more likely his son, decided to expose the story and target the culprits. The first detail aids in establishing who may have been additionally involved. It is not far-fetched to assume that both Yasin and Zu'bi were reassured and bolstered by the fact that the primary signatory of the contract would be an Alawite, hand-picked by the president in 1992 to be his minister of transportation. Nor is it unrealistic to assume that the $124 million could have been distributed amongst more than just four individuals. Given the vast amount being pocketed, it is hard to visualise this plan having been enacted solely by bureaucrats. A more likely scenario, therefore, is that an important Alawite figure (possibly a security officer) connected to 'Abd al-Karim was also involved, and that his involvement was what further encouraged Zu'bi and Yasin to go along with this dangerous plan. Even if no such figure existed, however, the involvement of 'Abd al-Karim is pivotal to understanding the dynamics of this story.

The second important point pertains to why the Syrian government would wait for four years before deciding to go after these officials. It was well-known amongst the inner circles of the regime that security agencies began investigating this story as early as 1997, and that a file had been prepared for submission to the courts for prosecution by later that year. In short, a delay of three additional years was unwarranted; a solid case had already been made. The decision was taken to turn against these officials not because this story suddenly came to light in 2000, or because additional information had been gathered, but rather because very different dynamics were now at play. The common explanation for the move against Zu'bi was that this was the way through which the President's son, who, given his father's health, was well aware that he was on the cusp of assuming the presidency, could convey that he would not tolerate this type of corruption in his government.

Shortly after Zu'bi's sacking in March 2000, Yasin and 'Abd al-Karim were arrested. Zu'bi was discharged from the Ba'th Party Regional Command and placed under house arrest. A warrant was also issued for the arrest of Madrid-based businessman Munir Abu Khudur, yet he avoided capture by remaining in Europe. Other junior officials who had signed, witnessed, and facilitated the deal were also arrested. When the officer charged with Zu'bi's arrest arrived at his home in the Damascus suburb of Dummar, Zu'bi chose to commit suicide rather than face the inevitable humiliation of being dragged through the courts.

The property of 'Abd al-Karim would be sequestered within a week of his arrest, and so too was the property of Yasin and his family. Yasin and 'Abd al-Karim were eventually charged with misuse of public office, receiving bribes, causing SyrianAir to incur heavy losses, and 'damaging the national economy'. The contract was found to be the result of Abu

Khudur's facilitation, Yasin's advice, 'Abd al-Karim's authorization, and Zu'bi's backing. On 8 December 2001, the verdicts were issued, around a year and a half after their arrests; Yasin, Abd al-Karim, and Abu Khudur (tried in absentia) were found guilty of embezzlement. Yasin and 'Abd al-Karim each received 10 years behind bars and, along with Abu Khudur, they were collectively fined $240 million.

* * *

The second important event that came back to Imady when recollecting the latter part of the nineties began shortly after he returned to Syria in 1985, and continued until a few weeks before president Hafiz al-Asad died. One of the first things Imady realised after his return to Syria was that the hard currency reserves were not adequate enough to cover even a single week of necessary imports. As though this was not sufficiently troubling, Imady had to also come to terms with the fact that not having enough dollars to import wheat did not mean that officials would stop expecting work to start on the Damascus Opera House or the completion of the Dummar housing suburb. No one seemed to understand the gravity of the situation. In a work entitled *The Concerns of Development – Events I Will Not Forget*,[9] Imady writes that not long after his return from Kuwait, Asad asked him why wheat had not been purchased. When Imady began to explain that the Minister of Economy was not responsible for the purchase of wheat, and that this was in fact the job of the Minister of Supply, Asad interrupted him: 'No, you are the sole official responsible to me for all such matters.'[10] It was then that Imady decided that something had to be done.

After weeks of silent deliberations, Imady decided he would identify someone he trusted at the Commercial Bank of Syria, which was administratively under the supervision of the Minister of Economy, to open a hidden account and begin to slowly deposit whatever foreign currency earnings the Syrian government acquired through the reform measures introduced in the tourism sector (1985), the agricultural sector (1986), and, subsequently, earnings that resulted from Law No. 10. To further conceal the account from Prime Minister Zu'bi, who in Imady's mind was far too generous with his use of precious hard currency reserves to fund various projects that had no real economic value, Imady asked that the books documenting the deposits use a foreign exchange value that deliberately made the deposits seem far less than their actual amount. A time would come in the late nineties, when Imady would have trouble sleeping, wondering what would happen if he were to suddenly die, leaving behind an account that had by then accumulated billions of US dollars, an account of which even the president was not aware. And so, finally, in late 1999, Imady decided it was time to share his secret. He asked to speak to the president and after he explained what he had done, Imady recalled that the president asked, 'So, what is the figure in this account, $100 million?' Imady responded, 'No, Mr President, it's far more than this.' 'One billion?' Again, Imady replied in the negative. The total figure was $9 billion. Imady recalled that Asad was silent. Imady was worried he had upset him because he had kept this a secret for so long. He was about to apologise when Asad said, 'Had you shared this account with anyone, it would have been spent. May God give you health [an Arabic/Syrian phrase expressing gratitude].'

On 13 March 2000, and in accordance with Decree 8 of 2000, a new cabinet headed by Dr Mustafa Miru was formed. This was the tenth cabinet during the presidency of Hafiz al-Asad, and it was also destined to be the last. In the midst of the events that followed, Imady was suddenly asked to meet with the president. When Imady arrived at the president's home, something in him felt as though this was the last time he would see the man who had selected him to be his minister of economy and, in the process, had changed his life. Imady's intuition was right. Asad would die less than two months later. The meeting was short, and surprisingly Asad didn't have anything he wanted to share with Imady. There were no instructions or requests. He said he wanted to thank him in person for what he had done for Syria's hard currency reserves. Imady recalled he could hear children playing from the floor above, and Asad smiled and explained that these were his grandchildren (the children of his daughter, Bushra, and her husband, Asif Shawkat who would himself be killed in the 18 July 2012 Damascus bombing of the National Security headquarters). A photographer walked in and took a picture of Imady as he embraced the president. As he walked out of the building, Imady was overwhelmed by the feeling that an entire phase of his life was about to end.

* * *

On Saturday, 10 June 2000, shortly after 4pm, Imady received a phone call from the prime minister's office, asking him to attend a special session at parliament. It was an unusual request, and Imady recalls dreading the possibility that it was related to yet another corruption scandal involving high-level officials. Though his meeting with Hafiz al-Asad had assured him he was not personally targeted, the mere thought that he would have to witness the humiliation of his colleagues was enough to put him in a sombre mood. When he arrived, he was seated next to the Minister of Health, Iyad al-Shatti, whom he found fighting back his tears. For a few seconds, Imady wondered if his colleague, whom he deeply respected, could have overheard a rumour that implicated him in a case of corruption. But his confusion quickly ended when Shatti whispered to him that the president had died, at which point Imady also started to weep.

A few minutes later, 'Abd al-Qadir Qaddurah, the Speaker of the People's Assembly, announced the death of Hafiz al-Asad. Before the session was over, the minimum age of the president was lowered from 40 to 34, to allow for the transfer of power from Hafiz al-Asad to his son Bashar who was only thirty-four at the time of his father's death.

TV footage of this event repeatedly showed Imady and Shatti crying, and photographs of them in their moment of grief became iconic symbols of how the death of Hafiz al-Asad was received. But, as is the case with the majority of events reported by the media, there is often a far more complex explanation for what the camera had captured. Imady wasn't the type of man who regarded expressing emotions as unbecoming of a man. He cried whenever he was overtaken by emotions. When an official knocked on his door in the middle of the night to deliver a confidential notification in which the decision to oust Zu'bi from the Ba'th party was proclaimed, Imady cried, even though his relationship with Zu'bi had never been friendly or warm. When he first heard about Hama he cried, and when his wife finally returned home after a long vacation in her hometown of Palisades, he cried.

But what exactly was the nature of Imady's emotions on 10 June 2000?

My emotions were a mixture of genuine sadness, and intense relief. I was sad to lose the man who had protected me for over thirty years, and I was relieved that I had finally passed the test – the most prolonged and intense test of my life – of working in a government led by Hafiz al-Asad.[11]

POST-UPRISING INTROSPECTIONS: IN THE CIRCLES OF KINGS

The works of classical Muslim scholars are replete with references to the dangers associated with proximity to those in power. *Iyyakum wa-al-dukhul 'ala al-salatin,* 'Never enter the palaces of sultans', is a common heading found in many early works on morals and etiquette. Some, like Suyuti, authored complete treatises on the subject.[12] To seek to be close to a king, we are told, is to be invariably compromised. Rather than pursue such proximity, religious figures should themselves be pursued for advice, and even then, they should be reluctant to provide this advice since it is inevitably a waste of time. In one account, we are told that the Sultan of Bukhara sent his messenger to Bukhari, the famous compiler of prophetic traditions, to invite him to recite his works in the palace. The response of Bukhari summarizes the classical approach: 'Say to the sultan that I will not degrade the sanctity of knowledge, nor visit the palaces of sultans. If you want something from me, visit me at the mosque or at my home.'[13] Some were even more extreme in their emphatic insistence that kings were to be avoided: 'If they ask you to visit them, even if only to recite a verse from the Qur'an to them, do not accept.'[14]

There were, of course, always exceptions: Reformers, who felt that proximity to a powerful figure may result in something positive, an added value that would be impossible to achieve without a powerful patron; and, of course, those who found in such proximity an opportunity for personal gain. As the modern state began to emerge, the exceptions increased, either due to the realization that no reform project could succeed if the modern state was opposed to it, or simply because of the dramatic centralization of power that was taking place, and the transformation of religious scholars into government employees.[15]

In the careers of Jamal al-Din al-Afghani (1838–1897)[16] and Muhammad 'Abduh (1849–1905)[17] we find fascinating examples of interactions with the leaders of the time. Both tried to co-opt Khedive Tawfiq[18], and supported his succession, believing he would enact the reforms they believed in.

'Abduh would describe him as: 'not greedy and covetous, rather he is kind-hearted and pious. There is much hope in him for those who want to reform the situation.'[19] Once he became the ruler, however, Tawfiq awoke from his reformist fantasy and turned against them. In no time, Afghani was expelled from Egypt. Afghani was no more fortunate with Sultan Abdülhamid II[20] who effectively placed him under house arrest. When told to stop playing with the beads of his *masbaha*, or string of prayer beads, in the presence of the sultan, the agitated Afghani responded, 'The Sultan plays with the lives of thirty million subjects, and I am not allowed to play with thirty beads?'[21] 'Abduh's relationship with Khedive 'Abbas[22] was no different. 'Abduh would agree to visit him, but he had an acute sense of the 'dignity' of that which he represented, far too much of it in the eyes of 'Abbas who would complain, 'He ['Abduh] enters my chamber as though he was pharaoh himself.'[23]

So much for the distant past. Let us zoom in now on Syria, my personal obsession. Ahmad Kaftaru (1915–2004), the late grand mufti of Syria, is perhaps most famous for being the Muslim scholar who decided to make an alliance with Hafiz al-Asad, long before Asad became the powerful 'king' of Syria.[24] This stand infuriated many of Syria's religious scholars who regarded Asad as an Alawite Ba'thist from rural Latakia (in essence combining everything they hated). Kaftaru's logic was that Asad was going to be president no matter what, and that an alliance with him would ensure that Muslim scholars were not entirely marginalized from society.[25] Eventually, most of those who disagreed with Kaftaru, including Al-Buti,[26] would emulate his approach and, by the late 1990s, numerous Syrian religious scholars had created some type of alliance with the regime. And it wasn't only religious scholars; merchants, technocrats, even philosophers, novelists and poets became part of this peculiar framework.

After completing my studies and returning to Damascus in 1993, I came to know many of these individuals personally. Some were relatives, and others were friends. For reasons not entirely clear to me, they would confide in me their close and private encounters with Syria's kings, the powerful figures with whom they became associated. Some were content to know the head of a security branch; others were more (or less) fortunate and became associated with a minister or prime minister, or (very rarely) with Asad himself. All had stories to share, as though driven by a hunger for catharsis. Their stories, shared over endless cups of tea and cigarettes, could go on for hours, leaving me exhausted and gasping for air. They weren't interested in my insights, though at times I felt I had to share a few words, words I knew they were far too consumed in their experience to hear. But I was listening, and learning. Looking back, I think I was silently writing in my head a manual entitled *One Thousand and One Reasons You Should Never Enter the Circles of Kings*.

Excerpts from *One Thousand and One Reasons You Should Never Enter the Circles of Kings*

(A book that was never written)

Do not attempt to befriend a king

Friendships imply reciprocity, and expectations of an even platform. None of this applies to kings. And if you happen to have been the friend of a king before he became one, abandon all such expectations the very moment he is crowned. Mustafa Tlas was once a friend of Hafiz al-Asad, but after 1970, Tlas understood that the most he could get away with was joking in the presence of Asad. He could tell a few animated stories about leaders Asad didn't like, such as Yasir Arafat, but that was about it. All the rules that applied to other political figures, applied to Tlas, and one error could send him on a fast train to Syria's twilight zone. Far more complex a scenario was to have been a person of accomplishment before your king assumed the throne. Tlas could move from friend to entertainer, but what was he to do with the president's son whom he had known as a child? How do you move from placing a child on your lap to nodding with approval at everything this child, now king, says?

Do not attempt to unfriend a king

Though you are barred from becoming the friend of a king, you must equally understand that once associated with a king, you cannot simply move on. You see, in the eyes of kings, your mere association meant that you benefited from this proximity, in return for which you are forever indebted. This is not a relationship you can put behind you. Even if you were a minister for a year, a spokesman for a month, or a mere personal barber for a week, that's it! Life as you previously knew it is over. From now on, you must always conduct yourself in a manner befitting of this relationship. I still remember the late 'Isam al-Za'im (1940–2007) who was Minister of State for Planning Affairs and, subsequently, Minister of Industry.[27] Not too long after he was encouraged to return to Syria to become Minister of Planning, this genuine reformer, with strong old-school leftist principles, found himself in a nightmarish maze from which there was no escape. When I would visit him at his office, as part of my work at the United Nations Development Programme (UNDP), he looked as though he was constantly consumed with a very different type of planning than that which his job entailed. The man looked as though he was planning his escape. 'Have you been to Mexico?' he would abruptly ask. 'I taught there for several years, it's a beautiful place.' His subsequent position at the Ministry of Industry brought with it more black comedy, and even a temporary hold on his assets. The very man who was at war with corruption now had to clear his own reputation. It took around seven years for Za'im's escape plan to finally succeed, but tragically, it came in the form of a fatal heart attack in December 2007.

Do not speak in the presence of a king

If there is a constant theme to the stories I once heard, it is the fact that kings, all kings, are genetically predisposed to anger. These poor creatures simply cannot help it. It appears to be something they are born with. So, in order to avoid the fits of anger being directed at you, the best possible policy is to say nothing. Anything you say can be misunderstood. If you provide advice, the implication is you know something the king does not know. Do you really think it is possible for you to know something that the king does not? If in doubt, ponder with me the fate of Faruq al-Shar'. In an interview with *Al-Akhbar* in 2012, Shar' provided unsolicited advice to Syria's president on the futility of using force to supress Syria's uprising.[28] This would mark his last interview before his rapid disappearance from all public life. I remember, too, a friend once shared with me how he travelled with an important government official. During a meeting with a foreign delegation, a question was asked and, since this important official clearly did not know the answer, my friend made the very unwise decision to provide it. For months, this was his only story. Not so much the actual event, but everything this official did to him after the event. 'He's out to get me,' he would whisper as he inhaled his cigarettes. 'And my only crime is answering a stupid question!'

Do not remain silent in the presence of a king

Even worse than speaking in the presence of a king is to remain silent when the king expects someone to say something. If the king asks a question, you cannot count on it being rhetorical. It may be, and it may not be. It's much wiser to say something, but it's equally wise to avoid sounding intelligent. You certainly don't want to end up patronizing a king. A close friend loved to share with me how every time the prime minister asked a question, he deliberately mumbled something incoherent. 'You have no idea how much he enjoys this. I am certain I am his favourite member of the cabinet!'

And always remember, kings die

This is by far the most difficult to comprehend. You see, even if you have mastered and perfected the art of survival with a king, this very king may die before you, leaving you in the hands of another king who may require and expect a very different art of interaction, and one which you are simply unable to learn fast enough. Driss Basri, the late Minister of Interior under Muhammad V of Morocco, went from being the second most powerful man in the kingdom to being detained and interrogated on the very same evening that King Muhammad V died.[29] After Hafiz al-Asad died, his vice-president, 'Abd al-Halim Khaddam, who in theory would have been Asad's successor, spent his thirty-six day period as Interim President of Syria,[30] ironically, almost entirely absent from public events. He had one task on which he was supposed to focus, his real job, which was to ensure the smooth transition of power from father to son.

A relative of mine, gentle and kind-hearted, and light years away from the sensibility of Driss Basri, felt that the whole system had turned against him after Hafiz al-Asad died. He would receive private messages from powerful men warning him that he was about to be arrested. 'If Asad were still alive, he would have protected me,' were the words he would share with me over and over, 'I gave up everything to serve my country, and this is how they repay me?' Unable to watch this kind man so sad and depressed, my hopelessly Sufi side got involved. 'You will find out that your true protector was not Hafiz al-Asad, it was (rather) *Al-Wahid al-Ahad* (God the One, the Unique),' I would repeat to him. Privately, however, I was truly concerned, often waking up in fear that he was in danger. When they finally left him alone, I made him promise to never, ever, regardless of intention or circumstance, enter the circles of kings again.

POST-UPRISING INTROSPECTIONS: IN THE CIRCLES OF KINGS – A PERSONAL SEQUEL

After I first shared my piece entitled 'In the Circles of Kings', I was encouraged by colleagues to pen a personal sequel. I had refrained from adding these stories originally, not only because it's always easier to talk about what others experience, but also because I felt my own stories were far too insignificant to warrant inclusion. It appears that, at least on the level of comedy, my colleagues thought otherwise. So, here they are uncensored.

My father had very strong feelings regarding shielding me and my sisters from the small world of Syria's political elite. And so, even though my father was a minister for far too long – thirty years in total (1971–2001) with a short (though important) interruption as the president of the Arab Fund – and even though he had known Hafiz al-Asad since the mid-sixties and had even taught him, and many other generals, economics and planning, I do not have any memory of meeting important officials, or sons of important officials for that matter. All of this changed, however, on one spring day in April 2000. Forty-five days before Hafiz al-Asad died, when his son was still the Head of the Syrian Informatics Society, I was asked by my father's secretary to attend an event at the Asad Library. 'Your father is not feeling well, and he would be very pleased if you attended,' were the words of my father's secretary, who was really far more than a mere secretary, and a man who had a talent for making you feel very guilty for not going along with his proposals.

A driver arrived at my UNDP office in Abu Rummaneh with the invitation card, but since it was walking distance, I decided to go by foot on that Tuesday morning. As I got closer to the library, I noticed that the security presence was heavier than normal. But in those days, it was easy to dismiss such signs. I kept walking until I reached the library, climbed up the marble steps and headed into the auditorium where the event was to take place. Now, it is important here to note that I am by nature introverted, an INFP (Introverted, iNtuitive, Feeling, Perceiving) to use the language of Myers-Briggs, and for those who know anything about INFPs it is not difficult to understand why I would automatically head to the back in search of a seat in some neglected corner where I could observe the event from a distance and leave if I felt it was not my kind of event, as I already suspected it wouldn't be. My attempt to head to the back of the auditorium, however, was abruptly stopped by a young woman with a very serious look. She asked to see my invitation card, and I shared it (big mistake) and she then asked me to follow her, which I did (an even worse mistake). You see, this young woman was leading me to where my father was supposed to sit. And as she walked towards the front row, I tried repeatedly to explain that this was not where I should be sitting. Finally, she reached her destination – the middle of the front row. She pointed at a seat and said, or rather commanded, 'Sit here.' One final time, I tried to explain, but she interrupted, 'I can only allow you to sit where your card says you should sit.' And she walked away, leaving me contemplating an empty chair in the still, as of yet, empty front row.

There is something about growing up in Syria that facilitates obedience even when you know what you are being asked to do makes no sense at all. And so, I sat. Don't ask me for how long; it may have been only for seconds. But suddenly, a group of men approached the front row, one of whom was very tall. They all shook my hand and sat down. The tall man, now sitting to my right, was Bashar al-Asad. I glanced to the back and noticed the important men of his circle, men who would soon become ministers and ambassadors, men who were probably wondering who on earth this young man sitting next to their king-in-waiting was. I felt I had to say something, something that could explain what I was doing in this chair before a security guard was asked to escort me out. And so, I turned to him and whispered something unintelligible about who I was and why I was here. He smiled, though I probably left him even more confused as to the identity of the impostor sitting next to him. And of course, there were numerous photographers taking numerous pictures, adding, in the process, to how surreal it all felt. At the very first intermission, I quietly walked out, and rushed back to my office, promising myself that from now on I would completely ignore the requests of my father's secretary.

The next day, pictures of the event were published everywhere, and for weeks I had to explain to acquaintances and, often, complete strangers, why and how I ended up sitting next to Bashar al-Asad. Needless to say, the story I have just shared was regarded as pure fiction. In the minds of the vast majority of those who witnessed this event, my presence meant I was being groomed for something far more important than words could share.

A far more pleasant experience took place shortly after the death of Hafiz al-Asad. The heads of state and various dignitaries who flooded Damascus to offer their condolences were assigned to various ministers. My father was asked to accompany President Muhammad Khatami (president of Iran from 1997–2005). I knew Khatami well through stories I had heard from my Sufi teacher, Bashir al-Bani. Al-Bani knew Khatami from the time he had been Iran's Minister of Culture, and they both shared a deep interest in philosophy and spirituality. My favourite story was when Al-Bani arrived at a mosque in Damascus for the Eid prayer. Khatami, who was by then president, noticed him and insisted on breaking all protocol and walked towards Al-Bani even as Khatami held Hafiz al-Asad's hand. Al-Bani tried to walk away, but Khatami caught up with him and for a few very awkward seconds, Khatami was holding on to both Al-Bani and Asad. 'I survived only by the *lutf* (grace) of God,' Al-Bani would conclude his story, as his students and I laughed. So, against this background, when I learned from my father that he was with Khatami at the Meridian hotel, I raced in my Peugeot 505 from my home in Mazzeh, arriving at the Meridian in a matter of minutes. As I walked in, I tried to think of what I would say, and how difficult it would be to speak to a man who was the very president of the Islamic Republic of Iran. When I reached the floor where my father had asked me to meet him, I found a very unexpected scene awaiting me. Khatami was surrounded by the hotel's workers, waiters, janitors, and others, all taking turns to have their picture taken with the ever-smiling president. I had expected spiritual depth, as Al-Bani had often emphasized, but I was not expecting this level of humility. When I reached him, my father, who was standing next to him, introduced me. 'So, you are this kind man's son,' he said. I smiled and replied, 'I am also the student of your friend, Bashir al-Bani.' He immediately embraced me, and said, 'You are, then, doubly-connected.'

No encounter was as inspiring, however, as meeting HRH Prince Hassan bin Talal at a special event held at the University of St Andrews in November 2018.[31] Listening to a Hashemite prince speak so eloquently, with an Oxfordian accent, about what he described as the crisis of 'human warming' and the need for a new global approach to human suffering and injustice had a profound effect on me. Memories of my elder family members sharing with me stories of the Kingdom of Syria and all the hopes that were crushed when King Faisal was forced to leave came back to me. Here I was, now sitting near the great nephew of King Faisal, wishing only that my father was here too to experience a very different type of royalty; one, sadly, that is as rare as desert rain.

I can add to these the many encounters that I aborted before they could materialise, but they are, in my mind at least, as boring as the pseudo-kings they involved. With only three actual encounters to my name, I think I can credibly claim to have faithfully lived the advice I shared in the previous section: to never, ever enter the circles of kings!

Chapter VIII

Life Beyond the Court

The period between the death of Hafiz al-Asad and the first cabinet formed under the presidency of Bashar al-Asad on 13 December 2001 spans a year, six months, and three days. During this time, Imady continued to serve as Minister of Economy, though upon the President's death it was instantly clear to him that this was not destined to last. The new president wanted new men and women in office, new approaches, new objectives; and though he didn't want to imply that he was at odds with his father's legacy, Bashar was clearly adamant at navigating his own path. In this vein, he wanted his own version of Muhammad Imady, and this, after a few experiments, he would find in 'Abdallah Dardari, a non-Ba'thist, western-educated technocrat from a prestigious Damascene family who would eventually be appointed as deputy prime minister for economic affairs and would remain in this position until 2011.

Dardari, unlike Imady, was mentally attuned to the pace and nature of the new economic reforms Bashar wanted to introduce. Though Imady was thoroughly opposed to and by the Ba'thist guardians of centralised economies, he was, as Raymond Hinnebusch once noted: 'no neoliberal ideologue… Imadi's middle position between vested interests suggests he can be seen as an autonomous technocrat looking out for the state's economically rational best interest, rather than, as some suggest, a representative of the bourgeoisie, who, in fact, do not see him as their man.'[32] Indeed, even the few measures which were introduced prior to his departure, like Law 28 of March 2001 which permitted the establishment of private and joint-venture banks, were measures designed to lay the initial foundations for the far more dramatic changes that would take place after Imady had left office.

As eager as Imady was to put his ministerial career behind him, it must have been difficult for him to hear a new cabinet formed without his name included for the first time since 1972. From 13 December 2001, he suddenly became a free man, free to leave Syria and use his savings to settle with his wife in Palisades, free to take up a hobby, free to go on a long vacation. And yet, at the age of seventy, Imady, the man hopelessly addicted to reform, decided on a very different way to live his post-ministerial life.

First, he applied himself to writing. When he left his ministerial position in 2001, he had only written a few works on economics that were taught at the university, and a book on his experiment at the Arab Fund which was published in 1985. By 2004, however, he had published three additional books on the various economic challenges he spent his life trying to address:

The Concerns of Development – Events I Will Not Forget (July 2002)
Syria and the March towards Arab Economic Integration (November 2002)
The Evolution of Approaches to Development in Syria (May 2004).

In 2001, Imady would also embark on a project to establish an orphanage (Dar al-Na'im) that would equip young Syrian girls and boys who had lost their parents with the training and skills required to become financially independent. He was chosen by the trustees of the orphanage to be the chairman of their board, a position he continues to occupy.

In 2004, Syria was on the verge of allowing the establishment of both private banks and universities, and in both these realms – financial and academic – officials and private investors would see in Imady a man capable of providing credibility and integrity to their newly established institutions. Imady thus became the Chairman of the Board of Trustees of the Arab International University (2005–present), and was also designated as the Chairman of the Board of the Commissioners, after Law 22 of 2005 establishing the Syrian Commission on Financial Markets and Securities was passed, though he would not officially assume his duties until February 2006. It would take until March 2009 for the Damascus Securities Exchange to be launched (with six companies initially listed), and by May 2010, 14 companies capitalised at nearly $1.2 billion dollars were listed. Imady's tenure as chairman would be renewed for a second term in 2010, before he officially retired in February 2014.

His reflections on his experience in Syria's stock market and in the Arab International University would be documented, respectively, in his works entitled *Syrian Commission on Financial Markets and Securities: Eight Years Since its Establishment* (2014), and *Selected Studies on University Teaching* (2015).

On 4 April 2015, the Friends of Damascus Society honoured Imady for a lifetime of service, and for all the contributions he had made to Syria's economy. Speakers at the event congratulated Imady for nearly sixty-four years of dedication; from March 1960, when he first joined the State Planning Commission, to February 2014, when his second term at the Syrian Commission on Financial Markets and Securities ended.

What this award failed to take note of was that, in addition to his achievements in the realms of economics, Imady had also succeeded in reviving the legacy of a family that had lain dormant since at least the eighteenth century. Status, once lost, is rarely revived; once it has disappeared, families that formerly enjoyed prominence and prestige usually fade into obscurity where they tend to remain. As such, not only had Imady achieved the difficult task of introducing his reforms, but he had accomplished the seemingly impossible task of reviving the significance of his family name too.

THE QUEST FOR JOSEPH

Of all the events that have taken place in Syria since my father left office in December 2001, none have been as significant as the event that came to be known first as the Syrian Uprising, and subsequently as Syria's civil war, or even wars. When my father's term as the Chairman of the Board of Commissioners was renewed in 2010, he could not have imagined that by the time this second term ended in 2014, Syria would be damaged in ways unprecedented in its modern history. For three years, my father was associated with a regime which had unleashed brutal violence against peaceful civilian protesters, besieged and bombarded towns and cities, even allegedly used chemical weapons against the residents of East Ghuta, and destroyed an economy that took decades to build. Yes, my father was far more removed from the regime than he had been when he was minister of economy. Yes, he was in effect a technocrat in charge of a very specialised and technical aspect of the Syrian economy, the stock market, but he was still on some level an official who carried out official duties.

How is one to understand my father's moral positioning during this period?

My last visit to Syria was in January 2012. During this visit, I argued with my father for hours over why he would continue to work in his position despite all that had taken place, that continues to take place? (Though in January 2012, the worst was yet to come.) Why, at the age of eighty-two would he not simply retire, invoke a health problem and withdraw to the privacy of his home? Would that not be morally superior to remaining associated with a regime that was seen, even as early as January 2012, in a far worse manner than during the height of the Hindawi affair?

It is necessary here to pause and briefly discuss the terms *state, government* and *regime*. While these terms have distinct meanings in accordance with which political thinker or analytic school employs them, many analysts of Syria tend to use these terms to denote the following: The state is the largest umbrella possible and it would encompass everyone who has an official duty in Syria, from an accountant at a cement factory to the president. The government is used to denote the prime minister and the cabinet of ministers who effectively carry out the president's policies. And the regime is used to denote the power pillars in the Ba'th party, the military and the security agencies which empower and sustain the presidency.

In my father's mind, he was never part of the regime, not even remotely, though he was, prior to December 2001, a member of the Syrian government. But from 2006 to 2014, he was only part of a broader framework, best described as the Syrian state. In his mind, he was one of the 2.2 million workers in the public sector who ensured, through daily contributions, that Syria's economy did not collapse. To my father, Syria's economy did not belong to any specific government or regime. It belonged to the people, and not just the current generation, but to future generations as well. As such, he was simply doing his part to preserve it.

Still, and though my father never actually shared this with me, I am certain that he was very uncomfortable, and morally challenged by the state of affairs from 2011 onwards. Perhaps this explains why during this period, he never took part in a media event in which he articulated a position for or against what was taking place.

My father, in short, did what every other Damascene reformer would do; he opted for what I described earlier as the 'fourth path':

> 'The path of those adamant at introducing meaningful changes to what appeared to be a meaningless setup. The path of allaying the regime's security fears and then proceeding to work quietly in the shadows. The path of signing an agreement, as it were, with the security pillars of the regime:
>
>> We will not work against you. We will say those things you like us to say in public. We will even allow others to regard us as your supporters. But in return, you will allow us to truly work for this country in a manner that reflects our own values and moral sensibility. And you will allow us to do so outside the framework of your politicised institutions. Furthermore, we will accept that we will be regularly harassed, especially when our achievements become too noticeable. You will harass us, yes, but you will not eliminate us.'[33]

So wholehearted was my father's commitment to this fourth route that even when, on 8 April 2013, he was injured after a bomb exploded outside his office in central Damascus, he still returned to his duties the moment he recovered. He could easily have used this event (which resulted in a head injury requiring thirteen stitches) to retire, as I in earnest wished he had. But he stubbornly remained committed to what he regarded as his life's mission, the mission of serving his country irrespective of who ruled over it.

Today, more than ten years after the Syrian Uprising began, and at least seven years after it mutated into something more akin to a civil war, I often reflect on how differently my father and I diagnosed what took place after 2011. In my mind, this was a battle for the soul of Syria, a battle for dignity, freedom and human worth. In my father's mind, on the other hand, this was, in the final analysis, a battle over power, and he was, at ground zero of his sensibility, not interested in a battle of this type. He was very cynical about the expectations I, and other idealists like me, attach to the outcome of power battles. In Egypt after all, the protestors won only for the very regime they attempted to overthrow to reproduce itself.

Perhaps his indifference was exacerbated by the fact that he had worked under very different regimes – from the 'democratic' experiment of post-independence, to the United Arab Republic, to the secessionist phase, moving on to the first Ba'th regime in 1963, and then finally to Hafiz al-Asad following the coup of 1970. My father, in a sense, had seen it all. And, having seen it all, he didn't seem to attach as much importance to who was in charge as he did to how much each respective political system allowed him to contribute in a meaningful way. In fact, the secessionist regime, which was, in theory, far more liberal and democratic, had somewhat side-lined him because of his Nasserite sympathies, whereas under the pseudo-Marxist Ba'th regime that took over after the 1963 coup he had been able to contribute meaningfully in various posts at the State Planning Commission.

Of course, it wasn't only me who was problematised by what I term here as my father's 'moral positioning'. Many thinkers, activists, and revolutionaries who are opposed to the Syrian regime would share my sentiment, and at times, to far more intense degrees.

On 18 August 2018, Fu'ad 'Abd al-'Aziz, a regular contributor to an important opposition media outlet named *Zaman al-Wasl*, published an article entitled: 'Dr Muhammad Imady, the honourable economist who loved Hafiz al-Asad with all his heart'. 'Abd al-'Aziz's article is significant because it is a rare example of a piece that both praises and criticises my father, and its author appears to be as perplexed as I am as to how to understand Imady's legacy.

> 'No one has been able to find a convincing explanation for why Imady cried upon learning of the death of Hafiz al-Asad, especially since Imady enjoys the genuine respect of all Syrians… and yet, regardless of the many question marks related to Imady's relationship with Hafiz al-Asad, we cannot ignore the role he played as minister of economy for many years… a role which many regard as having saved Syria's economy in crucial phases… Imady, in fact, according to many observers, was capable through his selfless dedication to his job and his love of his country, to infuse Hafiz al-Asad with a degree of compassion… And yet, the charge can be levelled

> against Imady for having been supportive of the regime of Hafiz al-Asad and for having not voiced his opposition even to the clear instances in which the regime's corruption was manifest... And yet, regardless of what can be said about Imady's performance, no one can deny his integrity and his patriotism and his dedication to his work, attributes which have qualified him by some to be known as the 'Father of the Syrian Economy.'[34]

To aid in unraveling the phenomenon my father represents, it is helpful to zoom out, out of Syria, even out of the Middle East, and to consider cases from other countries and regimes in which figures who share his approach to reform have worked. In a sense, it is the search for Damascene reformers outside of Damascus.

David Luban is a Professor of Law and Philosophy at Georgetown University. In his controversial work entitled 'Complicity and Lesser Evils: A Tale of Two Lawyers', he explores the ethical dilemma faced by a person of integrity, who is either already employed or has been offered a position by an authoritarian regime. He focuses on two lawyers, Bernhard Lösener and Helmuth James von Moltke, who remained part of the Nazi regime and, as a result of their positions, were able to save lives. Luban captures the crux of the issue:

> 'Government lawyers and other public officials sometimes face an excruciating moral dilemma: to stay on the job or to quit, when the government is one they find morally abhorrent. Staying may make them complicit in evil policies; it also runs the danger of inuring them to wrongdoing, just as their presence on the job helps inure others. At the same time, staying may be their only opportunity to mitigate those policies – to make evils into lesser evils – and to uphold the rule of law when it is under assault.'[35]

Luban uses the term *Spielraum* to identify the key component which facilitates the pursuit of this 'lesser-evilism' in authoritarian regimes. *Spielraum* denotes the scope for oppositional manoeuvring within a post or position; the more *Spielraum* one is permitted, or can negotiate, the greater one's capacity for effecting positive change within an otherwise corrupt institution. Without this manoeuvre room, one is essentially straight jacketed into the regime's structures and objectives, and the pursuit of any oppositional or positive change would result only in the termination of one's employment, or life. Luban proposes an analysis of the lives and actions of figures such as Moltke and Lösener through the lens of the *Spielraum* they enjoyed or manufactured, and the change they were able to enact as a result, largely in response to the views of Hannah Arendt, who advocated the maxim: obedience is support. In her analysis of the swift and shocking rise of Nazism in Germany, Arendt holds that to participate in authoritarian regimes under the guise of 'lesser-evilism' in any way is to commit two crimes: that of self-deception; and of perpetuating the greater evil. In respect of the first, she conveys her moral absolutist conviction that 'those who choose the lesser evil forget very quickly that they chose evil'.[36] The milieu of authoritarianism is pervasive and swift in its diluting of one's ability to distinguish between right and wrong.

Her second charge is based on the view that those who choose to stand beside the regime, regardless of how strong their internal opposition, erode the confidence of others in their own conviction to disobey and facilitate the regime's stay in power. In essence, the presence of the 'reformers' not only obstructs the clear view of the evil of these regimes that others may have otherwise had and acted upon, but by doing so they facilitate the pursuit of evil by those in power who enjoy the veil of normality or acceptability such reformists provide.

Such a crime of complicity is found in the example of Hjalmar Schacht, who opposed Hitler's policy of re-armament whilst serving in the Nazi government, first as President of the Central Bank (1933–1939) and subsequently as Minister of Economics (1934–1937). In the closing argument of the Nuremberg trials, Robert H. Jackson, appointed by President Harry S. Truman in 1945 as US Chief of Counsel for the prosecution of Nazi war criminals, is unequivocal in his articulation of Schacht's complicity:

> 'It was Schacht, the facade of starched respectability, who in the early days provided the window-dressing, the bait for the hesitant, and whose wizardry later made it possible for Hitler to finance the colossal rearmament programme, and to do it secretly.'[37]

In the example of Schacht, the crime of complicity is taken further than the mere veiling of evil; the skills and talents such individuals possess, at the same time as they are being used for good, are also being employed in the pursuit of the regime's own goals. As such, these individuals are inevitably tools in the facilitation of the greater evil. For surely that is how they found themselves in their official positions to begin with, for the potential benefits they represented in the eyes of those in charge. Jackson makes this point ardently clear in his remarks:

> 'It is doubtful whether the Nazi master plan could have succeeded without their specialized intelligence which they so willingly put at its command. They did so with knowledge of its announced aims and methods, and continued their services after practice had confirmed the direction in which they were tending. Their superiority to the average run of Nazi mediocrity is not their excuse. It is their condemnation.'[38]

As convincing as these arguments may appear, however, Luban argues against what Arendt herself termed this 'germ-proof moralism'. The thesis that obedience is support, and that appearance is reality he argues, is, in the final analysis, too simple, too stark, and too easy.[39]

In the instances when an individual is afforded *Spielraum*, the question is not one of comparing two evils – the evil of a regime's actions with or without their presence. Rather, it is the weighing of the good they were able to do against the evil which their assuming or remaining in a post may have facilitated. In his examination of the cases of Moltke and Lösener, Luban concludes that 'the intangible contribution to moral breakdown seems far outweighed by the concrete good these two did'.[40]

Furthermore, Luban argues against Arendt's firm position that choosing evil of any degree inevitably erodes one's ability to discern it from good in the longer term. In fact, he writes, the enactment of resistance can bolster and reaffirm one's moral commitments, particularly in the face of an authoritarian system. Rather than a corrosion of one's convictions, evil can serve to sharpen them. What Luban does not go so far as to mention, but which is clearly referenced in the piece by 'Abd al-'Aziz, is not only the possibility of maintaining one's own sense of morality in the midst of corruption, but also the potential for this to positively influence those in power themselves. 'Abd al-'Aziz, as aforenoted, ascribes to my father the capacity to have morally seduced the other side towards a degree of compassion and honesty:

> 'Imady, in fact, according to many observers, was capable through his selfless dedication to his job and his love of his country, to infuse Hafiz al-Asad with a degree of compassion…'[41]

Arendt's position of moral absolutism, and in turn the positions of Robert H. Jackson and numerous Syrian anti-regime figures, are all, according to Luban, right only in contexts in which no room for oppositional manoeuvring exists. Where it does, and where it is acted upon, our judgements must be based on carefully weighed evidence.

> 'Sometimes quitting is the right thing to do; but when there is *Spielraum*, and a genuine prospect of mitigating evil, staying at the desk can be the righteous path. But only for those who actually resist.'[42]

Ironically, though Luban's conceptual framework provides a layer of moral legitimacy to Imady's approach to reform, my father and his fellow Damascene reformers were not waiting for any such validation. They appear to be driven by an existential sense of what their mission is, rather than by the type of moral 'resistance' Luban invokes.

When asked how he regarded his own moral positioning, my father would respond instantly: 'As Joseph once did.' Both in the Biblical and the Qur'anic accounts, Joseph becomes a high-ranking official in a kingdom which was neither monotheistic nor known as a bastion of justice and compassion. Yet, Joseph explicitly asks the pharaoh (postulated by some scholars to be Amenemhat III (1841–1797 BCE)) to be made responsible 'for the treasures of the earth',[43] a job which my father equated with the modern position of Minister of Economy. As Joseph managed the drought Egypt underwent during his service, thus did my father regard his attempt to alleviate Syria's economic crisis during the 1980s.

Joseph was not inhibited by what the upper echelons of ancient Egypt stood for, nor by the practises and lifestyles of its officials. He wanted to make a contribution, and both the Bible and the Qur'an celebrate his achievements. And though Amenemhat III does indeed recognise the potential of Joseph, as Hafiz al-Asad would recognize my father's potential, neither the pharaoh nor Asad appear to be relevant to the larger narrative. Amenemhat III is not even mentioned by name in the Qur'an or Bible, and nothing is shared in either account to validate his moral legitimacy. In accordance with the scriptural approaches, to dwell on who this Egyptian king was is as much a distraction as it is to dwell on who Hafiz al-Asad was. The real story lies in the attempt of an individual to achieve something meaningful, however ultimately minimal, in a very meaningless, and often hostile, context.

I find peace in regarding my father as a modern manifestation of Joseph not because I could see myself making the same choices he made. I am certain that I would have been unable to be at peace with working for a regime with whom I did not morally identify. My idealism, probably implanted in me by my mother, would have inhibited me constantly. I find peace in this approach, rather, because it helps me understand not just my father's life, but also the lives of the many Damascene reformers I was blessed with knowing as relatives and close family friends. Joseph's story was about Joseph. It is shared through an individualised, human-centred lens, unencumbered by the moral status of other characters, larger questions of leadership legitimacy, and the interplay of person and context which, regardless of the route reformers take, will always be subject to scrutiny and criticism. Those are certainly valid and important discussions, but often distract from the focus on the individual lived experience of the Josephs involved. There is a need to examine the stories of the pharaohs; this was the story of Joseph.

And yet, even as I find peace in understanding how Damascene reformers regard themselves, there has never been a time when it was harder to assume such a position. To be a Damascene reformer today, as I once wrote, is 'to stand for the very first time stripped of the capacity to even contemplate reform; watching the country being torn at its seams, and waiting for the day when the last of the reformers will finally be eliminated for daring to believe that reform was ever possible.'[44]

Chapter IX

Nonsense and the Absurd

THROUGH MY OWN LENS

The surreal world my father dealt with following his arrival back in his country of birth in 1960 took on proportions and dimensions of a nature no one could have predicted after 2011. Just when one thinks events are as surreal as they can possibly get, another unfolds which makes the former seem normal by comparison.

The last time I met with my father in person was in 2017, when I travelled to Beirut and was able to talk to him directly. During that visit, I was able to ask him for his perspectives on the events that had transpired since the Uprising. As such, for the introspections I have hitherto shared relating to events prior to 2017 I have at least an idea of his response, careful and elusive as it may have typically been. Though I speak to my parents regularly, discussion of any topic of a political nature is, of course, impossible by phone or any other medium of communication. What follows in this part are my reflections on events post-2017. In order to articulate a position on these events, I often found myself adopting a satirical lens, perhaps because any other attempt to identify meaning or purpose in the continuing tragedy simply failed as the news headlines sound more and more like surrealist apocalyptic fiction. What is ironic is that, while the sharing of these thoughts, as I have done in the following chapters, would not have been condoned by my father, I often think that they are precisely the types of reflections that must cross his mind now as he observes the Syria he helped to build over the past forty years fall into chaos and turmoil.

ALL IN THE NAME OF SOVEREIGNTY

What most people don't understand about events in Syria is that everything that has taken place since the Uprising began has been done in the name of sovereignty. Yes, sovereignty. This is not a popular idea in the West. The West is addicted to freedom, elections, and the rule of law; meaningless things that often weaken the inner fabric of a country and diminish its stature and global standing. We are Arabs. Syrians. We understand the value of national honour.

You must be careful of those who try to misrepresent this story. To lure you into their flawed perception of things, they will share insignificant numbers. They will tell you over 500,000 were killed, millions were wounded, more than 5 million are now refugees, 6.5 million are displaced from their homes, and 13.5 million require humanitarian assistance. They will also bring up the economy. They will tell you the losses are in the hundreds of billions, cities are destroyed, infrastructure is shattered. They will bring up society. They will tell you there are so many wounds in Syria that it will take centuries to heal; that Syria's sects and ethnicities have never distrusted each other this much, hated each other this much; that we may not, in our lifetime, see children from the coast play with children from rural Damascus again; that there is so much thirst for vengeance that we may soon see walls dividing up Syrian towns and cities. In their desperation, they might even bring up psychology, and talk to you about a new generation of traumatized children, radicalized children, children who watched the aircrafts of their own government bomb their towns, kill their relatives, maim their friends. But we all know these are mind games they play. In the end, what are these except sacrifices, sacrifices made in the name of sovereignty and honour? Every country after all has had to make sacrifices. And these are the sacrifices Syria has had to make.

What were we supposed to do? Let some young men and women take over the country? Allow them to desecrate everything the Syrian Arab Republic stood for? To be sovereign is to have your land, sky and sea safeguarded, your borders approached as a sacred domain. Be careful of their arguments, their flawed logic. They will tell you that there are more foreign military bases in Syria now than there has ever been. They will tell you it is even worse now than it was during the French mandate. They will talk about the Russians in the west, the Turks in the north, the Americans in the northeast, and the Iranians in the south. They might even bring up the Israelis in the sky. Again, these are meaningless facts. The only relevant fact here is that all of this is temporary. So what if in one week American, Turkish and Israeli warplanes bombed different places in Syria? Nothing but a coincidence, and again, all temporary, all transient facts.

The same applies to land not presently under government control: the north, the east, the south, rural Damascus. All this geography is temporary. They should be bombed until they are obliterated. What are they full of except traitors and terrorists? They will show you footage of civilians killed. Be careful of these. Most, if not all, were filmed in makeshift cities. Have you watched *Wag the Dog*?[1] In fact, we don't even want the refugees to return, they are all cowards after all. Who other than cowards would leave their country? What were they escaping anyway? The rubble and destruction? The barrel bombs? Watching their family members killed? Does this justify abandoning your home? Does this justify seeking asylum in a hostile country? Regardless, in the end, we will have a Syria that is far purer. A Syria full of people who cherish their flag and admire their leadership. People who understand that everything their government has done was in the name of sovereignty.

STRANDED IN KABUL

More than a decade after the Syrian Uprising began, I now have an unexpected answer to the question I am repeatedly asked: 'Where is Syria today?' Without blinking, I respond: 'Stranded in Kabul!' My response generates the effect I am seeking, a combination of confusion and curiosity, followed by a request, by some, for me to elaborate. To those who are genuinely interested in an explanation, I proceed to share a story that began on the morning of 1 March 1994 in the basement of a building at the heart of the Damascene neighbourhood of Abu Rummaneh. This was where, back in the 1990s, the United Nations Development Programme (UNDP) office was based. My mother, too, once worked in this office, and she remembers the wounded pedestrians who rushed into the building, victims of the shrapnel from bombs dropped on Damascus by Israeli Phantoms in October 1973.[2]

But on 1 March 1994, the sky was clear, and the jacaranda trees glowed violet blue. I walked into this building as UNDP's new National Programme Officer, with the added description of Head of the Programme Support Unit. A few minutes later, I was introduced to the

Head of the Programme section, a man who looked far bigger than the small desk he was sitting behind. This was 'Abdallah Dardari who, by the end of the day, had convinced me that not only was he physically not well suited for his desk, but that he was also far bigger than his position at UNDP. This was not an easy feat, mind you. I'm not easily impressed, especially intellectually. Taught at Macalester by the likes of Mahmoud El-Kati, and at Penn by the late George Makdisi, and Alan Watson, I had high standards for what constitutes crisp and cohesive discourse. I remember 'Abdallah speaking non-stop on Syria's politics and economy, moving easily from Arabic to English. What captured me the most in his eloquent conversation was the faith he constantly reflected, faith that something could be done to make things better. This 'something' was not an actual plan, though it was thirsty to become one.

With time, it became clear that we both had a lot in common. We both came from old Damascene families and had fathers who had played an important role in modern Syria. Abdallah's father was General 'Abd al-Razzaq Dardari, commander of the Operations Division in the war of 1973,[3] and my father was the long-serving Minister of Economy. Both of us had also been educated in the West and had deep respect for its liberal values. And yet both of us were also deeply committed to Islam, though our understanding of it was far more 'enlightened', as we liked to describe it, than most of our acquaintances would have been comfortable with. We did, however, have a very important difference. Watching my father over the years, as he moved from one failed reform attempt to another, watching him having to deal with the dark side of Syria as he did his best to remain untainted, had left me unable to engage with the idea that reform, real reform, was possible. I was still very interested in studying and understanding how reform attempts were planned, organised and executed, but I was not in the least tempted to join such an attempt. 'Abdallah, on the other hand, was eager to do just that. At UNDP, we would both initiate a micro-finance program in rural Syria, and the first poverty alleviation program to openly use the term 'poverty' since 1963.[4]

It took around nine years for 'Abdallah to finally become one of Syria's new technocrats. Sometime in 2003, I recall him inviting me into his office. He closed the door and said he had something important to share with me. He then explained that he had been asked to be the new Head of the State Planning Commission. By then, he liked to refer to me as *al-Damir*, an Arabic word that can be translated as 'Mr. Conscience' or moral compass. 'Abdallah used it in jest to highlight what he regarded as my hyper-idealism. 'So, what does *al-Damir* think?' I smiled, and replied: 'Well, it's too late for me to think anything, you clearly can't say no to this, but my prayer is for you to be protected.'

'Abdallah understood my words to mean that I wished him to be protected from all the enemies of reform who had often driven my father and many others into despair and depression. And I did mean that, but I also was praying that the 'Abdallah I knew, the light, genuine, Damascene man I had met back in 1994, would not allow the circle of power and influence to change him.

Only two years later, 'Abdallah was appointed as Deputy Prime Minster for Economic Affairs, a post reserved during my father's tenure for hardcore Ba'thists. 'Abdallah was not only not a Ba'thist, he was also a strong believer in the market economy, though he would argue that his take on the economy was far more consistent with a Swedish take on capitalism, with strong emphasis on the role of the state in protecting the poor and fragile segments of society. After 2003, meetings with 'Abdallah became less frequent, partially because by then I was working at a university in Jordan, but also because his new duties meant he was consumed with work. But when I did meet him, I was always comforted by the fact that he was still the man I knew. In many ways, I felt sad for him. I regarded him as entrapped in a framework where, if things go wrong, as undoubtedly they would, he would be blamed by everyone, and if something happened to succeed, he would be the last to be credited with its success. Mostly, however, I was troubled on his behalf for all the contact he had with figures and officials with whom I could not imagine myself sitting in the same room.

And then March 2011 arrived. I remember at one point in Asad's infamous speech on 30 March 2011 reference was made to failed economic policies,[5] and I understood this as an implicit critique of 'Abdallah, and I actually felt relief. This to me meant that 'Abdallah would soon be relieved of his duties, and he would be out of what was bound to become a political and humanitarian nightmare. But the ever-believer in reform would not quit. In no time, 'Abdallah was creating an extensive network of Syrian researchers and experts from both loyalists and opposition circles to be part of a United Nations Economic and Social Commission for

Western Asia (ESCWA) sponsored program entitled National Agenda for Syria.[6] And sometime in late 2015, he asked me, and the Centre for Syrian Studies at the University of St Andrews, to be part of a team that would author *Syria at war: Five years on*.[7] During this phase I met and spoke to 'Abdallah more than I had had the chance to when he was working for the government. Many were troubled at the time by the fact that 'Abdallah did not openly attack the Syrian regime. He explained to me his logic, though I was already very familiar with it. It was not only his logic; it was also my father's and that of many others whom I had often described as Damascene reformers; figures who wanted to do something for Syria, and who understood that the quickest way to become irrelevant on Syria's reformers' map was to become entangled in an inflamed political battle.

Of course, in my mind there was, and continues to be, far more at stake than mere politics; there is a human aspect to what unfolded after March 2011 that I do not believe can be ignored. But as strong as my feelings are against the regime's brutal crushing of peaceful protesters, I also do not subscribe to the 'with us or against us approach' which both loyalists and opposition figures overwhelmingly employ. Ba'th party members, like Muslim fundamentalists, had produced a mindset where those who disagree or act differently are instantly branded as traitors, and ironically Syrians who hate the Ba'th and the Syrian regime are just as capable of using this tactic against those who do not publicly stand up against the regime as they do.

My dilemma is that I can understand both perspectives. After all, I was raised as a cultural bridge, constantly 'translating' to my mother, born and raised in New York, the Damascene ideas and perceptions that escaped her, and doing the same for my Syrian relatives when they seemed bewildered by my mother's words or actions. And so, when I listen to Samar Yazbek eloquently and powerfully describe the regime's brutality,[8] I sink into a deep mood and 'get it'; and when 'Abdallah speaks about all the reforms that need to be implemented in Syria, from the minute details to the larger frameworks, I smile, unsure of how much of this I can see unfolding in actual space and time, but I also 'get it'. I understand the need to believe that something rational can be done for Syria, and not for its regime, the need to believe that Syria is bigger than the transient government that rules over it; I get all of this because my father, like 'Abdallah, and like many other Damascene reformers I have met along the way, believed in this too. My dilemma becomes even more complicated because something in me thinks I can successfully 'translate' for both, if only given the chance; that I can demonstrate that in their raw essence, both Samar and 'Abdallah are after the same objective, a prosperous Syria where human worth is valued and no one, under any pretext, is empowered with the right to oppress others.

Even after 2011, 'Abdallah still wanted to do something, still believed that something could be done; and for this, some went as far as describing him as a fundraiser for the regime, a description which stood in deep contrast to 'Abdallah's strong moral position against what was taking place in Syria, a position he repeatedly shared with me and others in the clearest of terms, though not with media outlets. In 'Abdallah's mind, this was not the time to withdraw and allow Syria's dark side to fully take over. It was rather the time to try to do something, something however modest for those who really mattered, for those who were suffering in destroyed villages that lacked access to the most basic requirements of a healthy and dignified life. What would another anti-regime statement achieve exactly? He would rhetorically ask.

After ESCWA, 'Abdallah moved to the World Bank where he was the team leader of a project focused on reconstruction in the MENA (Middle East and North Africa) region, for which he was once again attacked, this time for allegedly trying to legitimise the regime's reconstruction efforts. Once again, the Centre for Syrian Studies was engaged, and I contributed *The Weaponization of Syria's Reconstruction*;[9] a piece which clearly contradicted the idea that whatever 'Abdallah or his team at the World Bank were after was research that supported the regime's approach to reconstruction. If anything, my colleagues and I thoroughly documented why regime practises were the very obstacle to fair and sustainable reconstruction – and I went even further, questioning the very purpose of the term 'reconstruction'. And yet, in the midst of all of this, I recall sitting and watching 'Abdallah on my computer screen as he spoke in a World Bank conference of his vision of what must take place in Syria, and I recall how he was able, in a manner very similar to 1 March 1994, the day I first met him, to inspire me, to make even the idealist sceptic in me believe that perhaps, just perhaps, something meaningful could still be done for Syria.

And then, last month, I received an email from ‘Abdallah which was sent to me and many of his other friends and colleagues informing us that he had been designated as the new UNDP Resident Representative in Kabul. The email was entitled ‘Goodbye’. It evoked an unexpected feeling, a feeling that it was not just ‘Abdallah who had, for the first time since 1994, shifted his energy to a project that was not purely Syria-related, but that somehow Syria, too, was now in a metaphorical Kabul: dangerous, beyond any form of political transition, and forgotten by the world. The suffering of its people has been normalised; the destruction of its towns and villages has been normalised; and its political nightmare has been normalised. Or perhaps somewhere in ‘Abdallah’s reformist Damascene mind, this new appointment constituted a specialised training session focused on learning the art of picking up the pieces and rebuilding, one tragic brick at a time.

ALL THE THINGS THAT STOPPED

The Arab International University (AIU) lies 35 km south of Damascus on the highway that leads to the Jordanian border. It was established in 2004, and at its height was home to seven thousand students studying in various fields. The AIU campus was very impressive, boasting a massive circular meeting hall that converged into the administrative building. For a period of two years, from 2008 to 2010, I served on the University’s Board of Directors. During this time, I was also working as the dean of an American university in Amman, but since AIU meetings were held at weekends and my weekends were always spent in Damascus, the arrangement worked well.

I remember clearly repeated invitations to leave my job in Amman for a position at AIU. I also remember how easy it was to decline these invitations. My decision wasn’t so much motivated by specific reasons as much as by a deep feeling that I should not return to live in Syria, at least not for the time being. Today, the AIU is confined to offices and classrooms in central Damascus. The campus, in which more than $250 million was invested, is now abandoned, as are other campuses that were established on the same highway. These include Yarmouk, the Syrian International University, and the International University for Science and Technology, all established between 2004 and 2007.

The AIU was not the first private university to be established in Syria. The University of Kalamoon, based in Dayr 'Atiyyah, was granted official status a year earlier and was known to be the only non-public university authorised to teach medicine. Kalamoon is owned and managed by Salim Da'bul, the son of the infamous Abu Salim (Mohammad Dib Da'bul) who served for a long time as the head of the office of President Hafiz al-Asad, a position he continued to hold under Bashar al-Asad. Kalamoon was initially more fortunate than other private universities around Damascus because of its location 88 km north of Damascus on the main highway leading to Homs. It survived the brief kidnapping of its founder back in July 2012,[10] but then found itself at the heart of the present battle over the area of Al-Qalamun. And so, like AIU, Kalamoon, too, retreated to central Damascus. It was not only universities that were affected in this way. The same pattern is found with private schools that were set up around the same period. Schools like Al-Wataniyyah in Saboura, The Little Village in Sahnaya, where two of my children once went, and the Modern Syrian School in the Ghuta, the green belt around Damascus destined to be the site of chemical weapons use against civilians. These were co-ed schools which, in addition to teaching the mandatory government curriculum, also taught various subjects in English. The largest of these schools was Little Village, which has today been reduced to a few classrooms in the Mazzeh neighbourhood.

It is indeed a daunting intellectual exercise to reflect on the various dynamics that were suddenly and unexpectedly suspended in March 2011. The story of this Uprising, along with its major subcategories, is largely known and documented. But underneath these main headings are fragments that are yet to be unearthed and shared. The story of how the Syrian Uprising changed, and ultimately stopped, various aspects of life in Damascus is one such fragment. The first student protest at AIU was held in October 2011.[11] The response came the next day, and it was quickly repeated at other campuses whenever student protests took place. *Shabihah*, or armed thugs, would suddenly arrive. They would walk into classrooms to the disbelief of professors and would call out the names of students who had clearly been reported by other students or security officers on campus. A vivid account of how this took place in Kalamoon was shared with me by my Damascene dentist who taught there at the time. As his various instruments drilled and poked into my teeth, he talked nonstop of how faculty members were humiliated by these thugs. What was surprising at first later became a pattern, which in turn became an established practice.

I also recall the sudden disappearance of young foreign women and men who had moved to Damascus to study Arabic. Until the 1990s, Cairo had been far more popular as a destination for those seeking to advance their knowledge of Arabic. However, the Centre for Teaching Arabic to Foreigners at the University of Damascus was slowly being discovered. By 2010, hundreds of foreign students were learning Arabic at this centre. Their presence in the city added something special to the coffee shops they were known to visit, like Nawfara, Beit Jabri, and Narenj. Another dynamic that was suspended was the weekly influx of families from rural Damascus to attend lessons given by popular Damascene religious teachers. On Fridays, the Abu al-Nur mosque, for example, in the neighbourhood of Rukn al-Din, would normally be surrounded by buses that had arrived from Jawbar, Duma, 'Irbin and other nearby towns. However, the Uprising would eventually cut these towns off from Damascus, and the buses that were once famous for blocking the roads were suddenly gone.

And then, of course, there was the change that affected my lifestyle the most. When I decided to stop working for the UN back in 2004 and search instead for an academic position, my decision to join the New York Institute of Technology (NYIT) in Amman rather than a university in the West was almost entirely based on my desire to remain close to Damascus. And so, for the next eight years, I would get in my car on Thursday evenings, tired from a long working week but eager to visit my family, and cross the 200 km of largely desert terrain. The most uncomfortable part was crossing the border, and all the processes that entailed – from the passport stamping to the 'voluntary' payment of one hundred Syrian pounds to the customs officer so he would be willing to process the entry of my car into Syria. After March 2011, I stopped traveling in my car and opted instead to use a reliable Damascene taxi service. Traveling the road alone had become too dangerous and unpredictable. My Damascene driver, with his various connections along the road, knew which detours to take and which checkpoints to avoid. The trip morphed into a tragic experience, a time when I would be updated by my driver on who had been killed, injured or arrested. I kept this up until early 2012, but then even my driver began to advise me to simply stay in Amman and travel if I must by plane to Beirut and from there by car to Damascus.

It was almost as though all of this was taking place in some type of insulated space that provided the illusion of permanence and continuity. Thousands upon thousands of people invested their time and energy into lifestyles that they never dreamed were as vulnerable as they proved to be beyond March 2011. None of this clearly compares, not by far, to the stories of death and destruction that Syria is so permeated with today. Yet, if there is a moral to this story, it is perhaps found in a Damascene proverb shared by my taxi driver during one of our eventful trips to Damascus: *Dab al-talj au ban al-marj*. 'The snow has melted, and the (true) field has appeared.'

RECONSTRUCTION & OTHER SYRIAN MYTHS

Joseph Campbell would speak of myths as constituting 'clues'.[12] When it comes to Syria, mythical narratives are precisely that; clues that point to what is really being said, to what is really being attempted. From the very beginning of the Syrian Uprising in March 2011, both the regime and the opposition have invested significant energy in the production of mythical narratives, and in the process have provided us with clues as to what they are truly after.

Take, for example, the first myth, that the spontaneous protests that emerged in February and swelled in March were manifestations of a foreign conspiracy. This wasn't difficult to discredit. After all, according to Syria's official media, Syria has always been the target of conspirators, a price it pays for its 'patriotic' positions against Israel and other enemies. Why would thousands of the inhabitants of Dar'a suddenly choose to join the enemies of Syria in an unprecedented show of popular resistance? Why would voices, deep inside the regime, from Faruq al-Shar' to Muhammad Salman, make it very clear that this is not a manifestation of a conspiracy?

But to dwell on discrediting the myth is a distraction. The point here is not whether or not this myth is easy to discredit, the point rather is what 'clues' this myth provides. In advancing this myth, the regime wasn't counting on people believing in it, the regime rather was providing regional and international players, and more importantly Syrians, with clues on how it planned on reacting. If a government accuses a certain movement of constituting the pawns of a conspiracy, then one should expect that it plans on fighting this movement till the very end. The president's speech on 30 March 2011[13] wasn't meant to be convincing in so far as the conspiracy narrative is concerned, rather it was meant to provide clear clues on how the regime planned to respond; clues, that were sadly ignored or cast aside by many.

Myth-production is by no means exclusive to the regime. Another myth which is very difficult to stay clear of is the personalization of what is taking place in Syria. This is all about Asad, we are constantly told: it's Asad's regime, Asad's army, even Asad's bombs – all terminology which I and many of my colleagues have used but which I am increasingly philosophically against. The problem with personalization is that it is an act of oversimplification. The implication here is that one person is behind all of this, when in fact the crimes committed by the regime are made possible only because of a 'system'; a system which is ready to be activated even if Asad is replaced tomorrow. As I tried to explain in a recent interview, it is dangerous to make this about Asad, because if a day arrives when Asad is replaced (without the initiation of a process that structurally modifies the system that makes such crimes possible) then it will be nothing more than a cosmetic change. In the same manner that the conspiracy myth provides clues, so too does the Asad myth. Here the clues point to the fact that what many in the opposition truly want is to remove a person, rather than to change a system. If they were to be in charge, they may leave the system intact, or even use it against their opponents. If this was about a system, then the emphasis would be on UN-monitored presidential elections in which all Syrians, including refugees, take part. Ironically, the Asad-myth is mutually cherished. The regime embraces it just as much as the opposition does. To the regime, it's far easier to respond to calls to exclude Asad as unacceptable and impinging on sovereignty than it is to respond to calls that emphasize fair presidential elections and place no conditions on who can participate. Here, the myth not only provides clues, it also sets a trap.

'Victory' is a more recent myth. We are now constantly told that the regime won, and the opposition has been defeated. Here the myth is based on the assumption that this was a story about a battle between the Syrian army, and the militias that support it and the various rebel groups on the ground, from the moderate to the fanatic and extreme. If this assumption is accurate, then it naturally follows that a military victory means the story is over. Early in the Syrian Uprising, the common word used by regime loyalists was '*khalsit*', meaning 'it's over' in the Syrian dialect. The counter response to this, of course, is that this wasn't about a military battle for it to 'end' in a military victory. This was about thousands of young protesters (who for the most part are not even represented by the armed rebels) who believed in a different Syria, a Syria where freedom, dignity and reform were possible. How then can a regime military victory in Idlib, or anywhere else for that matter, change any of this? The transformation of the Syrian Uprising into a myth about a military conflict provides clues on how the regime wants us to understand this. If this is a military conflict, then it will end when a military victory is achieved. Ironically, the myth of 'victory' is yet another that is cherished by both sides. Members of the opposition constantly speak in a manner that implies accepting that the armed rebels somehow represent them, and hence their defeat means the end of the story. To the thousands of young Sunni, Christian and even Alawite protesters framing the story as a military conflict is to marginalize everything they tried to achieve. Here the myth is an act of betrayal.

Finally, though the list of myths is far more extensive, we now turn to the myth of 'reconstruction'; a more recent myth, but one which appears destined to become more popular. The idea here is that Syria has been largely destroyed and now that the story is over (see previous myth) it is time for reconstruction. The myth immediately gives birth to two opposing groups, as it frequently does: those who are for reconstruction (now, and before a political settlement) and those who are against it (until a true political transition is agreed upon). Both sides ignore historical precedent and the lessons we have learned from Lebanon, and more recently Bosnia; namely, that reconstruction is seldom about the rebuilding of structures destroyed during the war. Reconstruction, rather, is about the recreation of identity, the invention of memory, and the reward and punishment of allies and enemies. Reconstruction may even constitute an act of violence using cement and tractors. An act of violence because of who it chooses to exclude, and what it deliberately chooses to give prominence to. To speak of reconstruction as though it is the mere act of rebuilding which either requires or does not require a framework of political transition, is to embrace the myth that there is a way for reconstruction to be inclusive and Syria-driven when in actuality, even under the best of conditions, reconstruction will involve regional and international companies making billions of dollars in profit as Syrians continue to suffer in refugee camps. Here the myth becomes a tragedy.

SYRIA'S RECONSTRUCTION – THE GOOD, THE BAD & THE UGLY

Let's begin with the 'ugly'. This would be the combination of laws, structures and projects, recently decreed and initiated by the Syrian regime. They range from the vulgar 'ugly', like the large-scale confiscation of the homes of the displaced and refugees, to the surreal 'ugly' with luxury housing projects announced at the very site where families were pressured to abandon their homes.[14]

Indeed, the regime understands reconstruction as a process through which allies are rewarded, communities are redefined, and, just in case the 'lessons' of the last decade have not been fully absorbed, reconstruction, or the lack thereof, is used to invent memory. Areas that were known to be staunchly against the regime, like the Khalidiyyah neighbourhood in Homs or Salah al-Din in Aleppo, appear to be deliberately ignored, as though constituting reminders on a grand scale of the fate of those who stand up to the regime. All of this is 'ugly' because of how indifferent it is to human suffering.

The 'bad' reflects frameworks and agents that intrinsically lend themselves to abuse, either because of an obsession with material gain, or out of sheer weakness. Foremost among the 'bad' are global actors and corporations that interact with reconstruction as though it was a guaranteed product that could be delivered if only conditions were met and the resources to pay the bills secured. Syria's tragedy will only end through a political settlement that leads to a genuine transition towards an inclusive and democratic Syria. This noble objective, however, should not be pursued as a way through which the international donor community, the West in particular, can be convinced to adopt and fund Syria's reconstruction. This massive project, estimated at anywhere between 200 and 400 billion dollars, will be a project through which Syria is further broken rather than rebuilt. All one has to do is to study recent precedents, from Bosnia, to Afghanistan and Iraq, to understand the way in which this inherently 'bad' option works.

Corporations want to sell their products; they do so regardless of whether their products are irrelevant or even counterproductive to the area being reconstructed. Read, if you wish, the story of how Kellogg Brown and Root (KBR) ignored studies that pointed to the fact that soil was not compatible with plans to have a pipeline buried beneath the Tigris River.[15] Three years later, after the bill had reached $100 million and nearly $1.5 billion in revenues had been lost, the digging was finally halted. Or read Bassam Yousif's account 'Coalition Economic Policies in Iraq' in which he described how, even as Iraq's unemployment rate was near 40 per cent, foreign workers were imported in the tens of thousands.[16] And, just in case you think this is confined to Iraq, please also read about similar experiences in Afghanistan[17] and Bosnia[18]. Not only do these grand projects fail, but there also seems to be a direct correlation between how much money is used and how significant the failure is. Indeed, top-down approaches that are guided and controlled by global corporations are bad, even when they intend to do good.

The UN is another variation of the 'bad', though in my mind, it is far more moderate on the scale of bad, and at times even potentially useful. As pointed out in a recent LSE conference I attended, the UN does not confront the regime when it restricts its access to areas requiring humanitarian assistance.[19] This is undoubtedly true, and it reminds me of how the UN acted during the siege of Madaya. Stationed in Damascus, and only forty kilometres away from where people were literally being starved to death, UN convoys stayed put.[20] Also very difficult to process is when the UN agrees to oversee the displacement of entire communities from areas like Homs, Darayya, and Idlib.[21] Such displacements were carried out under the theoretical pretext of protecting civilians in areas held by opposition forces from either continuous regime bombardment, or arrest and reprisal upon imminent government recapture of these areas. By overseeing such displacements, however, the UN becomes indirectly complicit in the purposeful demographic distortion of Syria. All of this seems to be reflective of weakness bordering on cowardice. And it is a trait that is contradicted at times even from within the UN when some UN reports describe in detail the regime's massive and systematized violence.[22]

The UN, however, is also a structure within which a level of monitoring and accountability exists, as does evidence of successful initiatives with local communities. I once took part in such an initiative in Syria, and later documented the unfortunate way this experiment in political and economic empowerment ended.[23] The weakness the UN exhibits when interacting with the Syrian regime can be partially explained by how restricted its current mandate is. As such, the UN is presently 'bad' but has the potential to become a more positive force if it was empowered with the mandate to work directly and without regime restrictions with the millions of Syrians whose communities have been severely damaged since the beginning of the Uprising.

This brings us to the last and most important category, the 'good'. The 'good', no doubt, are the Syrians themselves who alone, so far, have truly engaged in the process of reconstruction, a genuine variant of reconstruction that aims at rising above the deep wounds and damage that was caused by years of violence. It is a creative, resilient and ongoing process of reconstruction. The good are the inhabitants of towns under siege who found ways to reconstruct their lives even as they were attacked and bombarded. They identified alternative means to generate power, built hospitals, and stocked an underground library with books rescued from bombed buildings.[24] The good are Syria's children who found ways to reconstruct their own schools by having the older children take the place of teachers, caregivers and counsellors for friends and younger siblings.[25] The good are Syria's women whose stories far exceed 'survival', and who are indeed actively engaged in reconstructing a life for themselves and their families.[26]

What is fascinating here is the fact that as we continue to discuss reconstruction – how much it will cost, who will undertake it and under what conditions it will take place – those most in need of reconstruction efforts are neither waiting for help nor expecting it. This is far more about us than them. In identifying ways to provide assistance, whether through a UN with a very different mandate, or some other creative way that skids around the regime/global corporations trap, we are in fact demonstrating that even though we have totally failed in stopping the violence that was unleashed against the Syrian people, we can at least succeed in assisting them in reconstructing their lives.

SYRIA'S DAY AFTER: SEX, LIES, & VIDEOTAPES

Welcome to the new Syria, the Syria that defeated the cosmic conspiracy against it!

Those who stood by Syria's leadership are finally in a position to harvest the fruits of prosperity and progress. In fact, a survey of prominent loyalists' media outlets will leave you fully convinced of just how vibrant, how full of promise this new Syria is.

Start with *Yomyat Kzefeh Hawen Fi Dimashq* (Diary of a Mortar Shell in Damascus), a loyalist media news site established in early 2014.[27] Gone is the obsession with the sexual practises of the opposition, the infamous *jihad al-nikah*, or sexual jihad. Today, the focus is on the sexual practises of the victors. From wife swapping in Damascus, to sexual acts in public parks, and in public baths. From prostitution rings in Damascus, rural Damascus, Aleppo, Homs, and Tartous, to prostitution rings involving celebrities, Lebanese clients, and 'adult parties' organized in restaurants and night clubs. And just in case you think this has always been the case, *Yomyat* will remind you that incidents of sexual harassment, sexual assault and rape have increased by 50 per cent since 2011.[28] How dynamic and modern is this new Syria!

Yomyat is equally consumed with documenting lies, the lies it believes officials are constantly using to defraud Syrians from the prosperity they deserve. *Yomyat* finds corrupt officials everywhere – in the medical field, in the judiciary, public works, housing, agriculture, industry, tourism, academia, banking, customs, and even in sports. In the news items of *Yomyat*, we meet corrupt bakers, butchers, and makers and sellers of food products. If you read too many of these, it's hard to resist the conclusion that the entire country is now corrupt.

Because of the lies of corrupt officials, the new Syria, according to *Yomyat*, has significant urban and rural poverty. *Yomyat* doesn't hesitate to share a UN report which estimates that 80 per cent of the population live below the poverty line.[29] After all, asserts *Yomyat*, the average income of a government employee is SP50,000, even though a family of four requires at least SP325,000 a month to cover basic necessities of life. Even if you did have sufficient income, *Yomyat* will make sure you understand that you still have to deal with the shortages; various forms of shortages with various types of official explanations (more lies). Gas shortages, electricity shortages, which come with official reminders not to use gas to warm your home, and not to use electricity to warm your home! Perhaps the implicit message is to simply not attempt to warm your home at all. Then there is the new culture of queues. People literally dying as they wait in gas queues, bread queues, the unique Syrian phenomenon of queue-rage, and more.

Sahbit al-Jalalah (Her Majesty) another loyalist news site shares detailed and graphic reports of crimes, new crimes that are befitting of the new Syria.[30] Murders, at times for a mere mobile, in Damascus, Jaramana, Hama, Homs, Swaida, and Jableh. Decapitation was once the exclusive trademark of ISIS, but today even common criminals decapitate their victims. Aleppo is described as not only one of the oldest cities in the world, but also as one of the most dangerous.

And then we have the videotapes, videotapes documenting all kinds of 'new' and not-so-new behaviour. Maggie Khozam, a once fervent Christian loyalist with peculiar views on genetics and linguistics, is clearly disappointed.[31] Her videos bluntly attack what she regards as the regime's betrayal of Syria's secular values, official financial policies, and corruption at the Ministry of Reconciliation. But she reserves her most scathing attack for a video of Mohamed Qanbad, a member of the People's Assembly.[32] The video shows Qanbad while he is distributing water bottles to the displaced inhabitants of Eastern Ghuta. Qanbad made the thirsty men gathered around his truck repeat slogans praising the president and condemning Saudi Arabia before they could receive the water bottles. Khozam is disgusted. 'Are you supposed to represent the civilized generation?' she contemptuously asks. She adds, 'This video is proof that there is no such thing as reform in Syria […] and there is no doubt that the president has seen this video […] if Qanbad remains a member of parliament after this video it would mean that the entire state from its head to its base is corrupt and should be trashed.'[33]

It is this context that explains the president's latest speech; a 'new' speech that goes out of its way to de-emphasize victory: 'We have this romanticized perception at times that we were victorious, though the war is not over.'[34] Not only is the war not over, three additional wars are added to it, including a war against corruption. Perhaps the most significantly 'new' aspect of the speech, however, is its use of sarcasm (once reserved solely for enemies) to attack those 'who sink deep in flaunting their criticizing muscles…' The day has arrived when the loyalists are attacked. Commenting on the 30 interruptions of chants, poetry and applause in praise of the president, the loyalist celebrity Bashar Ismail posted on his Facebook account, 'The hypocrites who kept interrupting the president made me turn off the TV…'.[35]

The day has also arrived when even the loyalists have stopped listening.

IN CAME CORONA: NONSENSE AND THE ABSURD IN SYRIA'S UNFOLDING TRAGEDY

Back in the 1980s, when I was a student at Macalester College, I remember I once took a course entitled: Nonsense and the Absurd in Russian Political Discourse. I haven't thought of this course or of the Czechoslovakian professor who taught it in years, but when I came across an interview with Syria's Minister of Health, Dr Nizar Yazigi, I suddenly felt that I was back in that classroom reading excerpts of Nikolai Gogol's *The Nose*!

Lest you think that this is a grand exaggeration, this is a verbatim quote of Yazigi's message to all Syrians who were concerned about the coronavirus pandemic:

> 'Praise be to God, the Syrian Arab army has purified much of the microbes which existed on Syrian territory, and we, as a medical sector and a medical army, are very grateful to the army for what it has achieved.'[36]

The microbization of Syria's political opponents was not invented by Yazigi. This sophisticated simile was first introduced by the Syrian president in a speech in 2012:

> 'Conspiracies are like germs, after all, multiplying every moment, everywhere. They cannot be eliminated, but we can strengthen the immunity of our bodies in order to protect ourselves against them.'[37]

Approaching the coronavirus with the mindset of war, microbes and conspiracies unleashes yet another wave of absurd imagery. I imagine barrel bombs thrown over villages where corona cases are confirmed; patients tortured to confess that they are agents of a biological war against

Syria, and besieging areas where the coronavirus has been detected and proceeding to bar all food and medical supplies from entering so as to ensure the thorough 'purification' of Syria from this new enemy.

Underneath Syria's surreal political discourse are tragic realities that continue to be normalised and ignored by the world. The Syrian regime is no doubt taking advantage of the coronavirus crisis to ask for sanctions to be lifted for its own vested interests. Regardless, Syrians have and continue to suffer as a result of these sanctions, and the coronavirus pandemic is bound to make their suffering even worse.

A March 2020 update by the World Food Programme reminds us that 11.1 million people in Syria are in need of humanitarian assistance; 6.1 million people are internally displaced; 7.9 million people are food insecure; and 1.9 million people are at risk of food insecurity.[38] A 2019 WHO report confirms outbreaks 'of measles, acute bloody diarrhoea, typhoid fever and leishmaniasis [...] in various areas of the country throughout the year.'[39] The report also states that 10.2 million Syrians live in areas effected by explosive hazards. Perhaps most striking is the fact that attacks on health facilities 'have rendered 46 per cent of hospitals and primary health facilities in Syria as either partially functional or not functional, while in some areas humanitarian partners have been unable to secure sustained and predictable access to populations in need.'[40]

Notwithstanding these critical indicators, all one really has to do to capture the gravity of the current situation is reflect on the contrast: If Western officials can be seriously concerned about the collapse of their healthcare systems as a result of this crisis, how does one expect a country like Syria, where so many hospitals were destroyed, and where medical equipment and supplies were not able to address the medical needs of its citizens long before the coronavirus was even heard of, to have even a remote chance of protecting vulnerable citizens from the effects of this pandemic?

Imagining what this pandemic would do to Syrians living in crowded camps, and damaged neighbourhoods, with some estimates of deaths already in the hundreds of thousands, is perhaps the most surreal part of this entire subject.

In my mind at least, the lesson here is profoundly simple: Syria's tragedy should never have been ignored or normalised by the international community. Tragedies on this scale only get worse, and the arrival of the coronavirus in Syria provides ample proof of this reality. There is, now more than ever, a moral responsibility to protect Syria's already vulnerable population, who are now likely to be the victims of a vicious virus unless adequate medical assistance is urgently provided. Failing to do so is to only add material to the syllabus of The Nonsense and the Absurd.

SPLASH: THE INTRICATE ART OF WEAPONIZING FICTION

Yevgeny Prigozhin, a fascinating Russian figure known as 'Putin's cook', and an important 'investor' in Syria's oil industry, recently prepared a new and surprising dish.[41] On 15 April 2020, columnists at his Federal News Agency (FNA) suddenly announced that they had discovered that what was long regarded as Western propaganda was in fact true: the Syrian regime is indeed corrupt. This exquisite new platter, however, was far more than a mere accusation of corruption. It had a brilliantly crafted artistic twist:

> Асад купил своей жене картину за 23 млн
> фунтов на аукционе в Лондоне[42]
>
> Assad bought his wife a painting for 23 million pounds at auction in London
>
> СМИ: Президент Сирии Асад купил жене картину Дэвида Хокни за десятки миллионов фунтов[43]
>
> Media: Syrian President Assad bought his wife a David Hockney painting for tens of millions of pounds
>
> Асад купил на Sotheby's картину за 30 млн долларов для своей жены[44]
>
> Assad bought a $30 million painting at Sotheby's for his wife

As documented in *The Art Newspaper*, a well-established authority in the art world, it was, in fact, the Californian media magnate, David Geffen, who had purchased the artwork, *The Splash*; one of a trio that includes

A Little Splash and *A Bigger Splash*.[45] *The Art Newspaper's* article found the whole story linking the purchase with the Syrian president 'curious' inasmuch as it was 'spurious'.

How fascinating! For once, the Syrian regime was facing the same type of media campaigns it had long perfected: weaponized fiction. Various theories, insightful, and mutually reinforcing, on why and how this story was fabricated have since surfaced: (i) the President's uncle, Muhammad Makhluf, who now lives in Moscow along with at least one of his sons,[46] shared this story with Russian sources; (ii) the story is yet another manifestation of the apparent economic feud between the president's wife and Rami Makhluf, the president's cousin and arguably the wealthiest businessman in Syria;[47] (iii) the story reflects Russia's impatience with the Syrian president's unwillingness to arrive at any meaningful agreement with the opposition,[48] which would in turn allow the Russians to declare victory and close this file.

The weaponization of fiction is a sophisticated process that uses very real fragments to compose its fictional tapestry and seeks to flirt with our base psychological impulses by invoking the very things we fear or hate. To be effective, the process not only requires real fragments, but works best when a powerful patron is willing to adopt it. This explains why opposition-fiction, though not lacking when it comes to real fragments, never managed to reach the circulation level of regime-fiction. Though everyone who is anyone is in the business of weaponizing fiction, the grand prize to date – suspending our knowledge of the tragic consequences for a few seconds – must go to whoever it was who came up with the idea that Iraq possessed enough weapons of mass destruction to pose a strategic threat to the world.

Being a historian, and a detective at heart, I could not let go of how *The Splash* story could have been invented in the first place. I was primarily consumed with the 'real' fragments that lent themselves to such a process. Of the many advantages of being confined to my home during the pandemic and fasting long Ramadan days is the hours one can spend researching strange, and often meaningless topics, in this case, the 'curious' relationship between David Hockney and the Syrian regime. Shortly before sunset, when it was finally time for me to break my fast, I succeed in collecting enough scattered fragments to construct my own fictional account that explains, or rather invents, this relationship.

Fragment 1
The original news item (11 February 2020) on the purchase of *The Splash* made it clear that it was 'bought by an unknown buyer'.[49]

Fragment 2
The president's wife has a very specific taste in art, and emails that are part of the *Syria Files* – a collection of more than two million emails from Syrian political figures and ministries and from various Western companies, published by Wikileaks[50] – show her to have been interested in *Ornithop Callicore IV* by Nick Jeffrey, a young artist based in Battersea who produces three-dimensional pieces of butterflies.[51]

Fragment 3
David Hockney appears in 11 emails in the *Syria Files*. One of the emails is dated 4 January 2012 and was sent by *The Interview People* to shorufat@moc.gov.sy at the Ministry of Culture.[52]

Fragment 4
The late Patrick Seale, author of *Asad: The Struggle for the Middle East*, a biography of Bashar al-Asad's late father, was in fact an art dealer and 'ran a London gallery dealing in, among other things, David Hockney and Henry Moore limited-edition prints in the 1980s.'[53]

Fragment 5
David Hockney had a connection, via David Plante, with Claudia Roden, the well-known British cookbook writer, whose grandfather was the Chief Rabbi in Aleppo.[54]

Fragment 6
Brooke Allen, author of the *The Other Side of the Mirror: An American Travels through Syria*, notes that she made a connection between scenery in the north of Syria and landscapes painted by David Hockney of his native Yorkshire.[55]

Not bad for a few hours of research. Next comes the arduous task of putting these fragments together:

It must have all started with Seale who, on one of his many visits to Damascus, shared his admiration of David Hockney with the Asad family. We may even postulate that he presented Asad Senior with one of Hockney's artworks as a gift to thank him for all the long hours he spent sharing his stories with him. Seale is charismatic, and a fetish for anything Hockney is implanted in Asad's children. During Bashar's sojourn in London, he meets Hockney and invites him to visit Syria. At first hesitant, Hockney is reassured by his friend, Claudia Roden. He subsequently visits Syria in secret and is fascinated by its landscapes, which explains why some of his paintings resemble fields in the Syrian north. And finally, well aware of his wife's admiration of fine art, the Syrian president decides to buy *The Splash* for his wife as a gift to celebrate her full recovery from her latest ordeal, and then uses his connections to invent a story that identifies David Geffen as the real buyer. Voila!

I remind my readers that the story I just shared is a fictional account. Ironically, however, it is no less fictional than many stories produced during the last decade, including the one that advanced the idea that the inhabitants of the Ghuta had used chemical weapons against their own villages in August 2013;[56] the ingenious creation of the idea of sex-jihad; and the depiction of all those who protest against the regime as agents of a foreign conspiracy.[57]

In his first speech after the Syrian Uprising (30 March 2011), President Asad summarised the art of weaponizing fiction:

> 'The fact is that they follow the principle of lying. Repeat your lie until they believe you. So, they eventually believe their own lie and fall in the trap.'[58]

Who, one wonders, is in the trap now?

REFUGEE? BECOME AN ANARCHIST!

For years now, my mornings have begun the same way. Coffee, news updates on Syria, more coffee, more updates, followed by a walk; long enough – though no walk is truly long enough – to dispel the black cloud that has formed in my mind. It all starts with a headline:

> Man charged with rape, premeditated murder of Syrian child[59]

The headline is followed by a hesitant click:

> 'Last Saturday, a Criminal Court prosecutor in Amman charged a man with premeditated murder and rape in connection with the brutal killing of a Syrian child…'

This in turn invokes an instant connection in my head with yet another earlier headline:

> Refugee fled Syria violence only to die in the London fire[60]

And another:

> Syrian refugee brutally killed by gang of migrants in savage attack in Germany[61]

And yet another:

> Pregnant Syrian Refugee Raped And Murdered In Turkey[62]

At this point, the connections have become too overwhelming. I swallow the rest of my coffee, and head out for my walk.

At first, my anger is directed towards Syria's neighbours. I lived in Jordan for nearly eight years, and I truly felt at home. There is so much that I respect and admire about the Hashemite Kingdom, but none of my Jordanian friends have been able to convincingly explain to me why the majority of Syrians are confined to camps there. The logic shared is reminiscent of the logic Syrian officials would use to explain why Palestinian Syrians are only eligible to a travel document and have limited rights to ownership. 'We are protecting their distinct identity and ensuring that they would one day return!' In the same vein, my Jordanians friends explain that the camps ensure that Syrian refugees will return to Syria. More honest explanations speak about the enormous economic weight on a country with limited resources like Jordan. Security concerns, no doubt, are at the forefront of Jordan's interaction with Syrian refugees, and as much as I respect these concerns, something about how Syrians are being treated – about the dichotomy between the Western notables who visit these camps and the Jordanian notables who don't – is wrong.

Compared to Lebanon, however, Jordan seems like the land of opportunity. Syrian refugees in Lebanon, which has the highest concentration of Syrian refugees per capita in the world, are actually forbidden to live in formal camps and, rather than being allowed and helped to integrate into society, which is clearly the ideal scenario for a refugee, they are left to try to survive in unofficial settlements which only reinforce the fragility of the already fragile.

Turkey, by far, provides the best conditions for Syrian refugees, but even there, Syrians are often treated with fear and suspicion. The camps are far superior in their conditions, but they remain refugee camps with all that brings with it.

My anger then shifts to rich Arab countries which have spent billions on arms and rebel groups in Syria, and yet no states are harsher than these when it comes to welcoming Syrian refugees. The mere thought of what these billions of dollars could have done to help those who ran away from death and destruction is startling. At the very least, they could have supported countries like Jordan and Lebanon host them in a more honourable manner.

Towards the end of my walk, I find myself recalling all the times we had hoped for the US, and even later for Russia, to create some type of safe zone for Syrians in Syria. Years later, no such zone has been created, and we are still trying to understand what exactly 'deconfliction zones'[63] means. Will they guarantee that Syrians will no longer associate the sky with barrels and shrapnel? Will they guarantee that the most basic conditions for Syrian refugees to return are secured?

Where exactly is one to find comfort? What possible perspective or equation can help me see this in a more positive light?

I return to my desk and the first headline that appears on my screen provides a surreal ending to my morning:

> Anarchists offer a lifeline for refugees in Greece[64]

This time my click is less hesitant:

> '...conditions in the anarchist squats are much more humane. There's little violence or crime, and refugees have better access to food, sanitation, and medical services. Their kids are in local schools, and they feel like they are a part of society ... for the anarchists, their work with refugees is just one step toward their ultimate goal – wholesale revolution.'[65]

I am finally capable of smiling. Thank you, William Godwin, it didn't occur to me to look in your direction!

WHEN YOU'RE SHOVED FROM THE RIGHT, LOOK TO THE LEFT...

With the approach of every anniversary of the Syrian Uprising, I am reminded of a story I once heard from my late Damascene Sufi teacher, Shaikh Bashir al-Bani (1911–2008).[66] The story is about a man who was trying to concentrate on his *tawaf* (circumambulation of the Ka'ba) during the Hajj pilgrimage. As is required from men during this ritual, he wore only two white pieces of cloth, one around his waist, another around his shoulders, and a special leather belt with a pouch attached in which he kept his valuables. As he walked around this ancient monument of Islam, a child suddenly shoved him from his right side. Mindful that he should control his anger during Hajj, the man continued his *tawaf* in silence. Yet, with each time he circulated the Ka'ba this rude and abrupt act was repeated, filling him with anger and totally distracting him from his spiritual experience. His eyes were fixated on his right side in the hope that he could somehow avoid the child when he made his next sudden move. After a while, the exhausted man decided to take a rest. When his hand reached for his belt, he realized that the pouch, situated on his left side, had been cleverly cut off by another accomplice as he was being shoved from the right by the child. Al-Bani would end the story with this line:

> 'When you are shoved from the right, look to the left... the real story isn't where the noise is, and dramatic events are rarely what they initially seem to be...'

The way in which the Syrian Uprising is interacted with today is far more about ISIS, the PYD, Turkish or Iranian geopolitical concerns than it is about Syrians suffering. This ultimate distraction, the intrusive child of Al-Bani's story, has successfully distracted all the major players, and most interested observers, from the daily killing, from those still imprisoned and tortured, from the homeless and the refugees and, perhaps most importantly, from the maimed and psychologically traumatized new generation of Syrians being constantly manufactured amidst the rubble and refugee camps.

The distraction is not only very effective, it also has a way of demanding attention when it suspects our focus may shift elsewhere. When we appear to be on the verge of becoming numb to an individual beheading, we are confronted with scenes of collective beheading, and when those lose their magical effect, cages are produced and people are burned alive. Subsequently, the story shifts to Raqqa, and from there to Aleppo and today to 'Afrin. Everything about the Syrian Uprising now seems to be at odds with what it was first expected to be. This process begins with the very name I still find myself using, perhaps as some form of stubborn expression of faith: 'uprising'. Civil war, if not wars, seems far more accurate today, and yet still somehow difficult to use. Nor is this anymore about how far the regime can go, how radical the opposition fighters can become, or how much, and for how long, the world can ignore a tragedy of this magnitude. 'Indefinitely' seems to be the applicable word here.

Almost every major event from March 2011 until today was initially regarded as pointing in one direction, only for an overwhelmingly different redefinition to take place. Scenes of peaceful protesters sharing flowers and water with army soldiers around Damascus are replaced with scenes of armed 'moderate' fighters, which are subsequently replaced by scenes of radical fighters, who are in turn eclipsed by the rise of ISIS with scenes out of a medieval horror story. Scenes of officials trying to speak to peaceful protesters are replaced by scenes of triumphant soldiers from the Syrian army, which are systematically replaced by scenes of members of Shi'ite militias proudly proclaiming victories over the 'enemies of the Prophet's family'. Again 'indefinitely' seems to be the key word with regards to how many times events in Syria can mutate into something else, something not initially expected, something invariably worse.

My mother writes a daily journal from Damascus which she sends to close friends and family members. Though she mostly shares trivial events, such as how they spend their day and whom they happened to see, every now and then she allows herself to let go and say a few things about the sounds, the fighter jets, the checkpoints, and the suffocating cloud of depression which hovers over Damascus. And if there is one thing that comes out clearly from her journal, it is how utterly undistracted she is. Nothing anyone can do has distracted her from the very simple fact that Syrians are suffering and that, years later, there has still not been one adamant attempt by anyone to stop this.

Afterword

On 29 June 2022, I received a phone call from Damascus informing me that my father had passed away in the early hours of that morning at the age of ninety-one. In the days after his passing, I wrote the following words:

> It has never been easy to be the son of Dr Muhammad Imady. I discovered this early on when I would be stopped by passers-by who would want to speak to me about my father – how he had once taught them, or employed them, or helped them through various government processes that had been obstructed by others. At times, they would speak to me at great length about what my father had done for his country, how he had returned from Kuwait to work with those who were adamant at preventing him from achieving reform of any type, however minor or insignificant. I would be obliged to listen to story after story, though I was well aware of the minute details of each of them. Their words would invariably end with an ardent petition for me to emulate my father's example. But I knew then, as I know now, that I lacked the essential characteristic that had qualified my father in the first place to be the man he was.
>
> My father's secret does not lie in the fact that he was highly educated, extremely talented, and a man of noble character, despite how rare each of these qualities were. His secret, rather, lay in the fact that he was able to bring all of this to a world which was almost organically at odds with everything for which he stood. This, plus his capacity to remain loyal to such a world for over half a century.
>
> I have many memories of sitting in my father's office, watching him interact with gentleness and wisdom with people who were neither willing nor capable of understanding the ideas he was trying to explain. I was aware of the fact that my father was carrying the banner of reform in a world that was waiting for him to commit

just one mistake – intentionally or otherwise – so that it may turn against him.

Reform is both easy and impossible. Easy because you are, in essence, asked to place what would benefit people first. And impossible because you are incapable of placing what benefits people first unless you are willing to interact with anything else as nothing other than foam that will sooner or later dissipate. Yes, there were those with whom my father enjoyed working; men and women who believed, as he did, in the imperative of striving to elevate the status of their country, but they were like scattered trees in an ever-expanding desert.

My father's secret also lies in the fact that he did not regard himself as having another option, though in actuality he had many. Those who loved him would often speak to him of the possibilities of other places or positions which he could, if he wished, depart to away from a world that was causing him constant headaches, pain, and even fear from the threat of various types of enemies. In response, he would smile and change the subject, as though to say: I was created to be here, and I will serve my country to the very end.

Notes

Introduction

1. Abu-Ismail, K., Imady, O., Kuncic, A., et al. (2017). Syria at war: Five years on. Fife, Scotland: University of St Andrews. Available online at: https://www.unescwa.org/publications/syria-war-five-years

Chapter I

1. Mahmoud El-Kati is Professor Emeritus of History at Macalester College in St Paul, Minnesota. In recognition of his scholarly and community work, Macalester College has established the Mahmoud El-Kati Distinguished Lectureship in American Studies. For his biography, see the entry on his official website: www.mahmoudelkati.com/biography.html
2. On 'Imad al-Din al-Hanafi, see Ibn Ayyūb, S. Kitāb al-Rawḍ al-'āṭir fīmā tayassara min akhbār ahl al-qarn al-sābi' ilā khitām al-qarn al-'āshir, (*The Perfumed Garden of Assembled Notices of the People of the 7th to the End of the 10th Century*). Berlin, Staatsbibliothek, MS Wetzstein II 289, fol. 235b. Available online at: https://digital.staatsbibliothek-berlin.de/werkansicht?PPN=PPN689500920&PHYSID=PHYS_0505&DMDID=DMDLOG_0001 (henceforth Kitab al-Rawd); Ibn Tulun. (1999) Mut'at al-adhhan min al-tamattu' bi-l-iqran bayna tarajim al shuyukh wa-l-aqran, S. D. K. al-Shaybani a1-Mawsili (Ed.), Dar Sadir; Vol. 2, p. 885; Al-Burini, H. & Munajjid, S. (1959). Tarajim al-A'yan min Abna' al-Zaman. (*Biographies of the Notables from the People of the Time*). Damascus: al-Majma' al-'Ilmi al-'Arabi, Vol. 2, p. 302. Available online at: https://ia800306.us.archive.org/5/items/waq44457/02_44458.pdf (henceforth Tarajim al-A'yan); Al-Ghazzi, M. (1945) Al-Kawakib al-Saira bi A'yan al-Mia al-'Ashira (*The Orbiting Planets of the Notables of the 10th Century – 1624*). J. Jabbur (Ed.). American Press, Vol. 3, p. 35. Available online at: http://lib.eshia.ir/40258/3/35/%D8%B9%D9%85%D8%A7%D8%AF_%D8%A7%D9%84%D8%AF%D9%8A%D9%86_%D8%A7%D9%84%D8%AD%D9%86%D9%81%D9%8A (henceforth *Kawakib*); Abi al-Falah 'Abdul-Hayy Ibn al-Imad al-Hanbali. (1980). Shadharat al-Dhahab fi Akhbar man Dhahab (*The Particles of Gold in the Experiences of Those Who Have Passed On*), Vol. 10, p. 603. Available online at: http://lib.eshia.ir/40109/10/603; and Muradi, M. (1988). Sulk al-Durar fi A'yan al-Qarn al-Thani 'Ashr. [The String of Pearls of the Notables of the Twelfth Century]. Dar al-Basha'ir. Vol 2, p. 19. Available online at: http://lib.eshia.ir/40382/2/19/العنابي (henceforth Sulk al-Durar)
3. El-Rouayheb, K. (2008). al-Burini, Hasan b. Muhammad. Historians of the Ottoman Empire. https://ottomanhistorians.uchicago.edu/en/historians/22
4. Tarajim al-A 'yan, Vol. 2, p. 302.
5. Ibid.
6. Ibid., p. 159.

7. SBB Orient Digital. (2021). Sprenger 519 / 2r / 01 [Manuscript by Ibrahim ibn Kasbay]. Datenbank der orientalischen Handschriften der Staatsbibliothek zu Berlin. Available online at: http://orient-digital.staatsbibliothek-berlin.de/receive/SBBMSSecentry_secentry_00000632
8. Kitab al-Rawd, Berlin, Staatsbibliothek, MS Wetzstein II 289, fol. 235b.
9. Sulk al-Durar, Vol 2, p. 19.
10. Ghazzī, N., & Jabbūr, J. (1945). Al-Kawākib al-sā'irah bi-a'yān al-mi'ah al-'āshirah (Silsilat al-'Ulūm al-Sharqīyah. Jāmi'at Bayrūt al-Amīrīkīyah Manshūrāt Kullīyat al-'Ulūm wa-al-Ādāb; 18, 20). Bayrūt: Al-Maṭba'ah al-Amīrkānīyah. Vol 3, p. 40. Available online at: https://12c58cc3-195f-4978-5c0c-439c4c93eb97.filesusr.com/ugd/9f1309_cb3cbb079c08452aae062d8205e2719c.pdf
11. Candidates for "Kasbay" are found in the works of Mamluk historians including: Ibn Tulun, M. (1998), Mufakahat al-Khullan fi Hawadith al-Zaman (*Entertainment of Friends in the Events of Times*), Dar al Kutub al-'Ilmiyah; Ibn Taghribirdi, J. Y. (1929–1956). al-Nujum al-zahira fi muluk Misr wa'l-Qahira (*The Shining Stars in the Rulers of Egypt and Syria*). Maṭba'at Dar al-Kutub al-Miṣrīyah; Al-Sakhawi, S. M. (1992). Al-Daw'al-lami'li-ahl al- qarn al-tāsi' (*The Glowing Light on the People of the Ninth Century*). H. I. Marwa (Ed.). Dār al-'Urūba; al-Safadi, K. I. A. (1998) A'yan al-'Asr wa-A'wan al-Nasr (*The Notables of the Age and the Supporters of Victory).* Dar al-Fikr; Tarajim al-A'yan; Kawakib;
12. Al-Kawthari, (2001). "Tarjmat al-Sharih al-'Allamah al-Badr al-'Ayni (*The Biography of the Explicator, the Expert al-Badr al-'Ayni*)" in 'Umar, A. (Ed.). 'Umdat al-Qari fi-Sharh Sahih al-Bukhari. Dar al-Fikr, p. 9.
13. On Yashbak min Mahdi, see, for example, Ayalon, D. (1954). Studies on the Structure of the Mamluk Army--III. Bulletin of the School of Oriental and African Studies, University of London, 16(1), 57–90.
14. Ibid.
15. Conducted by Familytreedna.
16. El-Sibai, M., Platt, D., Haber, M., Xue, Y. et al. (2009). Geographical Structure of the Y-chromosomal Genetic Landscape of the Levant: A coastal-inland contrast. Annals of Human Genetics, 73(6), 568–581. Available online at: www.ncbi.nlm.nih.gov/pmc/articles/PMC3312577/
17. Balanovsky, O., Dibirova, K., Dybo, A., et al. (2011). Parallel Evolution of Genes and Languages in the Caucasus Region. Molecular Biology and Evolution, 28(10), 2905–2920.
18. Digitalisierte Sammlungen. (2021). [Manuscript by:] 'Abd-ar-Raḥmān Ibn-Muḥammad Ibn-'Imād-ad-Dīn. Staatsbibliothek zu Berlin. Available online at: https://digital.staatsbibliothek-berlin.de/werkansicht?PPN=PPN1014384605&PHYSID=PHYS_0176&DMDID=DMDLOG_0004
19. Al-'Imadi, A., (n.d.) Al-Rawdah al-Rayyah fi-man Dufina bi-Darayya. King Abd Allah ibn Abd al-Aziz Library. Available online at: https://www.alukah.net/manu/files/manuscript_2091/mhkitote.pdf
20. Al-Istwani, M. (1957). Ray al-Sadi min Fatawa al-'Imadi (*Quenching the Thirsty with the Legal Decision of al-Imadi*). King Saud University. Available online at: https://12c58cc3-195f-4978-5c0c-439c4c93eb97.filesusr.com/ugd/9f1309_c786a1f1cb644c1c88d2feb3a387b32d.pdf pp. 75–77.
21. Imady, M., (1994). Private interview.
22. Ibn Kannan al-Salihi, M. (1998). Al-Hawadith al-Yawmiyya fi Tarikh Ahad 'Ashar

wa-Alf wa-Miyya. (*Daily Events from the Year 1111*), MSS Ahlwardt 9479 and 9480, Staatsbibliothek zu Berlin, Berlin. Available online at: http://www.liillas.com/up/uploads/files/liillas-e65e782b92.pdf

23. Taqi al-Din, M. (1927). Kitāb muntakhabāt al-tawārīkh li-Dimashq. (*Selections of Histories of Damascus*). Damascus: al-Matba'ah al-Hadithah.
24. Rippey Imady, E. (2009) Road to Damascus. Hollister: MSI, 2009. p. 156.

Chapter II

1. Rippey Imady, E. (2009) Road to Damascus. Hollister: MSI, 2009. p. 18.
2. Ibid., p. 215.
3. Biographical information on Mildred Elaine Rippey can be found in her published works: Rippey-Imady, M.E. (2003). Postscripts from Palisades: Mildred Post Rippey's Story, MSI; and Rippey-Imady, M. E. (2009). The Road to Damascus, MSI.
4. For examples of the use of this term by Malcom X, see: Lomax, Louis (1963). "A Summing Up: Louis Lomax interviews Malcolm X". When the Word Is Given. TeachingAmericanHistory.org. Available online at: https://teachingamericanhistory.org/library/document/a-summing-up-louis-lomax-interviews-malcolm-x/
5. On Adib al-Shishakli, see: Britannica, T. Editors of Encyclopaedia (2021, January 1). Adib al-Shishakli. Encyclopedia Britannica. https://www.britannica.com/biography/Adib-al-Shishakli
6. Al-Halabi, M. (n.d.) Hakadha Qudiya 'ala al-Shishakli. […]. Al-'Umamah. http://www.al-amama.com/index.php?option=com_content&task=view&id=2041
7. On the Fatimids, see: Daftary, D. (2006). 'Fatimids'. Encyclopaedia Iranica. The Institute of Ismaili Studies. https://www.iis.ac.uk/encyclopaedia-articles/fatimids
8. Ahlul Bayt Digital Islamic Library Project. (n.d.) Men Expressing Fear for Al-Husayn: View of 'Umar al-Atraf. Al-Islam.org. https://www.al-islam.org/maqtal-al-husayn-abd-al-razzaq-al-muqarram/men-expressing-fear-al-husayn
9. Al-Jabiri, A. H. (2013, February 13). 'Umar al-Ashraf ibn Zayn al-'Abidin 'alayhima al-salam bayna hubb al-Muawalin wa-Ihmal al-Awqaf al-Shi'iyyah. Al-Katib 'Ali Husayn al-Jabiri. http://jabeire.blogspot.com/2013/02/blog-post.html
10. Hill, K. (2014, May 6). Was Yoda's Advice Any Good Psychologically. Discover. https://www.discovermagazine.com/the-sciences/was-yodas-advice-any-good-psychologically

Chapter III

1. Sources on Farhan al-Atasi are scare and information about his life and his execution is generally scattered and difficult to identify. The account shared here relies primarily on: Madani, S. Al-Tajasus al-Amriki 'ala Dimashq: Waqa'i' Muhakmat Jawsis Amrika bi-Dimashq, Farhan al-Atasi wa-'Abd al-Mu'in al-Hakimi (*American Espionage in Syria: Documents pertaining to the trials of American spies in Syria: Farhan al-Atasi and 'Abd al-Mu'in al-Hakimi*) Maktabat Dar al-Iman; Hanan, E. (1971). Our Man in Damascus: Story of Elie Cohen (First Edition). Robert Hale Ltd; Nachman-Tepper, N. (2017). אלי כהן – תיק פתוח (*Eli Cohen – open file*). Effie Meltzer - Research and Publishing. Hawrani, A. (2000). Mudhakarat Akram al-Hawrani (*The Memoirs of Akram al-Hawrani*). Maktabat Madbuli; Khayr, Hani. (2010). Eliyahu Kohen: Mashru' Jasus lam yuktamal, kayfa iktishafnah wa-kayfa-'itaqalnah (*Eliyahu Cohen: A Project of espionage which was not completed - How we discovered him and how we arrested him*). Manshurat Dar al-Fatat; Faluji, F. (2003). Al-'Amaliyyah 007: Ightiyal

al-Tayyarin al-'Iraqiyin al-Thalathah wa-hurub Awal Ta'irah Harbiyyah 'Arabiyyah li-Isra'il (*Operation 07 – Assassinating the three Iraqi Pilots amd the Escape of the first Arab Fighter Plane to Israel*). Caroz, Y. (1978). The Arab Secret Services. Corgi Books; "Syria: The Man from S.K.U.N.K." (1965, February 26). Time. Available online at: http://content.time.com/time/subscriber/article/0,33009,833485,00.html; "Syria: Of Hate & Espionage" (1965, March 5). Time. Available online at: http://content.time.com/time/subscriber/article/0,33009,839300,00.html.

2. Biographical information on Badr al-Din al-Siba'I can be found in: Hanna, A. (2018). Safahat min Tarikh al-Ahzab al-Siyasiyyah fi-Suriyyah al-Qarn al-'Ishrin wa-Ajwa'iha al-Ijtima'iyyah (*Pages from the history of political parties in Syria in the 20th century and their social context*). Al-Markaz al-'Arabi Lil-Abhath wa-Dirasat al-Siyyasat; "Kay la-Nansa: al-Daktur Badr al-Din al-Siba'i (*we may not forget: Dr Badr al-Din al-Siba'i*). (2018, August 20). Al-Nur. Available online at: https://alnnour.com/?p=56626; Hana, A. (2019). "Al-Daktur fi-al-Iqtisad Badr al-Din al-Siba'i: Mu'alif wa-Mutarjim wa-Nashir (*The Holder of a PhD in Economcis, Badr al-Din al-Siba'i: An Author, A Translator, and a Publisher*). Fenks. Available online at: https://www.fenks.co/index.php/%D8%A8%D9%84%D8%A7-%D8%B3%D9%8A%D8%A7%D8%B3%D8%A9/%D8%AB%D9%82%D8%A7%D9%81%D8%A9/32418-2019-12-22-18-02-11.
3. Habash, M. (2011). Al-Ba'th wa Thawrat Adhar (*The Ba'th and the March Revolution*). Self-published. p. 311. https://docs.google.com/file/d/0B1hVHp4YpIKobGxWOXRVb0YxQnM/edit?resourcekey=0-Zzel-5ogZdjZBBOgv0M7Pw
4. Shirbl, G. (2014, June 26). Rawa al-Qissah al-Sha'ikah li-Muhimmatihi al-Mustahilah fi Suriyah wa Mahattat Ukhra. (*The Thorny Story of His Impossible Mission in Syria and Other Postings*). Al-Jarida. https://www.aljarida.com/ext/articles/print/1462383891736409600/

Chapter IV

1. International Bank for Reconstruction and Development. (1976). 1976 Annual Meetings of the Boards of Governors: Summary Proceedings (English). Washington, D.C.: World Bank Group. https://documents1.worldbank.org/curated/en/101411468157501454/pdf/534130BR0board101Official0Use0Only1.pdf; p. 10.
2. Dale Jr., E. (1976, October 7). U.S. To Seek Shift In I.M.F. Gold Sales To A Weekly Basis. New York Times. https://www.nytimes.com/1976/10/07/archives/us-to-seek-shift-in-imf-gold-sales-to-a-weekly-basis-yeo-asking.html
3. Kennedy, C. (2017, December 6). Interview with Ambassador Richard W. Murphy. The Association for Diplomatic Studies and Training Foreign Affairs Oral History Project. Available online at: https://adst.org/wp-content/uploads/2019/02/Murphy-Richard-W.pdf
4. Extensive biographical information on Ahmad Kaftaru and Munira al-Qubaisi can be found in Imady, O. (2016). "Organisationally Secular: Damascene Islamist Movements and the Syrian Uprising." Syria Studies. Available online at: https://ojs.st-andrews.ac.uk/index.php/syria/article/view/1313 .
5. Kaftaru, A. (Summer 1990). Private lesson at the Mufti Ghuta Residence.

Chapter V

1. Imady, M. (2000). Private interview.
2. On the role of Badr al-Din al-Shallah, see, for example: Hinnebusch, R. (1993). State and Civil Society in Syria. Middle East Journal, 47(2), 243–257. Retrieved July 22, 2021, from http://www.jstor.org/stable/4328570
3. Kaftaru, A. (Summer 1990). Private lesson at the Mufti Ghuta Residence.
4. Naharnet. (2013, August 20). 'Marwan Hadid Brigades' Claims Responsibility for Weekend Hermel Rocket Attacked. Naharnet. http://www.naharnet.com/stories/en/94770
5. Mercer, D. (2018, February 22). Syria war: UN calls for end to 'hell on earth' violence in eastern Ghuta. Sky News. https://news.sky.com/story/syria-war-un-calls-for-end-to-hell-on-earth-violence-in-eastern-Ghuta-11260044
6. Maccallum, E. (1928). The nationalist crusade in Syria. New York (State): The Foreign Policy Association, 1928.
7. Fildis, A. (2011). The Troubles in Syria: Spawned by French Divide and Rule. Middle East Policy, 18(4), pp. 129–139. https://mepc.org/journal/troubles-syria-spawned-french-divide-and-rule
8. The Wall Street Journal. (2011, January 31). Interview With Syrian President Bashar al-Assad. The Wall Street Journal. https://www.wsj.com/articles/SB10001424052748703833204576114712441122894
9. Ebla Hotel & Omayad Palace for Conferences. (n.d.). http://eblahotel.com/
10. Bible Hub, 1 Kings 19:15. https://biblehub.com/commentaries/1_kings/19-15.htm
11. https://sunnah.com/abudawud/39/8
12. Imady, M. (2002). Humūm al-Tanmiyah: Hawādith Lan Ansāhā. (*The Concerns of Development: Events I Will Not Forget*). Dimashq: Dār Ṭalās lil-Dirāsāt wa-al-Tarjamah wa-al-Nashr.
13. Imady, M. (1985). Al-Takaful al-Tanmawi wa-Tajrubati fi-al-Sanduq al-'Arabi lil-Inma' al-Iqtisadi wa-al-Itima'i. (*Development Cooperation and My Experience at the Arab Fund for Economic and Social Development*). Kuwait: AFESD.
14. Imady, M. (1985). Al-Takaful al-Tanmawi wa-Tajrubati fi-al-Sanduq al-'Arabi lil-Inma' al-Iqtisadi wa-al-Itima'i (*Development Cooperation and My Experience at the Arab Fund for Economic and Social Development*). Kuwait: AFESD. p. 17.

Chapter VI

1. Arab Fund for Economic & Social Development (2020). About AFESD. http://www.arabfund.org/

Chapter VII

1. Biographical information on 'Abd al-Ra'uf al-Kasm can be found in Tlas, M. (2005) Mirat Hayati (*Reflections of my life*). 3 Vols. Dar Tlas; Moubayed, S. (2005). Steel & Silk: Men & Women Who Shaped Syria 1900 – 2000. Cune; Seale, P. (1989). Asad: The Struggle for the Middle East. University of California Press; Batatu, H. (2012). Syria's Peasantry, the Descendants of Its Lesser Rural Notables, and Their Politics Princeton University Press; Imady, O., Commins, D., & Lesch, D. W. (2021). Historical Dictionary of Syria (Historical Dictionaries of Asia, Oceania, and the Middle East) (Fourth ed.). Rowman & Littlefield Publishers; Sadiq, M.(1993). Hiwar Hawla Suriyyah (A Conversation About Syria). Dar 'Ukaz Lil-Tiba'ah wa-al-Nashr.

2. Information on the Hindawi affair is scattered in various sources that are often contradictory. They include, Levin, B. & Winslow, P. (1986, November 3). The Walking Bomb Affair. Maclean's. Available online at: https://archive..ca/article/1986/11/3/the-walking-bomb-affair; Hafez El Assad, Colpevole. (Hafiz al-Asad: Guilty). (1986, November 11). La Repubblica. Available online at: https://ricerca.repubblica.it/repubblica/archivio/repubblica/1986/11/11/hafez-el-assad-colpevole.html; Horovitz, D. (2006, November 24). Ignoring the lessons of the past. The Jerusalem Post. Available online at: https://www.jpost.com/opinion/columnists/editors-notes-ignoring-the-lessons-of-the-past; Erlanger, S. 4 Guilty in Fatal 1986 Berlin Disco Bombing Linked to Libya. (2001, November 14). The New York Times. A prosecutor said today two Jordanians accused of blowing... (1986, November 24). UPI. Available online at: https://www.upi.com/Archives/1986/11/24/A-prosecutor-said-today-two-Jordanians-accused-of-blowing/5174533192400/; Ann-Marie Murphy and the Hindawi Affair: a 30th anniversary review. (2016, April 13). Transport Security International. Available online at: https://www.tsi-mag.com/ann-marie-murphy-hindawi-affair-30th-anniversary-review/; Bomb suspect thought he was smuggling drugs. (1986, October 15). UPI. Available online at: https://www.upi.com/Archives/1986/10/15/Bomb-suspect-thought-he-was-smuggling-drugs/2275529732800/; Nezar Hindawi loses parole bid. (2012, December 17). BBC NEWS. Available online at: https://www.bbc.co.uk/news/uk-20757462; Jackson, S. Brit jail RIOT with six officers rushed to hospital after inmates rampage with pool cues. (2019, February 16). Daily Star. Available online at: https://www.dailystar.co.uk/news/latest-news/hmp-whitemoor-prison-riot-pool-16889609; Britain and Syria Restore Ties After 4-Year Break. (1990, November 29). The New York Times. Available online at: https://www.nytimes.com/1990/11/29/world/britain-and-syria-restore-ties-after-4-year-break.html?searchResultPosition=3; DeYoung, K. (1986, October 25). Britain Cuts Ties With Syria Over El Al Bombing. Links. The Washington Post. Available online at: https://www.washingtonpost.com/archive/politics/1986/10/25/britain-cuts-ties-with-syria-over-el-al-bombing-links/8cf37ff9-4443-4025-8eb9-2e4aa7ce6754/; Brother of Arab in Heathrow Case is Held in Berlin (1986, April 22). The New York Times. Available online at: https://www.nytimes.com/1986/04/22/world/brother-of-arab-in-heathrow-case-is-held-in-berlin.html; Lederer, E. (1986, April 23). Brothers Accused of Terrorism Said to Be from Jordan Valley. Associated Press. Available online at: https://apnews.com/article/b1584ff21d6399e86f0a28492ba4d678; L.A. Times Archives. (1986, November 10). Chirac Quoted on Bonn View of El Al Bomb Plot. Los Angeles Times. Available online at: https://www.latimes.com/archives/la-xpm-1986-11-10-mn-28789-story.html; de Borchgrave, A. (!986, November 6). Chirac told Syria was framed. The Washington Times. Available online at: https://www.cia.gov/readingroom/document/cia-rdp90-00965r000201460003-9; Jehuda, Y. (1992). Proceedings on the 4th International Symposium on Analysis and Detection of explosives. Kluwer Academic Publishers. Available online at: http://citeseerx.ist.psu.edu/viewdoc/download?doi=10.1.1.888.4278&rep=rep1&type=pdf#page=74; Pipes, D. (1989). Terrorism: The Syrian Connection. Daniel Pipes Middle East Forum. Available online at: http://www.danielpipes.org/1064/terrorism-the-syrian-connection; Scott, S. (2016). British Foreign Policy towards Syria: Its Importance, its Distinctiveness and its Relations to the Policy of other Actors in the Region. (Doctoral Thesis, University of St Andrews). Available online at: https://core.ac.uk/download/pdf/76986476.pdf

3. L.A. Times Archives. (1986, November 10). Chirac Quoted on Bonn View of El Al Bomb Plot. Los Angeles Times. https://www.latimes.com/archives/la-xpm-1986-11-10-mn-28789-story.html
4. Grunwald, H., Fischer, D., Prager, K., & Duncan, R. (2005, June 21). An Interview with Hafez Assad. Time. http://content.time.com/time/subscriber/article/0,33009,1075212-2,00.html
5. TOI Staff. (2021, April 10). 35 years after El Al bomb plot, security staff recount stopping unwitting bomber. The Times of Israel. https://www.timesofisrael.com/35-years-after-el-al-bomb-plot-security-staff-recount-stopping-unwitting-bomber/
6. On Syria's economic crisis during the 80s, see, for example: Perthes, V. (1992). The Syrian Economy in the 1980s. Middle East Journal, 46(1), 37–58.
7. Colvin v. Syrian Arab Republic, No. CV 16-1423 (ABJ) (D.D.C. Feb. 1, 2019). https://ecf.dcd.uscourts.gov/cgi-bin/show_public_doc?2016cv1423-59
8. Ibid.
9. Lucas, S. (2018, December 16). Syria Daily: Assad – Give Me $400 Billion for Reconstruction. EA Worldview. https://eaworldview.com/2018/12/syria-daily-assad-give-me-400-billion-for-reconstruction/
10. The Forgiveness Project. (n.d.) Kemal Pervanic. https://www.theforgivenessproject.com/stories/kemal-pervanic/
11. Sephton, C. (2017, June 6). Notre Dame attacker shouted 'this is for Syria' before being shot. Sky News. https://news.sky.com/story/paris-police-warn-public-to-stay-away-from-notre-dame-cathedral-10906298
12. France 24. (2017, May 24). Eight-year-old girl named among fatalities of Manchester bombing. https://www.france24.com/en/20170524-manchester-arena-attack-eight-year-old-girl-saffie-rose-roussos-terrorism
13. Gillett, F. (2017, June 7). Nursery worker beaten and stabbed by three girls 'shouting about Allah'. Evening Standard. https://www.standard.co.uk/news/london/wanstead-nursery-worker-beaten-and-stabbed-by-three-women-shouting-about-allah-a3559251.html

Chapter VIII

1. On Law No. 10, see: Barkei, C. L. (2004) Foreign direct investment in Syria an analysis of investment law no 10, Durham theses, Durham University. Available at Durham E-Theses Online: http://etheses.dur.ac.uk/3165/
2. Arslanian, F. (2015). Book Review: Mohammed Imady, The Evolving Concepts of Development in Syria: Damascus: Dar Tlas lil-Dirasat wa al-Nashr, 2004. Syria Studies. 7(3). 73–76.
3. Melhem, H. (1997). Syria Between Two Transitions. Middle East Research and Information Project. https://merip.org/1997/06/syria-between-two-transitions/
4. Alajaty, M., & Anchor, J. (2018). Transition economies in the Middle East: The Syrian experience. Post-Communist Economies, 30(3), 382–394. p. 386.
5. Hinnebusch, R. (1997). Syria: The politics of economic liberalisation. Third World Quarterly, 18(2), 249–266. p. 256.
6. Biographical information on Mahmud al-Zu'bi can be found in: Tlas, M. (2005) Mirat Hayati (*Reflections of my life*). 3 Vols. Dar Tlas; Moubayed, S. (2005). Steel & Silk: Men & Women Who Shaped Syria 1900 – 2000. Cune; Imady, O., Commins, D., & Lesch, D. W. (2021). Historical Dictionary of Syria (Historical Dictionaries of Asia, Oceania, and the Middle East) (Fourth ed.).

7. Moubayed, S. (2002, June 22). Corruption Trials in Damascus: A Popular New Trend? Washington Report on Middle East Affairs. https://www.wrmea.org/002-june-july/orruption-trials-in-damascus-a-popular-new-trend.html
8. Information on the Airbus scandal is scarce and found primarily in news clippings which were published during and after the event. Some of the insights into the event are based on interviews with officials who chose to remain anonymous. See: Airbus' secret past. (2003, June 12). The Economist. https://www.economist.com/special-report/2003/06/12/airbuss-secret-past; Moubayed, S. (2002, June 22). Corruption Trials in Damascus: A Popular New Trend? Washington Report on Middle East Affairs. https://www.wrmea.org/002-june-july/orruption-trials-in-damascus-a-popular-new-trend.html; Syrian ministers charged over $240 million Airbus deal. (2000, July 25). The Daily Star Lebanon. http://www.dailystar.com.lb/News/Lebanon-News/2000/Jul-25/28438-syrian-ministers-charged-over-240m-airbus-deal.ashx; Axon, A., & Hewitt, S. (2019). Syria, 1975/76-2018 (Contemporary archive of the Islamic world. 1). Brill: Leiden; Al Mulhem, N. (2000, July 24). Former Syrian Ministers on Trial for Fraud over Airbus Deal. Albawaba. https://www.albawaba.com/news/former-syrian-ministers-trial-fraud-over-airbus-deal; Suicide of a Prime Minister; An Egyptian Intellectual Criticizes Arab Regimes. (2000, June 13). MEMRI. https://www.memri.org/reports/suicide-prime-minister-egyptian-intellectual-criticizes-arab-regimes; Ziser, E. (2007). Commanding Syria: Bashar al-Asad and the first years in power. Tauris: London.
9. Imady, M. (2002). Humūm al-Tanmiyah: Hawādith Lan Ansāhā. (*The Concerns of Development: Events I Will Not Forget*). Dimashq: Dār Ṭalās lil-Dirāsāt wa-al-Tarjamah wa-al-Nashr.
10. Ibid.; and Ghusn, Z. (2006). Al-Rajulan yarwiyan ma yajdur qira'atahu al-an 'an tanfidh khuttah al-ra'is: Al-'Imady wa al-Mahayini rajulan Hafidh al-Asad alladhan a'ada bina' al-khazinah min al-sifr. (*Two men share what is worthy of reading today regarding the execution of the President's plan: Imady and Mahayini, the two men of Hafiz al-Asad who rebuilt the Syrian treasury from zero.)*. Syria Steps. https://syriasteps.com/index.php?p=131&id=178340
11. Imady, M. (June 2000). Private interview.
12. Al- Suyūṭī, A., & Sayyid, Majdī Fatḥī. (1991). Mā rawāhu al-asāṭīn fī 'adam al-majī' ilá al-salaṭīn; Dhamm al-qaḍā' wa-taqallud al-aḥkām; Dhamm al-maks. Ṭanṭā: Dār al-Ṣaḥābah lil-Turāth.
13. Ibid? http://islamport.com/w/sys/Web/191/4.htm
14. Abu Zaid, W. (2019). Mizan al-I'tidal fi Ta'amul al-'Ulama' ma'a al-Hikam. *(The Balance of Moderation in the Interactions of Scholars with Rulers)*. Muntada al-'Ulama'. https://www.msf-online.com/ميزان-الاعتدال-في-تعامل-العلماء-مع-الح/
15. Imady, O. (2005). The Rise and Fall of Muslim Civil Society. MSI Press.
16. Kedourie, E. (2021, March 5). Jamāl al-Dīn al-Afghānī. Encyclopedia Britannica. https://www.britannica.com/biography/Jamal-al-Din-al-Afghani
17. Kerr, M. H. (2021, January 1). Muḥammad 'Abduh. Encyclopedia Britannica. https://www.britannica.com/biography/Muhammad-Abduh
18. Britannica, T. Editors of Encyclopaedia (2021, April 26). Muḥammad Tawfiq Pasha. Encyclopedia Britannica. https://www.britannica.com/biography/Muhammad-Tawfiq-Pasha
19. Islahi, A. (2012). Economic Thought of Muhammad Abduh: An omitted aspect of his biography. Munich Personal RePEc Archive. Available online at: https://mpra.ub.uni-muenchen.de/68363/1/MPRA_paper_68363.pdf. p. 9

20. Britannica, T. Editors of Encyclopaedia (2021, February 6). 'Abbās II'. Encyclopedia Britannica. https://www.britannica.com/biography/Abdulhamid-II
21. Al-'Aqqad, M. (2012).'Abaqari al-Islah wa-al-Ta'lim: al-Imam Muhammad 'Abduh. (*The Genius of Reform and Education: al-Imam Muhammad Abduh*). Cairo: Mu'asasat Hindawi lil-Ta'lim wa-al-Thaqafah. p. 86.
22. Britannica, T. Editors of Encyclopaedia (2020, December 16). 'Abbās II. Encyclopedia Britannica. https://www.britannica.com/biography/Abbas-II-khedive-of-Egypt
23. Al-'Aqqad, M. (2012).'Abaqari al-Islah wa-al-Ta'lim: al-Imam Muhammad 'Abduh. (*The Genius of Reform and Education: al-Imam Muhammad Abduh*). Cairo: Mu'asasat Hindawi lil-Ta'lim wa-al-Thaqafah. p. 87.
24. Haddad, G. (2009). Shaykh Ahmad Kuftaro. Living Islam. https://www.livingislam.org/n/shk_e.html
25. Imady, O. (2016). Organisationally Secular: Damascene Islamist Movements and the Syrian Uprising. Syria Studies. 8(1). 66–91.
26. Sands, P. (2013, March 24). Thousands grieve for murdered Syrian imam who supported Assad. The National. https://www.thenationalnews.com/world/mena/thousands-grieve-for-murdered-syrian-imam-who-supported-assad-1.285732#page2
27. Al-'Amr, M. (2019, December 15). Isam al-Za'im al-Rahil bi-nawbah qahr wataniyy bi-imtiyaz. (*Isam al-Za'im - the one who departed on account of a nationalist embolism par excellence*) Snack Syria. https://snacksyrian.com/عصام-الزعيم-الراحل-بنوبة-قهر-وطني-با/
28. Al-Amin, I. (2012, December 17). Al-Shar' yakhruj 'an samtihi. (Al-Shar' emerges from his silence). Al-Akhbar. https://al-akhbar.com/Politics/80373
29. Al-Raysuni, S. (2013, June 11). Al-Jami'i: Na'am… *U'tuqila al-Basri wa-Uhin yawm bay'ah Muhammad al-Sadis* (*Al-Jami'i: Yes... Al-Basri was arrested and humiliated on the day of allegiance to Muhammad VI.*) Magress. https://www.maghress.com/almassae/184274
30. Reuters Staff. (2020, March 31). Syrian ex-vice president Khaddam, foe of Assad, dies in France at 88. Reuters. https://www.reuters.com/article/uk-syria-khaddam-idUKKBN21I1A4
31. University of St Andrews. (2018, November 27). Lecture by HRH Prince El Hassan bin Talal of Jordan. https://events.st-andrews.ac.uk/events/lecture-by-hrh-prince-el-hassan-bin-talal-of-jordan/
32. Hinnebusch, R. (1997). Syria: The politics of economic liberalisation. Third World Quarterly, 18(2), 249–266.
33. See above: Post-Uprising Introspections: The Damascene Reformer. pp. 63–65
34. 'Abd al-'Aziz, F. (2018, August 18). Al-Daktur Muhammad al-Imady: Al-Iqtisadi al-sharif, alladhi Ahabba Hafidh al-Asad min kull qalibih. (*Dr Muhammad Imady, the honourable economist who loved Hafez al-Asad with all his heart*). Eqtsad. https://www.eqtsad.net/news/article/21146/
35. Luban, D. (2021). Complicity and Lesser Evils: A Tale of Two Lawyers. Georgetown Journal of Legal Ethics. https://scholarship.law.georgetown.edu/facpub/2368/
36. Arendt, H., & Kohn, J. (2003). Responsibility and judgment (1st ed.). New York: Schocken Books. p. 36
37. Linder, D. (n.d.) Summation for the Prosecution by Justice Robert Jackson [July 26, 1946]. Famous Trials. https://famous-trials.com/nuremberg/1933-jacksonsummation
38. Harvard Law School Library Nuremberg Trials Project (2020). Transcript for NMT 2: Milch Case. The Nuremberg Trials Project. http://nuremberg.law.harvard.edu/transcripts/2-transcript-for-nmt-2-milch-case?seq=16

39. Luban, D. (2021). Complicity and Lesser Evils: A Tale of Two Lawyers. Georgetown Journal of Legal Ethics. https://scholarship.law.georgetown.edu/facpub/2368/
40. Ibid. p. 50
41. 'Abd al-'Aziz, F. (2018, August 18). Al-Daktur Muhammad al-Imady: Al-Iqtisadi al-sharif, alladhi Ahabba Hafidh al-Asad min kull qalibih. (*Dr Muhammad Imady, the honourable economist who loved Hafez al-Asad with all his heart*). Eqtsad. https://www.eqtsad.net/news/article/21146/
42. Luban, D. (2021). Complicity and Lesser Evils: A Tale of Two Lawyers. Georgetown Journal of Legal Ethics. https://scholarship.law.georgetown.edu/facpub/2368/ p. 53
43. Qur'an, Chapter 12, Verse 55. (Author's own translation).
44. See: Post-Uprising Introspections: The Damascene Reformer.

Chapter IX

1. Levinson, B. (1997). Wag the Dog [Film]. Baltimore Pictures.
2. Reuters. (1973, October 10). Casualties Placed at 100 In Raid on Syrian Capital. The New York Times. https://www.nytimes.com/1973/10/10/archives/casualties-placed-at-100-in-raid-on-syrian-capital-casualties-are.html
3. The Syrian Observer. (2015, January 7). Who's Who: Abdallah al-Dardari. The Syrian Observer. https://syrianobserver.com/who/31340/who_who_abdullah_dardari.html
4. Imady, O. (2014). How a Microfinance Network Could Have Preempted the Syrian Uprising. Syrian Studies. 6(1).
5. Al-Assad, B. (2011, March 30). Speech to the Syrian Parliament. Available online at: https://www.documentcloud.org/documents/2782925-Al-Assad-Speech-to-Syrian-Parliament-March-30-2011.html
6. UNESCWA. (n.d.). The National Agenda for the Future of Syria Programme. United Nations Economic and Social Commission for Western Asia. https://archive.unescwa.org/sub-site/national-agenda-future-syria
7. Abu-Ismail, K., Imady, O., Kuncic, A., et al. (2017). Syria at war: Five years on. Fife, Scotland: University of St Andrews. Available online at: https://www.unescwa.org/publications/syria-war-five-years
8. Flood, A. (2012, October 9). Syrian author shares PEN/Pinter prize with Carol Ann Duffy. The Guardian. https://www.theguardian.com/books/2012/oct/09/syrian-author-pen-pinter-prize
9. Imady, O. (2019). The Weaponization of Syria's Reconstruction. Syria Studies. 11(1). https://ojs.st-andrews.ac.uk/index.php/syria/article/view/1802
10. Zaman al-Wasl. (2012, July 9). Tafasil ikhtitaf 'Salim Da'bul' kama tarwiha safhat 'Facebook' (*The details of the kidnapping of Salim Da'bul as reported by Facebook)*. Zaman al-Wasl. https://www.zamanalwsl.net/news/article/28346
11. Tajammu' Ahrar Dimashq wa Rifiha. (2011, November 1). Mudhaharah al-Jami'ah al-'Arabiyyah al-Duwaliyyah 1-11-2011. (*The demonstration of the Arab International University*). [Video]. Youtube. https://www.youtube.com/watch?v=oXam1_1ieGk
12. Loar, C. (2010). The Meaning of Life: 'Joseph Campbell on the Power of Myth with Bill Moyers'. PopMatters. https://www.popmatters.com/132546-joseph-campbell-on-the-power-of-myth-with-bill-moyers-2496120081.html#:~:text="Myths%20are%20clues%20to%20the,of%20Myth%20with%20Bill%20Moyers.&text=The%20experience%20of%20eternity%20right,is%20the%20function%20of%20life."
13. C-Span. (2011, March 30). Syria President Bashar al-Assad Speech to Parliament [Video]. C-Span. https://www.c-span.org/video/?298760-1/syria-president-bashar-al-assad-speech-parliament

14. Goldsmith, J. (2018, April 6). After Decree 66, Some Residents Fear Reconstruction Means Eviction. The New Humanitarian. https://deeply.thenewhumanitarian.org/syria/articles/2018/04/06/after-decree-66-some-residents-fear-reconstruction-means-eviction
15. Smith, R. (2013, March 14). Waste, Fraud and Abuse Commonplace in Iraq Reconstruction Effort. The Center for Public Integrity. https://publicintegrity.org/national-security/waste-fraud-and-abuse-commonplace-in-iraq-reconstruction-effort/
16. Ibid.
17. Laber, J. (2018, April 19). Can We Admit Now That Afghanistan Reconstruction Failed? The American Conservative. https://www.theamericanconservative.com/articles/can-we-admit-now-that-afghanistan-reconstruction-failed/
18. Divjak, B. (2005). Corruption in post-conflict reconstruction Bosnia and Herzegovina case study. Transparency International BiH, Sarajevo. Available online at: http://ti-bih.org/wp-content/uploads/Documents/05-12-2007/Post-conflict_reconstruction_and_corruption_in_BiH.pdf
19. Imady, O. Syria's Reconstruction: The Good, the Bad, and the Ugly. In R. Turkmani, M. Theros, & S. Hadaya (Eds.). (2019, April). Political economy and governance in Syria: presentations from the Political Economy and Governance in Syria conference organised at LSE 3 – 4 December 2018. London School of Economics.
20. Orient Net. (2016, January 8). Starving Madaya: A story of shame. Orient Net. https://www.orient-news.net/en/news_show/99275/0/Starving-Madaya-A-story-of-shame
21. https://inthesetimes.com/article/syria-civil-war-assad-exile-displacement-siege-aleppo
22. Rosen, A. (2016, February 8). Massive and systematized violence: The UN released a horrifying report on Assad's human-rights abuses. Insider. https://www.businessinsider.com/massive-and-systemetized-violence-the-un-just-released-a-horrifying-report-on-assads-human-rights-abuses-2016-2?r=UK&IR=T
23. Imady, O. (2014). How a Microfinance Network Could Have Preempted the Syrian Uprising. Syria Studies. 6(1). https://ojs.st-andrews.ac.uk/index.php/syria/article/view/823; and United Nations Development Programme. (2006). Evaluation of UNDP Support to Conflict-Affected Countries. UNDP. http://web.undp.org/evaluation/evaluations/documents/thematic/conflict/ConflictEvaluation2006.pdf
24. Thomson, M. (2016, July 28). Syria's secret library. BBC News. https://www.bbc.co.uk/news/magazine-36893303; and Hajj Hamdo, A. (2014, November 28). With Diesel Scarce, Syrians Turn to Solar Power as an Emerging Energy Option. The New Humanitarian. https://deeply.thenewhumanitarian.org/syria/articles/2014/11/28/with-diesel-scarce-syrians-turn-to-solar-power-as-an-emerging-energy-option.
25. UNICEF. (2014, March). Under Siege: The devastating impact on children of three years of conflict in Syria. https://www.refworld.org/pdfid/531ecd534.pdf
26. Hilton, D. (2017, December 22). The Shifting Role of Women in Syria's Economy. The New Humanitarian. https://deeply.thenewhumanitarian.org/syria/articles/2017/12/22/the-shifting-role-of-women-in-syrias-economy
27. Yomyat Qadhifah Hawun fi Dimashq (*Mortar Shell Diaries in Damascus*). Home. [Facebook page]. Retrieved June 25, 2021 from: https://www.facebook.com/YomyatKzefeh
28. Yomyat Qadhifah Hawun fi Dimashq (*Mortar Shell Diaries in Damascus*). (2018, March 12). Irtifa' nisbah al-jara'im al-akhlaqiyyah khilal al-azmah bi-nisbah 50%.

(*50% rise in moral crimes during the crisis*). [Post]. Facebook. https://m.facebook.com/story.php?story_fbid=1498763380251125&id=469605269833613&p=30

29. Majesty News. (2019, March 3) Taqrir al-Umam al-Muttahidah: 80% min al-suriyyin tahta khatt al-faqr. [UN Report 80% of Syrians below the poverty line]. Majesty News. https://www.majestynews.com/ar/v-81803/تقرير-للأمم-المتحدة-80-من-السوريين-تحت-خط-الفقر#.YNX52i-ZNp8
30. Majesty News. (2021). https://majestynews.com/ar/home
31. Maggie Khozam. (n.d.). Home [Youtube Channel]. Retrieved from: https://www.youtube.com/playlist?list=PLBQCwakn0JSN1_nwp76ZiZlRSIJQGiTTB
32. Muhammad ibn 'Abd al-Qadir Qubnud. (n.d.). Man Hum. https://manhom.com/شخصيات/محمد-قبنض/
33. FMC World. (2018, March 23). Fadihah 'aduw majlis al-sha'b al-suriyy Muhammad Qubnud ma' al-i'lamiyyah Maggy Khuzam. *(Scandal concerning member of the Syrian People's Assembly, Muhammad Qubnud, with journalist Maggy Khuzam).* [Video]. YouTube. https://www.youtube.com/watch?v=JICI8Agdxl0
34. Perry, T. (2019, March 14). Syria's Assad struggles to reap spoils after military gains. Reuters. https://www.reuters.com/article/us-mideast-crisis-syria-analysis-idUSKCN1QV11P
35. Muhammad, H. (2019, Feb 20). Al-Fannan al-Suri, Bashar Isma'il. [Syrian Artist, Bashar Isma'il]. Al-Quds. https://www.alquds.co.uk/الفنان-السوري-بشار-إسماعيل-المنافقون/
36. Al-Modon Media. (2020, March 13). Wazir al-Sihhah al-Suriyy 'an Kuruna: 'Al-Jaysh Tahhara al-Bilad min al-Jarathim'. (*The Syrian Minister of Health on Corona: The Army has Purified the Land from Germs*). Al-Modon. https://www.almodon.com/media/2020/3/13/وزير-الصحة-السوري-عن-كورونا-الجيش-طهر-البلاد-من-الجراثيم
37. Chalati, N. (2020). Illness as Metaphor and Reality in Syria. Middle East Report 297. https://merip.org/2020/12/illness-as-metaphor-and-reality-in-syria/
38. United Nations Office for the Coordination of Humanitarian Affairs. (2020, April 17). WFP Syria Situation Report #3, March 2020. ReliefWeb. https://reliefweb.int/report/syrian-arab-republic/wfp-syria-situation-report-3-march-2020
39. United Nations Office for the Coordination of Humanitarian Affairs. (2019, March 1). 2019 Humanitarian Needs Overview. ReliefWeb. https://reliefweb.int/sites/reliefweb.int/files/resources/2019_Syr_HNO_Full.pdf
40. Ibid.
41. The Moscow Times. (2020, January 20). Russian Oil Deals in Syria Linked to 'Putin's Chef' – Novaya Gazeta. https://www.themoscowtimes.com/2020/01/20/russian-oil-deals-in-syria-linked-to-putins-chef-novaya-gazeta-a68964
42. Nezavisimaya gazeta. (2020, March 15). Асад купил своей жене картину за 23 млн фунтов на аукционе в Лондоне (*Assad bought his wife a painting for 23 million pounds at auction in London*). NG. https://www.ng.ru/news/676538.html
43. (2020, April 15). СМИ: Президент Сирии Асад купил жене картину Дэвида Хокни за десятки миллионов фунтов (*Media: Syrian President Assad bought his wife a David Hockney painting for tens of millions of pounds*). Rosbalt. https://www.rosbalt.ru/world/2020/04/15/1838586.html
44. Krasnova, E. (2020, April 16). Асад купил на Sotheby's картину за 30 млн долларов для своей жены (*Assad bought a $30 million painting at Sotheby's for his wife*). Versiya. https://versiya.info/politika/149654
45. The Art Newspaper. (2020, April 27). The curious, spurious tale of David Hockney's £23m pool painting and Syrian president Bashar al-Assad. https://www.theartnewspaper.com/blog/david-hockney-s-gbp23m-pool-painting-and-syrian-

president; Sotheby's. (2020, January 13). David Hockney's Iconic Masterpiece, "The Splash". https://www.sothebys.com/en/articles/david-hockneys-iconic-masterpiece-the-splash

46. Abdelrazak, A. (2020, April 21). Rami Makhlouf and His Father Respond 'With Two Scandals' to Asmaa al-Assad. The Syrian Observer. https://syrianobserver.com/news/57501/rami-makhlouf-and-his-father-respond-with-two-scandals-to-asmaa-al-assad.html; Global Witness. (2019, November 11). Assad Henchmen's Russian Refuge. https://www.globalwitness.org/en/campaigns/corruption-and-money-laundering/assad-henchmens-russian-refuge/
47. Mardam Bey, S. (2020, April 27). Exposing Assad's weak grip and corruption… Russian media reflect Kremlin's frustration. L'Orient Today. https://today.lorientlejour.com/article/1215911/exposing-assads-weak-grip-and-corruption-russian-media-reflect-kremlins-frustration.html; and Al-Modon 'Arab wa-'Alam. (2020, April 18). Ishta'alat bayna Rami Makhlouf wa-Asma' al-Asad… Fada'ih bi-l-Jumlah. […]. Al-Modon. https://www.almodon.com/arabworld/2020/4/18//اشتعلت-بين-رامي-مخلوف-وأسماء-الأسد-فضائح-بالجملة
48. Meyer, H., & Arkhipov, I. (2020, April 28). Putin has a Syria Headache and the Kremlin's Blaming Assad. Bloomberg. https://www.bloomberg.com/news/articles/2020-04-28/putin-has-a-syria-headache-and-the-kremlin-s-blaming-assad
49. Attitude. (2020, February 12). David Hockney's 'The Splash' Sells for £23.1 Million at Auction. The Attitude. https://www.attitude.co.uk/article/david-hockneys-the-splash-sells-for-231-million-at-auction/22815/
50. Wikileaks. (n.d.). Syria Files. https://www.wikileaks.org/syria-files/
51. Loughran Gallery. (n.d.) Nick Jeffrey Financial Times Butterflies. https://www.loughrangallery.co.uk/blog/2015/4/19/nick-jeffrey-financial-times-butterflies.aspx
52. Wikileaks. (2012, January 4). Syria Files. https://wikileaks.org/syria-files/docs/661356_stephen-hawking-david-hockney-jose-vazquez-abi-morgan-tom.html
53. Llewellyn, T. (2014, April 13). Patrick Seale, Syria specialist and former Observer correspondent, dies aged 83. The Guardian. https://www.theguardian.com/media/2014/apr/13/patrick-seale-observer-journalist-dies
54. Plante, D. (2013). Becoming a Londoner: A Diary. Bloomsbury. p. 244
55. Brooke. A. (2011). The Other Side of the Mirror: An American Travels Through Syria. Paul Dry Books. pp. 131–132
56. Herszenhorn, D. (2013, September 4). Putin Says Proof of Chemical Arms Attack Not Enough to Justify U.S. Attack. New York Times. https://www.nytimes.com/2013/09/05/world/europe/putin-says-proof-of-chemical-arms-attack-not-enough-to-justify-us-attack.html
57. Crocker, L. (2017, July 12). The Enduring Myth of 'Sex-Jihad' Still Sates the Media. The Daily Beast. https://www.thedailybeast.com/the-enduring-myth-of-sex-jihad-still-sates-the-media; and Shadid, A. (2012, January 10). Syrian Leader Vows 'Iron First' to Crush Conspiracy. New York Times. https://www.nytimes.com/2012/01/11/world/middleeast/syrian-leader-vows-to-crush-conspiracy.html.
58. Al-Bab. (2011, March 30). Syria: Speech by Bashar al-Asad. https://al-bab.com/albab-orig/albab/arab/docs/syria/bashar_assad_speech_110330.htm
59. Husseini, R. (2017, July 10). Man charged with rape, premeditated murder of Syrian child. The Jordan Times. https://www.jordantimes.com/news/local/man-charged-rape-premeditated-murder-syrian-child

60. Mackintosh, E. (2017, June 16). Refugee fled Syria violence only to die in the London fire. CNN. https://edition.cnn.com/2017/06/15/europe/syrian-refugee-first-victim-grenfell-london-fire/index.html
61. Bayliss, C. (2017, January 19). Syrian refugee 'brutally killed by gang of migrants in savage attack in Germany'. Express. https://www.express.co.uk/news/world/751750/refugee-kills-refugee-15-year-old-syrian-boy-migrant-attack-silvesternacht-bremen-germany
62. Agence France-Presse. (2017, July 8). Pregnant Syrian Refugee Raped and Murdered in Turkey. NDTV. https://www.ndtv.com/world-news/pregnant-syrian-refugee-raped-and-murdered-in-turkey-1722003
63. On Deconfliction-Zones, see: Bridgeman, T. (2017). About that "Deconfliction Zone" in Syria: Is the United States on Firm Domestic and International Legal Footing? Just Security. https://www.justsecurity.org/42183/deconfliction-zone-syria-united-states-firm-domestic-international-legal-footing/
64. Kailath, R. (2017, July 12). Anarchists offer a lifeline for refugees in Greece. Marketplace. https://www.marketplace.org/2017/07/12/world/anarchists-offer-lifeline-refugees-greece/
65. Ibid.
66. On Shaikh Muhammad Bashir al-Bani, see: Makki, M. (2008). Shaykh Muhammad Bashir Albani. [Ahmad, S. Translator]. Marifah. Available at: http://www.marifah.info/articles/bashiralbani-majdmakki.pdf

Bibliography

Abu Ismail, K., Al-Kiswan, B., Araji, S., Dahi, O., Hinnebusch, R., Imady, O., Nehme, M., & Shikh Ebid, A. (2020). *Syria at War: Eight Years On*. UN – ESCWA.

Abu Ismail, K., Imady, O., Kuncic, A., Nojoum, O., Walker, J. (2020). *Syria at War: Five Years On*. UN – ESCWA.

Al-'Aqqad, 'A. (2012). 'Abaqari al-Islah wa-al-Ta'lim: al-Imam Muhammad 'Abduh (The Genius of Reform and Education: al-Imam Muhammad Abduh). Mu'asasat Hindawi lil-Ta'lim wa-al-Thaqafah.

Al-Ghazzi, M. (1945). Al-Kawakib al-Saira bi A'yan al-Mia al-'Ashira [*The Orbiting Planets of the Notables of the 10th Century – 1624*]. J. Jabbur (Ed.). American Press.

Al-Ghazzi, M. (1981). Lutf al-Samar wa-Qatf al-Thamar min Tarajim A'yan al-Tabaqat al-Ula min al-Qarn al-Hadi 'Ashar [*The Sweetness of Nightly Conversation and the Fruitful Harvest of the Biographies of Notables of the First Class of the 11th Century*]. (M. al-Shaykh Ed.). Manshurat wizarat al-thaqafa wa'l-irshad al-qawmi.

Al-Muhibbi M. A. (1284/1867–68). Khulasat al – Athar fi a`yan al-Qarn al-Hadi `Ashar [*Summary of History of the Eleventh Century*], Bulaq.

Al-Munajjid. S. (1959). Al-Burini, Hasan, Tarajim al-A'yan min Abna' al-Zaman [*The Biographies of Notables from the People of the Times*]. Ed. , Salah al-Din (Damascus: al-Majma' al-'Ilmi al-'Arabi, 1959–63).

Al-Shallah, B. (1990). Lil-Tarikh wa-al-Dhikra, Qisat Jihad wa-'Umur [*For History and Memory, the Story of a Struggle and a Life*]. Self-Published.

Al-Shar', F. (2015). Al-Riwayyah al-Mafqudah [*The Lost Narrative*]. Arab Center for Research and Policy Studies.

Alajaty, M., & Anchor, J. R. (2018). Transition economies in the Middle East: the Syrian experience. *Post-Communist Economies*, 30(3), 382–394.

Barkei, C. L. (2004). Foreign direct investment in Syria an analysis of investment law no 10. Durham theses, Durham University. Available at Durham E-Theses Online: http://etheses.dur.ac.uk/3165/

Ben-Hanan, E. (1971). *Our Man in Damascus: Story of Elie Cohen* (First Edition). Robert Hale Ltd.

Chirac, J. (1987). American Reactions are a Little Primitive. *MERIP Middle East Report*, (144), 39–43.

Gray, M. (1997). 'The political economy of tourism in Syria: state, society, and economic liberalization.' *Arab Studies Quarterly*, vol. 19, no. 2, 1997.

Hinnebusch, R., & Imady, O. (2018). Introduction: Origins of the Syrian uprising-From structure to agency. In R. Hinnebusch, & O. Imady (Eds.), *The Syrian Uprising: Domestic Origins and Early Trajectory* (pp. 1–11). (Routledge/ St Andrews Syrian Studies Series). Routledge.

Hinnebusch, R., & Imady, O. (2018). Syria's reconciliation agreements. *Syria Studies*, *9*(2).

Hinnebusch, R., & Imady, O. (2018). *The Syrian Uprising: Domestic Origins and Early Trajectory (Routledge/ St Andrews Syrian Studies Series)* (1st ed.). Routledge.

Hinnebusch, R., Imady, O., & Zintl, T. J. (2016). Civil resistance in the Syrian Uprising: from democratic transition to sectarian civil war. In A. Roberts, M. J. Willis, R. McCarthy, & T. G. Ash (Eds.), *Civil Resistance in the Arab Spring: Triumphs and Disasters*. Oxford University Press.

Hinnebusch, R., Zartman, I. W., Parker-Magyar, E., & Imady, O. (2016). *UN Mediation in the Syrian Crisis: From Kofi Annan to Lakhdar Brahimi*. United Nations International Peace Institute.

Hopfinger, H. & Boeckler, M. (1996). 'Step by step to an open economic system: Syria sets course for liberalization', *British Journal of Middle Eastern Studies*, 23:2, 183–202.

Ibn Ayyūb, S. (1590). Kitāb al-Rawḍ al-ʿāṭir fīmā tayassara min akhbār ahl al-qarn al-sābiʿ ilā khitām al-qarn al-ʿāshir, [*The Perfumed Garden of Assembled Notices of the People of the 7th to the End of the 10th Century*]. Berlin, Staatsbibliothek, MS Wetzstein II 289.

Ibn Taghribirdi, J. Y. (1929–1956). al-Nujum al-zahira fi muluk Misr wa'l-Qahira [*The Shining Stars in the Rulers of Egypt and Syria*]. Maṭbaʻat Dar al-Kutub al-Miṣrīyah.

Ibn Tulun, M. (1998). Mufakahat al-Khullan fi Hawadith al-Zaman [*Entertainment of Friends in the Events of Times*], Dar al Kutub al-ʿIlmiyah.

Ibn ʿAbidin, M. A. (1270/1853–54). Al-ʿUqud al-durriya fi tanqih al-fatawa al-hamidiya, Dar al-Tibaʿa al-ʿAmira.

Imady Rippey, E. (2003). *Postscripts from Palisades – Mildred Post Rippey's story*. Dar Tlass.

Imady Rippey, E. (2009). *The Road to Damascus*. MSI Press.

Imady, M. (1985). Al-Takaful al-Tanmawi wa-Tajrubati fi-al-Sanduq al-'Arabi lil-Inma' al-Iqtisadi wa-al-Itima'i [*Development Cooperation and My Experience at the Arab Fund for Economic and Social Development*]. AFESD.

Imady, M. (2002). Humūm al-Tanmiyah: Hawādith Lan Ansāhā. [*The Concerns of Development: Events I Will Not Forget*]. Dimashq: Dār Ṭalās lil-Dirāsāt wa-al-Tarjamah wa-al-Nashr.

Imady, M. (2003). Suriyah wa-Masirat al-Takamul al-Iqtisadi al-'Arabi [*Syria and the March Towards Arab Economic Integration*]. Dar Tlass.

Imady, M. (2014). Hay'at al-Awraq wa-al-Aswaq al-Maliyyah al-Suriyyah: Thamani sanawat 'ala al-ta'sis [*Syrian Commission on Financial Markets and Securities: Eight Years Since its Establishment*]. Dar Tlass.

Imady, M. (2015). Dirasat Mukhtara hawl al-Ta'lim al-Jami'i [*Selected Studies on University Teaching*]. Dar Tlass.
Imady, O. (1994). Muhammad Imady – Biographical Interview.
Imady, O. (2000). Muhammad Imady – Biographical Interview.
Imady, O. (2014). How a microfinance network could have preempted the Syrian Uprising. *Syria Studies*, *6* (1), 81–122.
Imady, O. (2017). Muhammad Imady – Biographical Interview.
Imady, O. (2018). Organisationally secular: Damascene Islamist movements and the Syrian Uprising. In R. Hinnebusch, & O. Imady (Eds.), *The Syrian Uprising: Domestic Origins and Early Trajectory* (Routledge/ St Andrews Syrian Studies Series). Routledge.
Imady, O. (2019). The Weaponization of Syria's Reconstruction: A Preliminary Sketch. *Syria Studies*, *11*(1), 6–21.
Imady, O. (2020). Sufism and the Preservation of Syrian Spiritual Identity. In D. Shahi (Ed.), *Sufism: A Theoretical Intervention in Global International Relations* Rowman & Littlefield / Scarecrow Press.
Imady, O. (2019). Syria's Reconstruction: The Good, the Bad, and the Ugly. In R. Turkmani, M. Theros, & S. Hadaya (Eds.). (2019, April). *Political economy and governance in Syria: presentations from the Political Economy and Governance in Syria conference organised at LSE 3–4 December 2018*. London School of Economics.
Imady, O., & Hinnebusch, R. (2014). The UN and the Syria Crisis. *EURO Atlantic Quarterly*, 9(1), 24–25.
Imady, O., & Hinnebusch, R. (2018). Conclusion: The early trajectory of the Syrian Uprising: From agency to structure. In R. Hinnebusch, & O. Imady (Eds.), *The Syrian Uprising: Domestic Origins and Early Trajectory* (United Kingdom ed., pp. 329–335). Routledge.
Imady, O., Commins, D., & Lesch, D. W. (2021). *Historical Dictionary of Syria* (Historical Dictionaries of Asia, Oceania, and the Middle East) (Fourth ed.). Rowman & Littlefield Publishers.
Imady, O. (2005). Rasa'il al-Bashir [*Letter of al-Bashir*]. Dar Tlass.
Imady, O. (2005). *The Rise and Fall of Muslim Civil Society*. MSI Press.
Luban, D. (2021). Complicity and Lesser Evils: A Tale of Two Lawyers. *SSRN Electronic Journal*. Published. https://doi.org/10.2139/ssrn.3817495
Moubayed, S. (2005). *Steel & Silk: Men & Women Who Shaped Syria 1900–2000*. Cune.